Xingni Zhou, Zhiyuan Ren, Yanzhuo Ma, Kai Fan, Xiang Ji

Data structures and algorithms analysis – New perspectives

Also of interest

Big Data Analytics Methods, Analytics Techniques in Data Mining, Deep Learning and Natural Language Processing
Peter Ghavami, 2020
ISBN 978-1-5474-1795-7, e-ISBN (PDF) 978-1-5474-0156-7,
e-ISBN (EPUB) 978-1-5474-0158-1

Data Mining
Jürgen Cleve, Uwe Lämmel, 2016
ISBN 978-3-11-045675-2, e-ISBN (PDF) 978-3-11-045677-6,
e-ISBN (EPUB) 978-3-11-045690-5

Regularization Algorithms for Ill-Posed Problems
Anatoly B.Bakushinsky, Mikhail M. Kokurin, Mikhail Yu.Kokurin,
2018
ISBN 978-3-11-055630-8, e-ISBN (PDF) 978-3-11-055735-0
e-ISBN (EPUB) 978-3-11-055638-4

Machine Learning and Visual Perception
Baochang Zhang, 2020
ISBN 978-3-11-059553-6, e-ISBN (PDF) 978-3-11-059556-7
e-ISBN (EPUB) 978-3-11-059322-8

Deep Learning, Research and Applications
Siddhartha Bhattacharyya, Vaclav Snasel, Aboul Ella Hassanien,
Satadal Saha, B. K. Tripathy, (Eds.), 2020
ISBN 978-3-11-067079-0, e-ISBN (PDF) 978-3-11-067090-5
e-ISBN (EPUB) 978-3-11-067092-9

Xingni Zhou, Zhiyuan Ren, Yanzhuo Ma,
Kai Fan, Xiang Ji

Data structures and algorithms analysis – New perspectives

Volume 1: Data structures based on linear relations

DE GRUYTER   Science Press
Beijing

Authors

Xingni Zhou
School of Telecommunications Engineering,
Xidian University
Xi'an, China
xnzhou@xidian.edu.cn

Zhiyuan Ren
School of Telecommunications Engineering,
Xidian University
Xi'an, China
zyren@xidian.edu.cn

Yanzhuo Ma
School of Telecommunications Engineering,
Xidian University
Xi'an, China
yzma@mail.xidian.edu.cn

Prof. Kai Fan
School of Cyber Engineering,
Xidian University
Xi'an, China
kfan@mail.xidian.edu.cn

Xiang Ji
kloeckner.i GmbH
Berlin, Germany
hi@xiangji.me

ISBN 978-3-11-059557-4
e-ISBN (PDF) 978-3-11-059558-1
e-ISBN (EPUB) 978-3-11-059318-1

Library of Congress Control Number: 2020930224

Bibliographic information published by the Deutsche Nationalbibliothek
The Deutsche Nationalbibliothek lists this publication in the Deutsche Nationalbibliografie;
detailed bibliographic data are available on the Internet at http://dnb.dnb.de.

© 2020 China Science Publishing & Media Ltd. and Walter de Gruyter GmbH, Berlin/Boston
Cover image: Prill/iStock/Getty Images Plus
Typesetting: Integra Software Services Pvt. Ltd.
Printing and binding: CPI books GmbH, Leck

www.degruyter.com

Contents

Preface —— XI

1   Introduction —— 1
1.1   Let's begin with programming —— 1
1.2   The data to be processed by the program —— 7
1.3   The introduction of data structures —— 17
1.4   Basic concepts of data structures —— 18
1.4.1   Basic terminologies of data structures —— 18
1.4.1.1   Data —— 18
1.4.1.2   Data element —— 18
1.4.1.3   Data item —— 18
1.4.1.4   Data structure —— 18
1.4.2   The three key elements of data structures —— 19
1.4.2.1   Logical structure —— 19
1.4.2.2   The storage structure of data —— 20
1.4.2.3   Operation on data —— 23
1.5   How to design algorithms —— 24
1.5.1   The definition of algorithm and representation methods —— 24
1.5.1.1   Algorithm —— 24
1.5.1.2   Features of algorithms —— 24
1.5.1.3   Representation of algorithm —— 25
1.5.1.4   Key elements to describing algorithms —— 25
1.5.2   The relation between algorithm design and function design —— 25
1.5.2.1   Concepts related to function —— 25
1.5.2.2   The relation between algorithm design and function design —— 26
1.5.3   Software design method —— 27
1.5.3.1   Test case design —— 27
1.5.3.2   Description of data structure —— 27
1.5.3.3   Function interface and function structure design —— 27
1.5.3.4   Pseudocode description of the algorithm —— 27
1.5.3.5   Program implementation —— 28
1.5.3.6   Algorithm efficiency analysis —— 28
1.5.4   General steps of algorithm design —— 28
1.6   How to evaluate algorithms —— 31
1.6.1   The design requirements of algorithms —— 31
1.6.1.1   Correctness —— 31
1.6.1.2   Readability —— 31
1.6.1.3   Robustness —— 32
1.6.1.4   Efficiency —— 32
1.6.2   Measurement methods of algorithm efficiency —— 32

1.6.2.1	The after-execution analysis of algorithm performance —— 32	
1.6.2.2	The pre-execution analysis of algorithm efficiency —— 34	
1.7	The pre-execution analysis methods of algorithm efficiency —— 34	
1.7.1	The size of the problem and the strategy of the algorithm —— 35	
1.7.2	The upper and lower bounds of algorithm efficiency —— 37	
1.7.2.1	Best case —— 37	
1.7.2.2	Worst case —— 37	
1.7.2.3	Average case —— 37	
1.7.3	The asymptotic upper bound – the time complexity of the algorithm —— 41	
1.7.4	The comprehensive discussion on the time complexity of algorithms —— 43	
1.7.4.1	The practical implications of the time complexity of algorithms —— 43	
1.7.4.2	Function values with significant meanings to algorithm analysis —— 45	
1.7.4.3	Computation rules for time complexity —— 47	
1.7.4.4	General methods for algorithm efficiency analysis —— 48	
1.7.5	The analysis methods on the space efficiency of the algorithm —— 49	
1.8	Comprehensive evaluation of algorithm performance —— 55	
1.9	Chapter summary —— 57	
1.10	Exercises —— 58	
1.10.1	Multiple-choice questions —— 58	
1.10.2	Practical problems —— 59	

2	The data structure whose nodes share a linear logical relation – linear list —— 61	
2.1	Viewing the linear list from the perspective of logical structure —— 61	
2.1.1	The sequential relations that exist in practical problems —— 61	
2.1.1.1	The one-to-one correspondence relation that exists in queuing —— 61	
2.1.1.2	The representation method of alphabetical table —— 61	
2.1.1.3	The structure of phone number tables —— 62	
2.1.2	The logical structure of linear lists —— 63	
2.1.2.1	The definition of linear list —— 63	
2.1.2.2	The logical features of the linear list —— 63	
2.1.2.3	Major operations on the linear list —— 63	
2.2	One of the storage structures of linear lists – sequential list —— 64	
2.2.1	The design of storage structure of a sequential list —— 64	
2.2.1.1	The definition of sequential list —— 64	

2.2.1.2   The storage characteristics of sequential list —— 65
2.2.1.3   The design of the sequential list storage structure —— 65
2.2.1.4   Think and discuss on the application of "struct" —— 67
2.2.2   The operations on sequential list —— 69
2.2.2.1   The insertion operation of ordered list —— 69
2.2.2.2   Deletion operation on sequential list —— 73
2.2.2.3   Lookup operation of elements in sequential list —— 77
2.2.2.4   Accessing data element from sequential list —— 78
2.2.3   Discussion on the sequential storage structure —— 79
2.3   The second storage method for linear list – linked list —— 80
2.3.1   Introduction 1 – the story of word —— 80
2.3.2   Introduction 2 – linked lists in mobile phones —— 82
2.3.3   The storage of singly linked lists —— 84
2.3.3.1   The structural design of nodes of linked lists —— 84
2.3.3.2   How are the nodes in the linked list linked together in the
             storage space? —— 84
2.3.4   Operations on the singly linked list —— 90
2.3.4.1   Initialization of singly linked lists —— 91
2.3.4.2   Construction of singly linked lists —— 94
2.3.4.3   Lookup operation on singly linked list —— 101
2.3.4.4   The insertion operation on singly linked lists —— 106
2.3.4.5   Deletion operation on singly linked lists —— 111
2.3.5   Discussion of singly linked lists —— 115
2.3.6   Circular linked lists —— 115
2.3.6.1   Structural design of circular linked lists —— 115
2.3.6.2   Operations on circular linked lists —— 116
2.3.7   Doubly linked list —— 119
2.3.7.1   Structural design of doubly linked lists —— 119
2.3.7.2   Operations on doubly linked lists —— 121
2.3.8   Summary on linked lists —— 121
2.4   Examples of the application of linear lists —— 122
2.4.1   Algorithm design —— 122
2.4.2   Program implementation —— 122
2.5   Comparisons between sequential list and linked list —— 123
2.5.1   Considerations based on storage —— 124
2.5.2   Considerations based on operations —— 125
2.5.3   Considerations based on the environment —— 125
2.6   Summary of the chapter —— 125
2.7   Exercises —— 126
2.7.1   Multiple-choice questions —— 126
2.7.2   Algorithm design exercises —— 129

3	**Linear list with restricted operations – stack and queue** —— **133**	
3.1	Stack – a linear list managed in a first-in–last-out manner —— 133	
3.1.1	Introduction to the operation pattern of stack —— 133	
3.1.1.1	Introduction to stack 1 – erroneous operation in Word —— 133	
3.1.1.2	Introduction to stack example 2 – bracket matching —— 134	
3.1.1.3	Introduction to stack example 3 – the recursive invocation of functions —— 135	
3.1.1.4	Introduction to stack example 4 – the embedded invocation of functions —— 136	
3.1.2	The logic structure of stack —— 138	
3.1.2.1	The definition of stack —— 138	
3.1.2.2	The differences and connections between stack and linear list —— 140	
3.1.2.3	Operations on stack —— 140	
3.1.3	The design of the storage structure of stacks —— 140	
3.1.3.1	Sequential stack – use a piece of continuous space to store stack elements —— 140	
3.1.3.2	Linked stack – storing stack elements in noncontinuous space —— 141	
3.1.4	Operations on stack —— 142	
3.1.4.1	Basic operations on sequential stack —— 142	
3.1.4.2	Basic operations on linked stack —— 157	
3.1.5	Comparison of various stack structures —— 164	
3.1.6	Examples of the application of stack —— 164	
3.1.6.1	Base conversion —— 164	
3.1.6.2	Implement recursive functions with stack —— 166	
3.1.6.3	Evaluating expressions —— 171	
3.1.7	Recursion – a "first-in–last-out" process —— 172	
3.1.7.1	The concept of recursion and its key elements —— 172	
3.1.7.2	Analysis of features of recursion —— 174	
3.1.7.3	Summary of recursion —— 176	
3.2	Queue – linear list managed in a "FIFO" manner —— 177	
3.2.1	Introduction to the queue processing model —— 177	
3.2.1.1	Introductory example to queue 1 – asynchronous processing of data in computer —— 177	
3.2.1.1.1	Buffered queues in e-commerce systems —— 177	
3.2.1.1.2	Mail queues in mail servers —— 178	
3.2.1.2	Introductory example to queue 2 – solution to Pascal's triangle using queue —— 179	
3.2.2	The logical structure of queue —— 181	
3.2.3	The sequential storage structure of queue —— 182	
3.2.3.1	Sequential queue —— 182	

3.2.4   Basic operations on sequential queue —— 192
3.2.4.1   Basic operation on sequential queue – set queue as empty —— 192
3.2.4.2   Basic operation on sequential queue – check emptiness
               of queue —— 193
3.2.4.3   Basic operation on sequential queue – get the head element —— 194
3.2.4.4   Basic operation on sequential queue – insert element —— 195
3.2.4.5   Basic operation on sequential queue – delete element —— 196
3.2.5   Linked storage structure of queue —— 197
3.2.6   Basic operations on linked queue —— 199
3.2.6.1   Basic operations on linked queue – initialize and set the queue
               as empty —— 199
3.2.6.2   Basic operation on linked queue – checking emptiness of
               queue —— 200
3.2.6.3   Basic operation on linked queue – retrieve the head node —— 201
3.2.6.4   Basic operation on linked queue – enqueuing —— 202
3.2.6.5   Basic operation on linked queue – dequeuing —— 204
3.2.6.6   Destroying the linked queue —— 206
3.2.7   Comparison of different queue structures —— 208
3.2.8   Examples of the application of queue —— 209
3.2.8.1   Application of queue 1 – radix sort —— 209
3.2.8.2   Application of queue 2 – card game —— 213
3.3   Chapter summary —— 215
3.4   Exercises —— 217
3.4.1   Multiple choice questions —— 217
3.4.2   Practical questions —— 219
3.4.3   Algorithm design —— 219

4   Sequential list with special contents – multidimensional arrays and
               strings —— 221
4.1   Multidimensional arrays —— 221
4.1.1   The concept of arrays —— 222
4.1.2   The storage structure of arrays —— 223
4.2   The compressional storage of matrices —— 226
4.2.1   The compressional storage of symmetric matrix —— 228
4.2.2   The compressional storage of triangular matrix —— 230
4.2.3   The compressional storage of diagonal matrix —— 231
4.2.4   Compressional storage of sparse matrix —— 232
4.2.4.1   Definition of sparse matrix —— 232
4.2.4.2   The compressional storage of sparse matrix —— 235
4.2.4.2.1   Triple list —— 236
4.2.4.2.2   The linked list storage method of sparse matrix —— 236
4.3   String —— 238

4.3.1   The definition of string ── **240**
4.3.1.1   Substring ── **240**
4.3.1.2   The position of the substring ── **241**
4.3.1.3   Equivalence of string ── **241**
4.3.2   The storage structure of string ── **241**
4.3.2.1   The sequential storage of string ── **241**
4.3.2.2   The block link storage structure of string ── **243**
4.3.2.3   The indexed storage method of string ── **245**
4.3.3   Search on strings – pattern matching ── **248**
4.3.3.1   BF algorithm ── **249**
4.3.3.2   KMP algorithm ── **258**
4.4   Chapter summary ── **268**
4.5   Exercises ── **271**
4.5.1   Multiple-choice questions ── **271**
4.5.2   Applied problems ── **273**
4.5.3   Algorithm design ── **273**

Appendix A Relation graph of data ── 275

Appendix B How to add custom header files ── 277

Appendix C Format of software design manual ── 279

Appendix D Answers to selected exercises ── 283

References ── 285

Index ── 287

Preface

Looking at old problems with new perspectives, requires creative thinking —— Einstein

My experience in teaching and learning data structures

When I was teaching the course on data structures six or seven years ago, I advanced with the methods I've always used in this course. After a few lectures, I received an email from a student in which he said: "I myself like programming a lot. On one hand I am familiar with the computer, both software and hardware, thus I never lack an understanding of the foundational knowledge (for example, I know memory, address, circuits etc. very well); on the other hand, I seem to find your way of lecturing easy to adapt to and likable ... But it seems that many of my classmates are still having difficulties in studying data structures ... "

I have taught data structures for more than ten years. From my experience, students always treat data structures as a hard course to take. "Among many discipline courses of computer science, data structures is deemed by many students as a very difficult course" [8]. Although I didn't learn data structures when I was an undergraduate, and only learned data structures by myself later because of the need to teach, I have never thought of it as something difficult. Why?

Reflecting upon my study and work experience carefully, maybe it's indeed like what the email says – it was because I already had a strong grasp of programming and some understanding of the applications of data structures. For example, the first software development project I undertook already involved applications of concepts such as multithreading, linked list, queue and hash. Although I didn't learn them at school, I was able to easily understand the corresponding data structures and algorithms via dealing with concrete problems first. Therefore, when I started to learn the theoretical knowledge on the textbooks later, I was able to get up to speed pretty soon. Another reason is that I learned software testing methods during the project development. By tracing the programs, it is easy to see their execution paths and results, and thus helping to understand the design and implementation of algorithms.

I think of the textbooks available to students nowadays: they introduce the concepts in a highly abstract way. However, there isn't enough perspective on the relationship between the theoretical abstraction and the real-world application. If there isn't enough hands-on knowledge, it would be hard to understand or accept the abstraction. "There is a bad tendency nowadays: textbooks and lectures focus too much on abstract knowledge and ignore actual applications. Textbooks on data structures typify this tendency. Such a situation is harmful for entry-level students, as they can't walk into the abstract world, and thus eventually don't get what the courses are talking about" [7].

https://doi.org/10.1515/9783110595581-203

I think of my students again: they have neither experience on software development nor solid foundation in software testing. They don't have hands-on knowledge of data structures. When they start only with the abstract concepts, no wonder they encounter difficulties in understanding and accepting them. Zou Hengming pointed out in the book *Data Structure: Sparkling Strings of 0 and 1* [8] that the concepts on data structures are actually not hard, the real difficulties are:

1. How to make the leap from data structure concepts to program implementations (how to implement a data structure):
2. How to make the leap from actual application to data structure abstractions (how to make use of data structures to solve actual problems).

I myself only learned a little bit of programming as an undergraduate (no more than 20 h of lab in total), and I didn't have any knowledge on data structures. But as soon as I graduated, I took part in a large-scale software development project that eventually won the third prize of the National Award for Science and Technology Progress. Subsequently, I also participated in the software installation, testing and maintenance of multiple telecommunication companies, and thus experienced first-hand the most vivid cases that actuated the above two "leaps." Although the development process was very demanding – working late into the night every day for more than half a year at the client's office, dealing with the enormous pressure of memory leak on a 24-h online system, finding bugs urgently after a system crash on both the production and backup machine . . . – I shall say that I was lucky. Although I didn't learn much programming at school, I was able to learn by myself and from my colleagues many new skills, knowledge and experience in my work. Such tempering by practice was very conducive to my later understanding and teaching of courses related to program design.

The cruxes in learning data structures

Upon reflection and summarization, I believe the reason why the students struggle to make the two "leaps" mentioned above is because of the disconnection between the teaching method of the traditional textbook and the practical demands.

Nietzsche once wrote: "One can't understand what he hasn't experienced." In other words, people only accept information related to something already understood in the past. This is a process of learning via comparison. In this process, the brain seeks to find the connection between each piece of information, leaning on past experiences to understand new things [4].

"Euler believed, if the instructor is unable to teach the thought process behind the mathematical problems, math education will be meaningless. The de facto inventor of modern computer Leibniz also said: according to me, nothing is more important than exploring the source of the invention; this is much more important than the invention itself. Growing up, our math textbooks are almost all Euclidean: from definition to theorem, then to lemma. Such books completely distort the real process of mathematical discoveries. Currently, almost all algorithm books adopt a Euclidean instruction style: every step of deduction aims precisely at the target of data structures, but this actually completely reverses the natural process of creation and invention of the human brain. To the readers, this is equal to directly telling you the conclusion and the methods, then asking you to verify that the conclusion stands and that the methods work. However, there are few books that explain well how the conclusion and the methods are arrived at, and what kind of thought process is involved between the question and the answer. There have long been criticisms about such (Euclidean) method of instruction in the west (especially in the field of mathematics)" [3].

Traditional textbooks on data structures usually just list the question, and then directly give out the algorithm. But to actually solve problems with the computer, one has to consider: how to analyze the known information in the question, how to mine the connection among data (the logic structure of data), how to choose the appropriate storage method (the storage structure of data) to save the logical structure into the computer and then arrive at the algorithm top-down, from the storage structure. This is the real thought processes and steps for solving actual problems, and also the methods employed in software development. The problem of traditional textbooks is the lack of guidance and analysis on the thought process, which causes a surplus in concept illustration and implementation details, yet a lack of description on the process of design and implementation. This leads the students to only see the detailed solution of one problem after another, yet unable to grasp the general method and principles of algorithm design.

This book attempts to give the knowledge background and the application background of the questions and algorithms from the perspective of "apply what one has learned," adding in examples from actual software development. It focuses on the methods of analysis and thought flows of design, and illustrates the testing and analysis process of important algorithms, making up for the shortcomings of traditional textbooks. It teaches the students to solve problems with "methods of software development." This allows the students to comprehend and grasp them easily and to flexibly choose the appropriate logic structure, storage structure and the corresponding algorithms, design programs that have high performance and efficiency, and that are easy to read and maintain, thus fulfilling the aim of the data structures course.

The relationship between program design and data structures

Before learning data structures, one should have foundational knowledge about program design. Let's look at issues related to programming first.

What is programming? Programming is not only about understanding of the grammar, but also involves the various aspects mentioned below:

1. The flow of thought for problem solving: algorithms are complete problem-solving steps constituting basic computations and specified computational sequences. They are the soul of the program. The quality of the algorithms has a direct impact on the efficiency of the program. The conventions used by this book to describe algorithms are illustrated later.

2. The execution speed of the program: the execution speed of the program depends on a lot of factors. The user usually has requirements on the execution speed of the program, for example, real-time response systems.

3. The memory usage of the program: the execution of the code needs the corresponding memory space and runtime environment. In some occasions, there are limitations for the memory usage of the program, for example, embedded systems.

4. Coding standards: the code needs to be written according to certain standards to ensure the consistency of the code, for the purposes of communication and maintenance.

5. The structure of the program: a complex program consists of multiple relatively independent modules. High intramodule cohesion and low intermodule coupling is the standard to use on whether the program structure is reasonable.

6. Module interfaces: the communication between modules is done via interfaces. The parameters for passing information between modules should be reasonable and effective.

7. Testing and tuning of the program: use well-designed test cases to test whether the program is correct. Testing is an effective way to finish a software product with high efficiency. A proficient programmer is also a testing expert. The majority of experience and methods of testing are obtained via practice.

One should have foundations in program design before learning data structures. Then, what is the relationship between data structures and program design? It can be said that data structures is the foundation for writing huge and complex advanced programs. Table 0.1 lists the features of program design and advanced programming.

The crux of program design is module division and related issues. Another important aspect is to convert the information for solving the problem to data that can be understood and received by the computer. This conversion process is the abstraction process of data. To deal with large-scale and complex problems, one must grasp the thought pattern of data abstraction, while at the same time grasp various skills such as standardized declaration of algorithms, performance analysis of algorithms and performance evaluation of algorithms.

Table 0.1: Program Design and Advanced Programming.

	Related Courses	Main Contents	Course Goal
Structured Program Design	Basic Program Design Courses	Syntax, Rules, Modular Design	Write simple programs which solve simple problems
Advanced Programming	Data Structures	Abstracted Thinking about Data	Write large-scale, logically complex programs
		Formal Declaration of Algorithms, Performance Analysis and Evaluation of Algorithms	
	Software Engineering	Modular Design Methods, Software Engineering Methods	
	. . . . . .		

The relationship between data structures and other courses

As an important core discipline course, "Data Structures and Algorithms" is both a deepening and extension of previous courses, and a foundational course for in-depth study of other discipline courses. The sorting algorithms and basic data structures such as trees and graphs are basic skills for computer science. Advanced data structures such as B+ tree and hash are also foundations for important discipline courses such as database, operating system, compiler and computer networking. The relationship between this course and other courses in computer science is shown in Fig. 0.1:

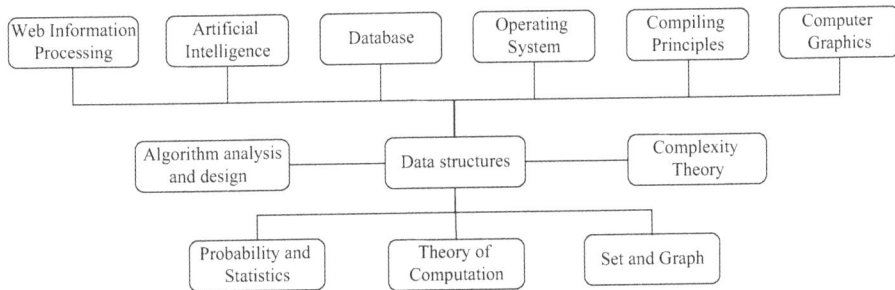

Fig. 0.1: The important position of "data structures and algorithms" course in computer science.

The importance of data structures

Commercial programmer Xiao He wrote in his blog: "During so many years, I've worked on projects related to games, communication, industrial control, education, VoIP, server cluster etc. It's really diverse."

However, I know that I've actually always been writing programs with one sole method: starting from the most low-level data structures and algorithms, using the most basic C and C++. No matter what, it's always those few data structures, queues, stacks and others.

This is just like inner strength in martial arts novels. Once the inner strength is worked on well, it's very easy to learn concrete martial arts skills. If you don't have inner strength, no matter how delicate the skills look like, you'll immediately be defeated in the face of a real master. "One inner strength defeats ten trickeries" is exactly talking about this. In the face of absolute ability, any trickery will be rendered useless [6].

A survey on the graduates and graduate students of Tsinghua University shows that almost all the surveyed students agree that "data structures" is among the most useful courses ever learned in school. Data structures is one of the fundamental courses checked by many software developing institutions; in interviews the majority of the exam concerns itself with data structures and algorithms; it is also a mandatory subject for the entry exam of any master's degree in computer science/software engineering in China.

Will data structures be outdated

Since computers were born in the 1940s, hardware has been ceaselessly advancing, and software advances simultaneously as well. As a branch of software studies, programming languages have also developed from machine languages to the fourth generation. But no matter how software develops, and no matter how developing tools advance, as long as our computers are still based on von Neumann machine, then data structures and algorithms will still be the core of programs, and will never be outdated.

Learning data structures and algorithms doesn't only require us to learn how to use and implement certain data structure, the more important thing is to learn the ability and methods to analyze and solve problems.

Additional contents in this book about the implementation of algorithms and programs

In this book, the following contents are specifically added:

1. Addition of design of test cases

From the point of view of program robustness, the design of test cases is an important thing to be considered from the beginning of program design. Normal textbooks on program design and data structures rarely consider issues on test cases. This book gives the design of test cases of the basic program in the earliest algorithm design process; this is to let the learners learn program design in a professional way, and form good design habits.

2. Addition of design of function structures

For beginners, when learning data structures, their foundation in the programming language is usually not very solid. They are especially unfamiliar with the design of function structures. There are usually various choices when functions input and output information according to a given functionality. The beginners usually get confused when trying to decide what are the reasonable types of parameters and functions, and thus face difficulties in programming. In view of this, this book particularly lists various implementations of typical data structure computations. Through the comparison of various function structure implementations, the readers will be able to find the features of various information passing mechanisms, solidify programming knowledge and skills, and achieve the unification of theory and practice.

3. Addition of testing of important programs

The process of program design is also a process of testing and tuning. The development and testing of a program are inseparable. For beginners, if they are not familiar with testing, it's easy for them to lose confidence in continuing learning. According to my experience in teaching over multiple years, if there is demonstration on program testing, then it's easier to grasp the related programs, especially when learning concepts such as linked lists. If the teacher only explains data structures, the linkage between nodes, the students will find it abstract and hard to understand. If there is testing on observing how the linkages between nodes are dynamically created and eliminated, then it will be much more vivid and straightforward. However, since there are various steps during the testing process, the student might understand in the classroom, but find it much harder to recall and retrace the process again on his own. Therefore, this textbook records some tracing process for important sample programs to facilitate the learning of students. All source codes of this book are programmed in C and tested in VS IDE.

Description of the algorithms

Description of the algorithms are given in the following order (mainly applied to the most basic part of programming):
1. Design of function interfaces and test cases: ascertain the input and output of the problem.

2. Pseudocode description of the algorithms: describes the functionality of the task.
3. Description of the data structures: gives the description of the appropriate storage structure in C types.
4. Design of function structures: ascertains function types, parameters, return values and so on.

Sample function structures are given in Tables 0.2 and 0.3.

Table 0.2: Example of Function Structure 1.

Description	Input	Output
Find the given value in the sequential list	Address of the sequential list SequenList *	Normal: index value int
LocateElem_Sq	Node value ElemType	Abnormal: −1
Function name	Parameters	Function type

Table 0.3: Example of Function Structure 2.

Description	Input	Output	
Get the value at the given index from the sequential list	Address of the sequential list SequenList *	Return	Normal: 1
GetElem_Sq	Index int		Abnormal: 0
	(Node value ElemType)		Node value ElemType
Function name	Parameters		Function type

Note: When the input and output of the function are the same, the return information is expressed via passing the address of the parameter, instead of using return statements. For example, in Table 0.4 sample 2, both the input and output are listed as "Node value ElemType," which denotes that "pass by reference" is used.
5. Program implementation: gives implementation in code.
6. Analysis of algorithm efficiency: analyzes the time complexity of the problem.

Note: For the code in this book, we assume #define TRUE 1 #define FALSE 0

A brief introduction to the course "data structures"

Solving concrete problems using the computer, the first thing one shall do is to store the information related to the problem into the computer, that is to say, represent the information in the problem as computer-readable data format. Then, one shall process the data stored in the computer according to specifications of the problem. In one sentence, solving problems using the computer is first about representing data with reasonable structures, only then can one process the data using corresponding algorithms. Data representation and data processing are exactly what the data structures discipline is about.

"Data structures" mainly introduces how to reasonably organize the data, efficiently store and process the data, correctly design the algorithms and the analysis and evaluation of the algorithms.

Through taking this course, the students will be able to deeply understand the basic concepts of logic structures and physical structures of data structures, and the related algorithms. They will also learn to analyze the features of the data objects and grasp data organization methods and representation methods of computers, in order to flexibly choose the appropriate logic structures, storage structures and algorithms in actual software development processes. They will design programs that are highly performant, easily readable and maintainable to solve concrete problems.

Basic aims

1. Understand data structures and their classification, the close relationship between data structures and algorithms.
2. Familiarize themselves with various basic data structures and their operations, learn to select data structures according to the actual requirements of problems.
3. Grasp the steps of algorithm design and algorithm analysis methods.
4. Understand the application of data structures in common algorithms such as sorting and searching.
5. Have a basic understanding of indexing technologies.

Organizational structure of this book

This book is divided into two volumes. The first chapter introduces the basic concepts of data structures and algorithms, as well as the analysis method of algorithms. The second chapter to the fourth chapter, together with the first and second chapter of volume two, introduce stages such as data analysis, function design, algorithm design, testing from the perspective of software development and via application background or knowledge background. It analyzes and discusses basic data structures such as sequential table, linked list, stack, queue, string, array, tree, graph. The third chapter of volume two, "sorting techniques", introduces common data sorting methods. The fourth chapter of volume two, "indexed searching methods", introduces methods for searching data. The contents of the third and the fourth chapter of volume two are introduction to typical operational methods of data.

The introduction, chapters one to four of volume one, and chapters one to two of volume two are written by Prof. Xingni Zhou. The third chapter of volume two is written by Prof. Zhiyuan Ren. The fourth chapter of volume two is written by Prof. Yanzhuo Ma. Prof. Kai Fan provided some sample cases in the fields like telecommunication. Xiang Ji provided localization support and revised the whole book.

There are columns such as "think and discuss," "Knowledge ABC." In "think and discuss" questions are raised to encourage the readers to think about and discuss the questions raised, and thus help the readers deepen their understanding of related concepts, and extend their minds. "Knowledge ABC" mainly introduces the knowledge background, the background story on the invention of the algorithms and stories, in order to enrich the knowledge of the readers and understand the application background of the algorithms. Some knowledge might be relatively deep, on which it suffices to have a rough understanding and refer to further materials if interested.

Acknowledgments

The inspiration for this book comes from my students – some students suggested that my way of teaching as well as thought process are good, and that a book might help understand the related concepts while studying this course. The detailed story is mentioned in my book *New Perspectives on Programming Design in C Language*.

My inspiration also comes from the encouragement of my father and the support of my family. I thank Professors Tie Manxia and Chen Huichan for their guidance as well as the enduring support of Qu Yucheng. I thank my students Sun Meng, Ding Yu, Sun Shu, Sun Yaping, Zhang Ke, Yang Hengjie, Wu Weiji, Huang Chao and Zhang Ping for the conducive opinions and advice on the first draft of this book.

All discussions with students and colleagues helped me a lot. Such discussions either widened my horizon or induced me to think deeply. Everything was a journey of growth and improvement.

I thank my colleagues who helped me a lot and worked hard together as well as to all who cared for and helped me.

I am grateful for April by Bandari. Every morning, such beautiful music helped me to start a day of writing with a pure, calm and warm mood.

I'm grateful for everything.

Zhou Xingni
xnzhou@xidian.edu.cn
Spring 2020 in Chang'an

1 Introduction

Main Contents
- The concept of data structures
- The basic requirements of algorithm design
- The methods to analyze algorithm efficiency in terms of time and space complexities

Learning Purposes
- Understand the importance of data structure courses
- Comprehend the concept of data structure
- Comprehend the steps for algorithm/program design
- Comprehend the methods for analyzing and evaluating algorithm efficiency

1.1 Let's begin with programming

Everybody who has learned program design would know that programming is the way by which the human brain drives the computer. The famous Swiss computer scientist, the creator of Pascal, Niklaus Wirth proposed a famous equation regarding the concept of programming. He won the highest honor of computer science, Turing Award, with it. The equation only has one line of text:

$$Algorithm + Data\ Structures = Program$$

Nicklaus Wirth published a book in 1976 named *Algorithm + Data Structures = Program*. It explains the function of data structures in program design. Before starting to program, two issues will have to be solved first: the design of algorithm and the design of data structures. Algorithms are strategies to solve problems, while data structures describe the data model of the information to be processed. A program is then a set of instructions used by the computer to process information based on the strategies.

The aim of program design is to let the computer help human to finish the complex tasks at hand automatically. The fundamental focus of computer science and technologies is – "what can be automated and efficiently automated?", "What is the process of transforming the concrete problem to an eventual solution via computers?", "What is the role played by data structure and algorithms in that?"

To solve problems via computers, the general steps are shown in Fig. 1.1. In the squares there are the steps or results of problem solving, in the ovals there are the processes, in which:

https://doi.org/10.1515/9783110595581-001

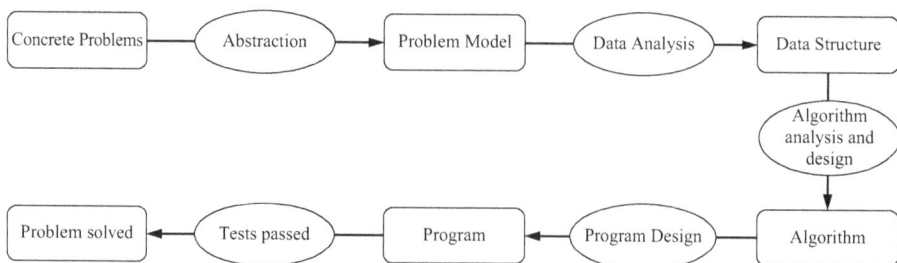

Fig. 1.1: Processes of problem solving of computer.

- Concrete problem: There must be known conditions and descriptions about the eventual requirement in the problem description.
- Model of problem: By analyzing the problem qualitatively as well as quantitatively, extract the functionalities to be fulfilled and the information to be processed, and find out the relations between the information. Extract the two key elements of the problem – information and functionality – and establish the problem model. The establishment of the problem model is for converting the concrete problem to a form that is "understandable" and "receivable" by the computer.
- Data structures: Analyze what is the data contained in the problem model, what are the relations between the data and in what form should the data be stored in the computer. Data structures are formed after such analysis.
- Algorithms: Analyze what are the input/output, functionalities and steps of implementation of the problem. Analyze the speed and space performance of the algorithm. Design a data processing plan after such analysis.
- Program: Program design "translates" the algorithm to the corresponding instructions and codes.
- Solution of the problem: Test the program with various professional testing methods. The solution should be obtained if all the tests are passed.

Think and Discuss How is "saving data to computer and processing it" implemented from a program design perspective?

Professor Zhou Yizhen of Carnegie Mellon University states in his explication of "computational thinking" concept: "Computational thinking is to use the basic concepts of computation to solve problems, design systems, and understand human behaviors. Computational thinking is based on the abilities and limitations of computational process." The most fundamental content of computational thinking, that is, its essence, is abstraction and automation. Concretely in program design, computational thinking can be described by the "thinking of programs" below; see Fig. 1.2.

The abstraction of information in program design is using identifiers, constants, variables, data types, arrays, structs, files and so on.

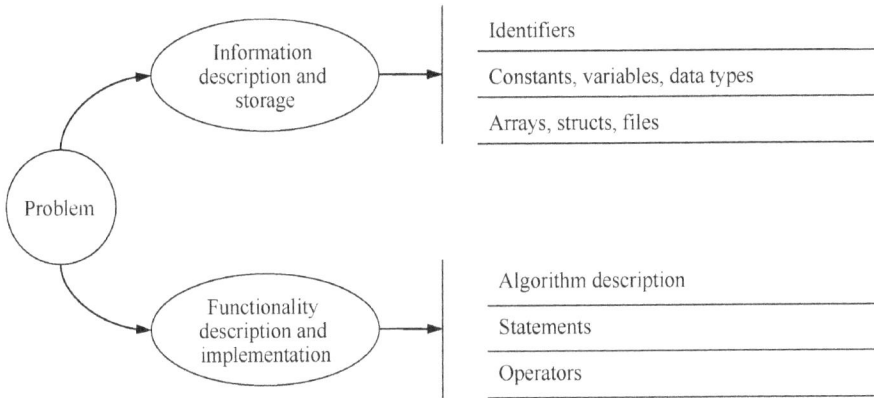

Fig. 1.2: Thought flow of programming.

Knowledge ABC "Top-down stepwise refinement" program design method
Structured Programming is a basic principle for detailed design focused on module functionality and process design. This concept was first proposed by E. W. Dijkstra in 1965. It was an important milestone for software development. Its essence is to adopt a top-down, stepwise-refined program design method. It employs three basic control structures to construct programs: any program can be constructed from *sequence*, *branch* and *loop*.

Top-down means one should first consider the entirety before considering the details; consider the global purpose before considering local purposes. Don't pursue too many details from the beginning, but start from the design of top-level purpose, and gradually make the problem more concrete. Gradual elaboration means using some subpurposes as transition when dealing with concrete problems.

Centering on modulized design means dividing the software system being developed into several independent modules. This makes the job of finishing each single module straightforward and clear, thus laying the foundation for designing large-scale software.

Designing complex software needs scientific construction and maintenance methods, that is, treating software development as an engineering project. This involves knowledge from the software engineering discipline. From the viewpoint of software engineering, software development constitutes of multiple stages, that is, requirement analysis, design, coding, testing and so on. Table 1.1 lists the normal steps of solving a programming problem and their correspondence with software engineering stages.

Table 1.1: Stages of program development.

Problem solving	Software engineering	Actual tasks
Modeling	Requirement analysis stage	Abstract the functionalities to be achieved by the problem; analyze the data objects involved in the problem; find out the relations between data objects
Designing	Designing stage	Data structure design, software structure design, algorithm design
Programing	Programming stage	Write program code
Verification	Testing	Software testing and tuning

i **Knowledge ABC** Software Engineering

Software engineering is an interdisciplinary engineering subject. It applies the basic principles of Computer Science, Mathematics, Engineering Science, and Management to the development and maintenance of software. Its focus is on the analysis, design, evaluation and specification of large-scale software. It involves various aspects including management, quality control, innovation, standardization, personal skills, teamwork and professional practice.

From the viewpoint of software engineering, the life cycle of a software from creation to end-of-life involves the following stages:

1. Problem definition and planning stage
   The developer and customer discuss together to ascertain the development purpose of the software and its feasibility.
2. Requirement analysis stage
   After establishing that the development of this software is feasible, there needs to be detailed analysis on the various functionalities to be realized by the software system.
   Specifically, the job is to describe the purpose, range, definition and functionality of the new system. Requirement analysis is a key process in software engineering. During it, the system analyzer and software engineer ascertain the need of the customer. Only after ascertaining such needs can they analyze and find the solution to building the new system.
3. Software design stage
   According to the result of the requirement analysis, design the whole software system, for example, data structure design, system architecture design (using object-oriented design as an example, there are module division, module communication, module workflow and so on), database design and so on. Software design is usually divided into generic design and detailed design, laying a solid foundation for writing the software program later.
   The basic flow for object-oriented system architecture design is by using the method of top-down, stepwise refinement to divide the system into modules. And then separately design the communication method and module workflow. The principle of module division is "high cohesion, loose coupling," that is, let the modules possess independent functionalities and have few interworkings with other modules. Modules divided according to this principle would have complete and independent functionalities, simple data interfaces, easy-to-implement programs and be easy to understand and maintain. The independence

limits the range of potential errors and makes errors easy to remove, thus making software development fast and reliable.

4. Coding stage
    Transfer the result of software design into computer-runnable program code. In the coding process, there must be a unified and standard-conforming coding standard to ensure the program's readability and maintainability, and improve the running efficiency of the program.

5. Software testing stage
    Once the software design is completed, it has to undergo rigorous testing to discover the problems of the software during the entire design process and rectify them. The whole testing process normally consists of unit testing, integration testing and system testing. There are mainly whitebox testing and blackbox testing methods. During the testing, a detailed testing plan is needed and the process should follow the plan closely, so that the randomness of the testing is reduced.

6. Maintenance stage
    Software maintenance is the long-lasting stage of the software life cycle. After the software is finished developing and is in use, because of multiple reasons, the software might not be able to continue satisfying the users' needs. To further the life span of the software, maintenance is needed. Two aspects, that is, error correction and functionality improvement, are involved.

The concrete steps in solving a problem with computer/developing a program are as follows:

1. Modeling
    Models are used to describe the necessary information to complete the system functionalities, that is, what are the given conditions (inputs) and results produced (outputs). The functionality of the software system is ascertained.

2. Design
    The design phase involves the following three types of design:
    –   Data structures design: analyze the data object, the relations between data objects, ascertain the storage method for the data objects and ascertain the operations to perform on the data objects.
    –   Software structures design: using the "top-down" method, divide the problem into medium-sized and easy-to-process modules according to the functionality. Software structures include constituent modules, the layer structure of modules, the invocation relations between modules, the functionalities of each individual module and so on.
    –   Algorithm design: concrete descriptions about the finished functionalities of each module. One needs to transform the functionality description into precise, structured process description.

3. Coding
    Use the programming language decided in the project to implement the algorithms.

4. Verification

   Verification includes testing and error correction.
   - Testing: use "test cases" to test the code.
   - Error correction: find the reason for errors through testing and correct them.

Knowledge ABC Test case and its design principles

Test cases are also called test samples. They are a set of test input, execution conditions and expected results created to verify whether the program satisfies specific needs.

When designing test cases, one should include the functionalities to test, the data to input (including reasonable and unreasonable inputs) and expected outputs. One should try to discover as many errors with the fewest test cases possible. Design the test cases that are most likely to discover software errors, and avoid using test cases that target the same kind of errors. The principle for designing test cases is: test data should be few, effective and as complete as possible.

The common methods used for designing cases include:
- Boundary analysis: ascertain the boundary conditions (exactly equal, slightly smaller than or slightly bigger than, just bigger than equivalent boundary value). Targeting the system, mainly introduces some legal/illegal data, chosen near the boundary value.
- Equal partition: partition all possible input data (legal and illegal) into several equal-potency classes.
- Error prediction: mainly based on testing experience and intuition and referring to previous software systems, find potential errors.

The test cases should be designed before the code design. According to requirement specifications and design specifications, understand the real needs of the customers in detail, and accurately comprehend the functionalities achieved by the software, before starting to design test cases.

Think and Discuss Which one costs more: design, programming or testing?

Discussion: The focal point of programming is actually not "coding," but testing. A theoretically perfect design will encounter a lot of issues in detail in implementation, which must be solved via testing.

Professor Wirth mentioned above once said in a report that he only spent 10% of the time in designing a certain architecture, and the rest 90% of the time was spent in development and testing. It was especially costly when the program encountered all kinds of runtime problems, some of which have easy clues to follow and some others are entirely out of the blue. It really drove them crazy.

1.2 The data to be processed by the program

In the 1930s and 1940s, the initial purpose of inventing computers is to deal with scientific and engineering calculations. The information being processed was purely numerical. Usually people call such problems "numeric calculation."

Nowadays, computers are developing extremely rapidly. This not only manifests itself in improvements in computer performance, but more importantly in the widening of the range of data able to be entered into the computer. For example, various types of information including symbols, sounds and images can all be stored on the computer via some encoding scheme. Correspondingly, the objects processed by computers also develop from simple purely numeric information to nonnumeric, structured information. The fields to which the computer can be applied are also rapidly expanding.

Knowledge ABC Numeric calculation and nonnumeric calculation

Numeric calculation, concretely speaking, is the method and process of effectively using the computer to get approximate solutions to mathematical problems. It can be achieved by abstracting the appropriate mathematical models, and then designing the corresponding algorithms. The algorithms are especially mature about floating-point algebraic calculations, for example, solving linear formulas, calculus and initial value problems for calculus formulas.

The so-called nonnumeric calculation problems are named to distinguish themselves from the previously mentioned "numeric problems."

In order to more concretely comprehend the concept of "numeric" versus "nonnumeric" and familiarize yourselves with steps of program design, let's look at some of the examples below:

Example 1.1: Example of numeric problem

From the infinite sequence below, calculate the value of π. Output a table, which shows the approximate value of π obtained from the first, second, third items in the sequence. Before we first obtain 3.14, how many items from the sequence must we use? To obtain 3.141? 3.1415? 3.14159?

$$\pi = 4 - \frac{4}{3} + \frac{4}{5} - \frac{4}{7} + \frac{4}{9} - \frac{4}{11} + \cdots$$

Solution:

Step 1: Establish the model

To deal with numeric problems, we must first find or establish the corresponding mathematic model. The mathematical model for this problem is the mathematical formula. We can find the relation between the data object and data, and establish the initial value of the data. See Figure 1.3.

Common formula	\multicolumn{2}{c}{$(-1)*m*4/(2*i+1)$}	
Data object	m	Scalar: Controls the sign of the sequence item
	i	Item number: The number of items being used currently
Relation between data	\multicolumn{2}{c}{}	
	Value of i	Value of m
	Odd	1
	Even	-1
Initialization of data	\multicolumn{2}{c}{$m=1;\ i=1$}	

Fig. 1.3: Parameters for the model in Example 1.1.

Step 2: Design

For the design of the algorithm, we follow the program design principle of "top-down, gradual refinement." We first describe it with pseudocode. When the algorithm is detailed enough to program, it will be easy to convert it to code. We can give the pseudocode implementation of the algorithm according to the functionality specification of the question. See Table 1.2.

Step 3: Coding

```
int main()
{
    float x=4;
    int i=1,m=1;

    while (1)
    {
        x = x +(float)(-1)*m*4/(2*i+1);
        i++;
        m=m*(-1);
        if (x>=3.14-0.000001 && x<=3.14+0.000001)
            break;
    }
    printf("i=%d,x=%f\n",i,x);
    return 0;
}
```

Table 1.2: Algorithm design.

Top-level pseudocode description of the algorithm
Value Initialization: Sum x = 4; m = 1; Item number i = 1;
Based on the common formula, perform iterative addition on x
Stop the iteration when x = 3.14
Output the values of x and i
Detailed description of the algorithm
Sum x = 4; m = 1; i = 1;
do
x = x + (−1)*m*4/(2*i + 1)
Add 1 to i;
m = m*(−1)
until x = 3.14 Stop the iteration
Output the values of x and i;

Note:

1. `while (1)`
   The design of infinite looping is because we can't ascertain the number of loops before-hand. We control the breaking of the loop with condition, not numbers.
2. `if (x≥3.14-0.000001 && x≤3.14+0.000001) break;`
   The design of break condition is because we can't directly compare real numbers in C programming language, thus we adopted a workaround. [You may refer to Chapter 2, storage of floating point numbers, in *New Perspectives on Programming in C.*]

Example 1.2: Example of nonnumeric problem
Querying phone numbers
    Telecom company records the various information about customers via phone number record table (see Fig. 1.4). Design a program that can query the phone number of a given customer. It requires finding the number quickly for any given name. If there's a number, return the number, otherwise return "no number found" token.

Let's first introduce some concepts in Fig. 1.4.
    One row of a table is called a "data element" or "node": an item in one row, for example, "customer name," "phone number," is called "data item." If we can distinguish data elements according to the certain data element, then we call this data element "keyword."

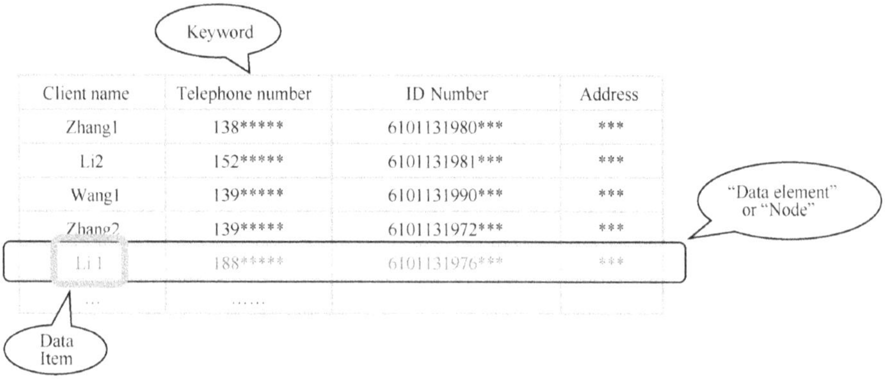

Fig. 1.4: Phone number record table.

i   **Term Explanation** Keyword, main keyword, subkeyword

Keyword: the data item used to identify data elements.

Main keyword: the keyword that can uniquely identify a data element. For example, the "phone number" in Fig. 1.4, each phone number is unique.

Subkeyword: a keyword that can identify some data elements. For example, the "name" in Fig. 1.4 – people sometimes have the same name.

Method 1 Sequential construction and sequential search

Step 1:   Build the model

According to the sequential storage of phone information in Fig. 1.4, the data objects involved in the problem and the relation between data elements are shown in Fig. 1.5.

Objects involved in the problem	Each customer and the corresponding data items
The relations between the objects	Data elements listed one by one according to the order of addition

Fig. 1.5: Example 1.2 model parameters 1.

Step 2:   Design

1.   Data storage: to solve this problem, we need to first construct a registration table of phone numbers. The table should include name, phone number, ID number, address. We save the data elements into the array according to the order of their additions.

2.   Algorithm design: sequentially search for the "client name" data item in the whole data table. If it's found, return the corresponding "phone number" data item. If it's not found, return the pre-agreed value.

Step 3: Coding

Omitted. Interested readers can finish it on their own.

Think and Discuss Is the algorithm described in method 1 efficient?

Discussion: This method that searches for a record one-by-one from head to tail in a list is called sequential search.

Apparently, in a sequential search, if the record being searched is at the beginning of the list, then we need relatively fewer numbers of comparisons. If the record being searched is at the end of the table, we need more numbers of comparisons. Especially when the data item to be searched is exactly the first item in the list, then the search succeeds with only one comparison. But when the data item to be searched is exactly the last item in the list, then every item in the list will be compared with. When the list is huge, sequential search costs a lot of time. This might be feasible for a list containing only entries for a company or a university, but is impractical for a city with tens of thousands of phone numbers. Since the sequential search costs a lot of time when the list is huge, we design the second method instead.

Method 2 Ordered structure, binary search

To improve the search efficiency, we can reorganize the record table of phone numbers, and arrange the data elements according to the order of the surname of clients.

Objects involved in the problem	Each customer and the corresponding data items
The relations between the objects	Data elements listed in order

Fig. 1.6: Example 1.2 model parameters 2.

Step 1: Build the model. The content is shown in Fig. 1.6.

Step 2: Design

1. Data storage: store the data elements from Fig. 1.4 "Phone number record table" orderly into the array, according to the order of clients' surnames. See Table 1.3.

2. Algorithm design: use binary search to find "customer name" data item. If it is found, return the corresponding "phone number" data item. If it is not found, return the preagreed value.

Step 3: Coding

Omitted.

Table 1.3: Ordered structure of phone number registration table.

Customer name	Telephone number	ID number	Address
Li 1	188*****	6101131976***	***
Li 2	152*****	6101131981***	***
Wang 1	139*****	6101131990***	***
Wang 2	138*****	6101131986***	***
Li 1	138*****	6101131980***	***
Zhang 2	139*****	6101131972***	***
. . .	. . .	. . .	. . .

Knowledge ABC Binary search algorithm

Binary search requires the list to be searched to be ordered, that is, the nodes in the list are ordered according to the main keyword.

Suppose the elements are stored in ascending order, then the design of the algorithm is as follows:

Compare the main keyword of the data item in the middle of the list with the keyword being searched. If the two are equal, then the search is successful; otherwise divide the list into two sublists from the middle of the list. If the keyword of the data item in the middle of the list is larger than the keyword being searched, then we search the first sublist, otherwise we search the second sublist. Repeat the above process. If we find the data item matching the condition specified, then the search succeeds. On the contrary, if no sublists exist anymore, then the search fails.

Think and Discuss What are the pros and cons of the algorithm in method 2?

Discussion: The pros of binary search are relatively few numbers of comparisons, fast speed of search and good average performance. Its drawback is that it requires the list to be queried to be ordered, thus making it hard to insert or delete. Therefore, binary search is more suitable to ordered lists that rarely change but are frequently searched. In order to let the algorithm apply to situations with huge amounts of data, we designed the third method.

Method 3 Index structure, layered search

Step 1: Build the model

In the phone number record book we listed all clients with the same surname together, and built another index table on surname, as shown in Fig. 1.7. Our analysis of the objects of the problem and the related connections is shown in Fig. 1.8.

Data list

Client name	Telephone	ID Number	Address
Li 1	188*****	6101131976***	0x2000
Li 2	152*****	6101131981***	***
...	......		
Zhang 1	138*****	6101131980***	0x4000
Zhang 2	139*****	6101131972***	***
...	......		
Wang 1	139*****	6101131990***	0x6000
Wang 2	138*****	6101131986***	***
...	......		

Index list

Surname	Address	Quantity
Li	0x2000	***
Zhang	0x4000	***
Wang	0x6000	***
...	......	

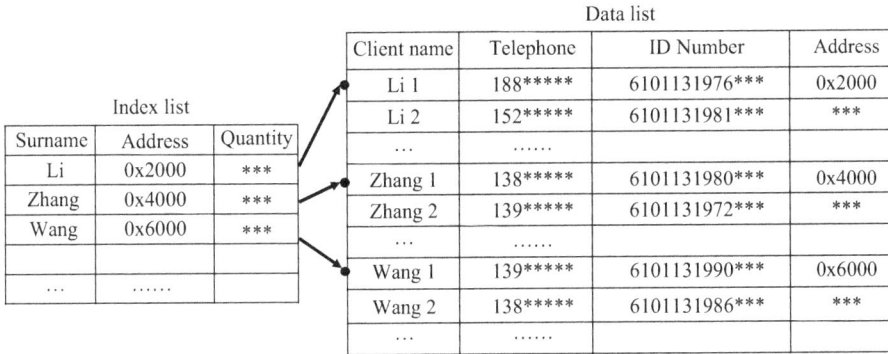

Fig. 1.7: Index structure of the telephone number registration table.

Objects involved in the problem	Index table	Customer surname & number correspond to the first address of the same surname in the data table
	Data table	Each customer and the corresponding data item
Relations between objects	Index table	Data elements listed in order
	Data table	Data elements listed sequentially or in order

Fig. 1.8: Example 1.2 model parameter 3.

Step 2: Design
1. Data storage: store the index table in Fig. 1.7 and the data table, respectively, using the corresponding data arrays.
2. Algorithm design: corresponding to such an index structure, the search process is to first search for the corresponding surname in the index table, and then search for the name in the data table according to the address and number in the index table. In this way, we don't need to search for names with other surnames, when searching for the data table. Therefore, the search algorithm built on this new structure is more efficient.

Think and Discuss In the search problem for phone numbers, what kind of impact does the structure of the table have on the efficiency of the algorithm?
Discussion: From the above three methods, we can tell that the efficiency of the search algorithm depends on the structure as well as on the storage method of the table. More detailed analysis on the search efficiency of index structures can be seen at the chapter "index and search techniques."

! To generalize, when processing data, we can organize data into different forms according to the computations required by the functionalities, in order to facilitate such computations, and thus improve the efficiency of data processing.

Conclusion
Both the organization method and storage method of data will impact the algorithm's efficiency.
Example 1.3 Example of nonnumerical problem 2
Problem of management of traffic like at crossroads.

At crossroads, how many colors of traffic light must be set up to maintain normal traffic order?

Solution:
Analysis: In everyday lives, we are familiar with the traffic lights at crossroads. The solution to the problem is that it is enough to have red and green, two colors. However, if we ask the computer to solve this problem, it won't be easy. The first problem to solve is how to store the information in the question into the computer. On this basis, we can then design algorithms to find a solution.

Step 1: Construct the model
        Suppose the crossroads are, respectively, ABCD, as shown in Fig. 1.9. The objects involved in the problem and the relations between the objects are shown in Fig. 1.10.

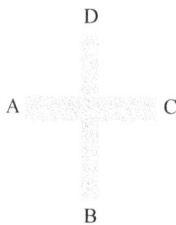

Fig. 1.9: Illustration of crossroads.

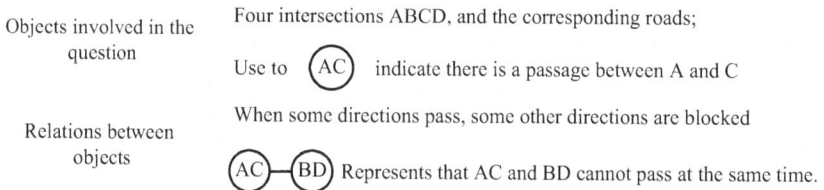

| Objects involved in the question | Four intersections ABCD, and the corresponding roads;
Use to (AC) indicate there is a passage between A and C |
| Relations between objects | When some directions pass, some other directions are blocked
(AC)—(BD) Represents that AC and BD cannot pass at the same time. |

Fig. 1.10: Example 1.3 model parameters.

Suppose the rule for turning left is the same as the rule for going straight, and turning right is permitted all the time, then, based on the objects given by the model and the relations between the objects, we can draw a figure as shown in Fig. 1.11, where each circle represents a data element.

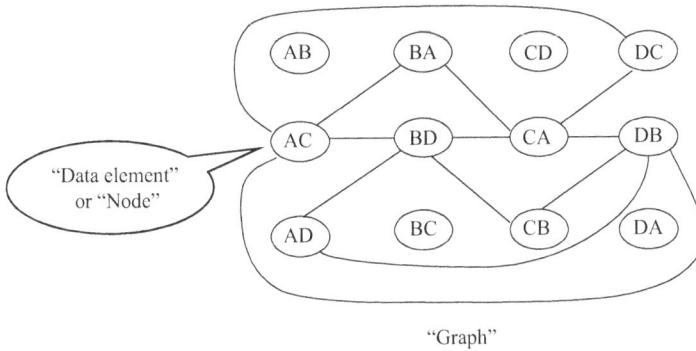

Fig. 1.11: The graphical representation of the crossroad problem.

Think and Discuss Why are the data elements in this example very different in format compared with the data elements in Example 1.2?
Discussion: Although the data elements here are very different in form compared with the data elements in Example 1.2, if we look at their essence, they are both basic units of data of the problems to be dealt with. They are a refinement and abstraction of the problem.

Step 2: Design
Data storage: how to store the information in Fig. 1.11 into the machine. This information can be referred to in the chapter "Graph."
Functionality of the algorithm: color the circles in the graph. The two circles at two ends of the same line segment should have different colors, and the number of colors should be minimized.
According to the requirements of the algorithm, we can obtain the results as shown in Fig. 1.12.

Step 3: Coding
Source codes for similar types of problems will be given in the chapter "Graph."

Example 1.4: Example of nonnumerical problem 3
The representation and management of the structure of computer file system.

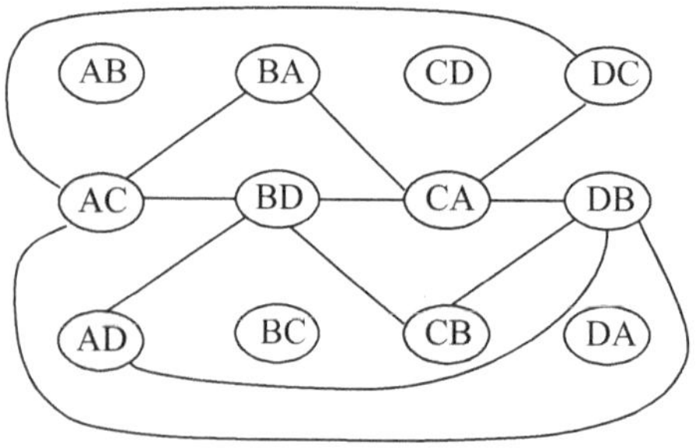

Fig. 1.12: The result of crossroads problem.

The management of files in the computer is achieved via the format of multi-level directory. For example, the file system structure of UNIX file system is as shown in Fig. 1.13. In this format, if we abstract each file directory into a data element or node, then the file directory structure is like a tree. The directory root is the root of the tree. The management of and operation on file directory include lookup, insertion and deletion.

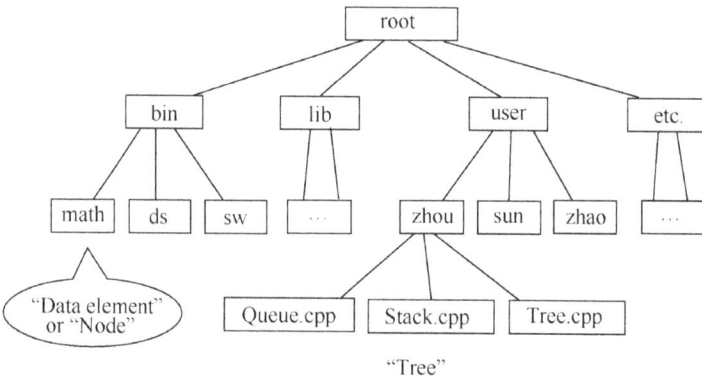

Fig. 1.13: The file system structure of UNIX.

Step 1: Construct the model. See Table 1.4.
Step 2: Design
　　　　Data storage: refer to the chapter "Tree."
　　　　Functionality of the algorithm: the lookup, insertion, deletion and so on of file directory nodes.
Step 3: Coding
　　　　Omitted. Implementation of relevant operations will be introduced in the chapter "Tree."

Table 1.4: Example 1.4 model parameters.

Objects involved in the problem	Each file directory node
Relations between the objects	Except for the root node, each node has a previous-level node

1.3 The introduction of data structures

As we can see from the previous examples, the models for structures such as list, tree and graph in nonnumeric problems cannot be described using formulas. Therefore, the key to solving such problems is no longer analyzing mathematics and calculation methods. It instead requires finding the data to be processed in the problem as well as the relations, organizational forms, methods of storage, methods of representation, and then designing the models appropriate for computers to work on. Only then the problems can be effectively solved.

Since the organizational form and methods of representation are directly related to the processing efficiency of the program on data, and system programs as well as many applications are large scale and complex in structure, and mainly process nonnumeric data, it is really hard to design efficient and reliable programs only relying on the experience and skills of coders. Therefore, there is a need for systematic studies of the objects processed by computer programs. Studies on the characteristics of nonnumeric data and how to represent and implement the operations on them – data structures – have then become a specific research field in computer science.

> **Knowledge ABC** The relation between mathematics, algorithms and data structures
>
> When we directly face and solve the problems from the perspective of mathematics and machines, data structures and algorithms are born. Algorithm and data structures are cross-disciplinary subjects across three subjects: mathematics, computer software and computer hardware. Algorithm can be interpreted as "the concrete solutions to general programming problems."
>
> Actually, data structures and algorithm solves the most limited, most fundamental problems in the whole programming process. It only solves limited problems such as the organization of memory and the support of operations on data stored in such memory (e.g., sorting and lookup).
>
> As an important branch of computer science, the study of data structures and algorithm involves constructing the two building blocks of problem-solving process of computers: data structures describe the information in practical problems and its inherent relations; algorithms describe solutions to problems.

Normally, data structures are connected and organized according to the inherent logic of data elements. The description of the logic relation between data elements is called the logical structure of data. Data must be stored on the computer; the storage structure of data is the form of implementation of data structure and is their internal representation in the computer. Besides, the discussion about a data structure is only meaningful when the operations on this type of data are also discussed at the same time. A logical data structure can have multiple storage structures. Based on different storage structures, the efficiency of data processing can vary a lot.

In many types of program design, the choice of data structure is a basic factor to consider. The experience of constructing various large-scale systems shows that the difficulty of system implementation as well as the quality of system construction both depend on whether good data structures are chosen. In many cases, after the data structure is ascertained, the algorithm will be easy to obtain. Sometimes it will also be the reverse: based on specific algorithms, we select the corresponding data structures. No matter which is the case, it is very important to choose the appropriate data structures.

This book only introduces classical data structures.

1.4 Basic concepts of data structures

1.4.1 Basic terminologies of data structures

Via the previous example about numeric and nonnumeric data processing, we already have an abstract understanding of the concept of data structures. The following are the related terminologies:

1.4.1.1 Data
In computer science, data represents the entirety of the symbols that can be input to the computer and processed by computer programs. They are distinguished by their ability to be recognized, processed and stored by the computer.

1.4.1.2 Data element
This is the basic unit of data, which is also called "element" or "node." It is usually considered as a whole in computer programs for processing. One element can include multiple data items.

1.4.1.3 Data item
Data item is the smallest unit with independent meaning. It is the most basic, indivisible data unit.

1.4.1.4 Data structure
It is composed of a certain data object and the relation between all the data elements in this object.

Data structure includes three key elements: the logical structure of data, the storage structure of data and operations on data.

1.4.2 The three key elements of data structures

The three key elements of data structure are, respectively, the logical structure, storage structure and operations on the data, as shown in Fig. 1.14.

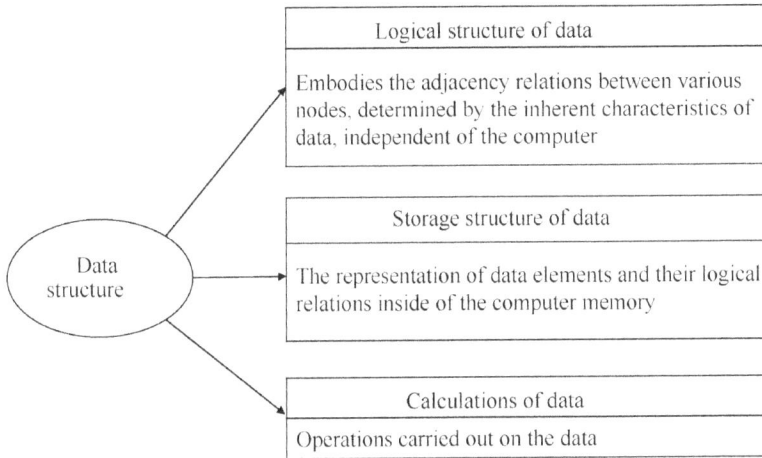

Fig. 1.14: The three key elements of data structure.

1.4.2.1 Logical structure

The logical structure of data reflects our explanation about the meaning of "data." It can be represented by a group of data and the relation between these data. The logical relation of data is a data model abstracted from concrete problems, is irrelevant to the form and content of the data element itself and is also irrelevant to the way the data is stored. The logical structure of data can be divided into the following types (see Fig. 1.15).

The data elements in a set do not have other relations aside from being in the same set and having the same type.

The various data members in the linear structure have a linear relation among themselves, that is, one can perform pairwise comparison on any pair of nodes (except for the foremost and the last element, every node has an immediate predecessor node and an immediate successor node). The nodes in the linear structure have a one-to-one correspondence, that is, except for the first and the last data element, all other data elements are connected. Seeing intuitively from the figure, all nodes are connected by one straight line. This structure is most widely applied in program design.

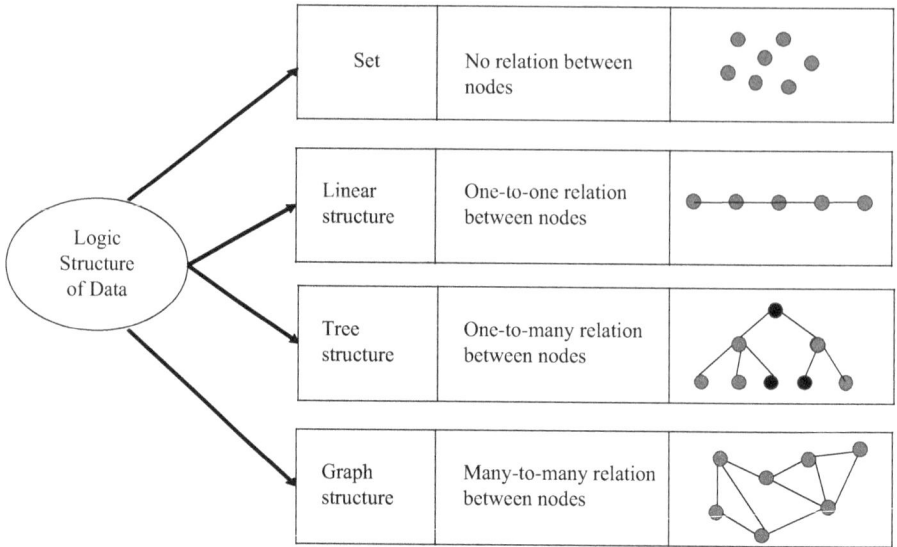

Fig. 1.15: The classification of logical structure of data.

In tree-like structures, the relation between nodes is one to many. Except for the root node, each node only has one predecessor node, but can have many successor nodes. Tree-like structures are abbreviated as tree structures, or leveled structures. Its relation is called leveled relation, or "parent–child" relation.

In graph-like structure or network-like structure, the relation between nodes is many to many.

Both tree-like structure and graph structure are nonlinear structures. The predecessor or successor of a node might number more than one.

Mathematically speaking, the basic difference between linear structure and tree-like structure is "whether each node only has one direct successor." The difference between tree-like structure and graph structure is "whether each node only belongs to one direct predecessor."

1.4.2.2 The storage structure of data

The storage structure of data is also called the physical structure. It is the way of representation in the computer of data and their logical structure. It refers to how data should be stored in the computer, and in essence it refers to the allocation of memory units. In actual implementations, it is described by the data types of programming languages.

Think and Discuss When storing data, what should be stored? How?

Discussion: To store data, first, one not only has to store the values of the data themselves, but also the relations between data. Only then can one completely store all the information regarding the relevant problem. The purpose of preserving interdata relations is so that one can find relevant elements through such relations. Second, the purpose of storing data in the computer is to process them. If we store them into the machine but can't find them when we want to use them, the storage doesn't make any sense. The meaning of "finding" here, on the one hand, refers to finding the data element needed, and on the other hand refers to finding the data elements related to it. Therefore, the design of data storage structures should be based on the following two principles:

(a) Data storage principle A: store the values and store the relations

(b) Data storage principle B: be able to store data and be able to retrieve them.

There are four common data storage methods currently (see Fig. 1.16).

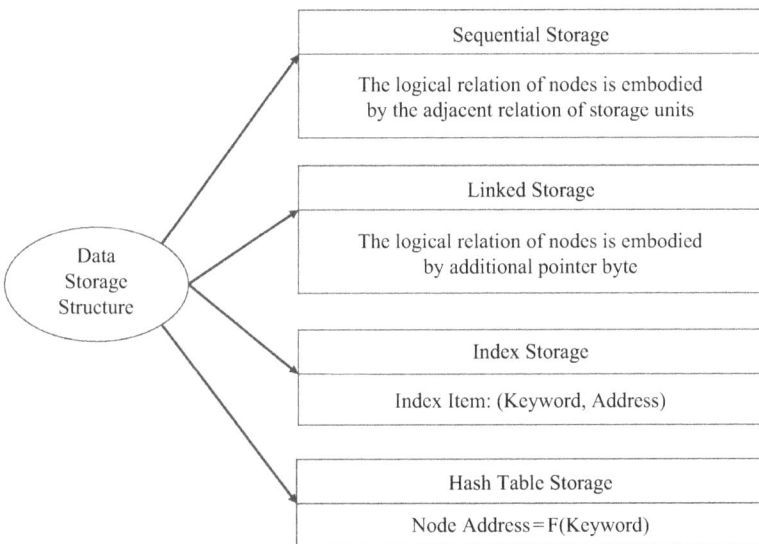

Fig. 1.16: Classification of storage structure of data.

1. Sequential storage structure
    Use a group of contiguous storage units to store data elements sequentially. The logical relations between data elements are embodied by the adjacent locations of elements. The features of sequential storage structure are as follows:
    – Store data elements consecutively.
    – If the logical structure of data is also sequential (linear), then the logical structure is completely unified with the storage structure. Continuously stored data elements can be easily found in the memory.

2. Linked storage structure
   Add a pointer field in each data element to record the logical relations between data elements. The features of linked storage structure are as follows:
   - The elements are not necessarily continuously stored in the memory.
   - Pointers are added within the elements, through which logically adjacent data elements can be physically located.

3. Index storage structure
   Index storage method is to construct an additional index table when storing node information. Each item in the index table is called an index item. The common form for an index item is: (keyword, address).
   Through the index table, one can find the location of the corresponding data element.

4. Hash table storage structure
   The hash table storage structure uses the keyword of the node as the variable. The storage address of the node is calculated directly via a function relation F:

$$\text{Node address} = F(\text{keyword})$$

The storage structure of data is also called the physical structure. It is the representation of the logical structure of data within the computer. The storage structure of data depends on the programming language, and is described using the "data types" in the language. Data type refers to the type of data able to be selected by variables in high-level languages.

Think and Discuss

1. Why set different data types?
Discussion: Data type is divided according to the characteristics, representation forms, size of memory space occupied and structural features. Every data structure has a unique name, which limits the valid range of data.
   Different data occupy different space in the memory and require different ways of operation. Differentiating data based on the concept of data type, and adopting the appropriate methods when using the data, one can make sure that both the data storage and operation are done in the optimal way. It avoids wasting space and improves runtime efficiency of code.

2. Why can't the logical structure and storage structure of data be completely unified?
Discussion: The logical structure of data is problem oriented and reflects the internal way of composition of data. The logical structure of data is independent from the computer. The implementation of the storage structure of data must be described by the data types in programming languages, thus depends on specific programming languages. It is concretely implemented in a computer-oriented manner.
   The four basic storage methods mentioned above can either be used independently or together, to store and reflect data structures.

Employing different storage methods to the same logical structure, one might obtain different storage structures. The choice about using which storage structure to represent the corresponding logical structure depends on specific needs. The considerations are mainly about ease of operation and efficiency of algorithms.

1.4.2.3 Operation on data

There are two aspects of meaning to operation on data: the definition of operation and the implementation of operation; see Fig. 1.17.

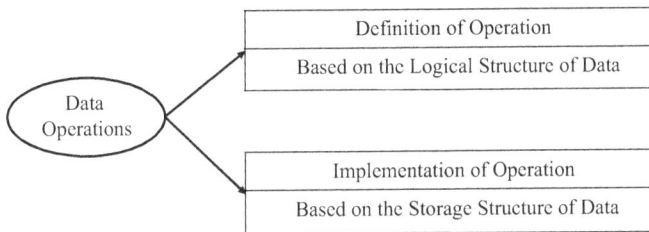

Fig. 1.17: Operations on data.

The definition of operation depends on the logical structure of data. After one knows the data and relations between data in the problem, they can proceed to design the corresponding data processing methods. The following are the common operations:
– Initialization: set the initial value for the data structure, or apply for storage space.
– Null check: detect whether the storage space is at a state without a valid value.
– Length querying: count the number of elements.
– Searching: detect whether the designated element is included.
– Iteration: visit all elements according to a certain order. Each element should only be visited once.
– Value querying: get the value of the designated element.
– Value setting: set the value of the designated element.
– Insertion: add the designated element.
– Deletion: remove the designated element.

For example, in Example 1.2 (phone number querying), after we get the registration list of customer phone numbers, we can perform operations such as customer information querying, new customer information insertion, customer information updating and so on. However. the concrete implementation methods of these operations are closely related to the storage form of the registration list. Different storage methods will necessitate different operation methods. This is why we say the implementation of operations on data is based on the storage structure of data.

1.5 How to design algorithms

The previously mentioned analysis of logical structure and design of storage structure among the three basic elements of data structures solve the analysis and storage of information in the problem to be dealt with. That is to say, we have converted the information to process from concrete problem to something that the computer can receive and understand. The upcoming work is to process the data, that is, operate on the data, in order to fulfill the functionalities required by the problem. The operation on the data is described by algorithms.

Since the logical structure and storage structure of data are not unique, the design ideas and skills of algorithms are also not unique. Therefore, algorithms addressing the same problem are also not unique.

The aim of learning the course data structures is to learn how to choose the appropriate logical structure and storage structure for the data to be processed, and then design satisfactory algorithms.

Discussions on algorithms are an important part of the data structure course.

1.5.1 The definition of algorithm and representation methods

1.5.1.1 Algorithm
There must be some specific steps to doing anything. Such steps are ordered, and each of them is essential. Therefore, broadly speaking, algorithm is the steps and methods toward solving problems. In program design, algorithm refers to the process by which computer solves problems. It requires accurate and complete descriptions of the solutions.

Specifically, algorithm is a set of clearly defined operation sequence used to solve a particular problem in finite steps. It can obtain required output from well-formatted input in finite time.

1.5.1.2 Features of algorithms
1. Finiteness: an algorithm must be guaranteed to end after executing finite steps. It cannot be infinite.
2. Decidability: each instruction in the algorithm must have some clear meaning, and cannot be unclear or ambiguous.
3. Feasibility: each operation step must be finished in a limited time.
4. Input: an algorithm can have multiple inputs, one input or no inputs.
5. Output: an algorithm can have one or multiple outputs. An algorithm without output has no practical meaning.

1.5.1.3 Representation of algorithm

We can use various forms to describe algorithms. Common forms include natural language, flow chart, N-S chart, pseudocode and programming language.

Normally speaking, the appropriate language to describe language is pseudocode, between natural language and programming language. Its control structure is similar to programming languages like Pascal and C, but we can use any expressive description to make the expression clearer and more concise, and avoid focusing on certain details of specific programming languages. This makes the algorithm more adaptable to different programming languages. This book uses pseudocode to describe algorithms.

1.5.1.4 Key elements to describing algorithms

See Section 1.5.3.

1.5.2 The relation between algorithm design and function design

In the ensuing algorithm implementation, concrete programming will be involved. The following is a recap of relevant important concepts.

1.5.2.1 Concepts related to function

Functions in C appear in three forms: declaration, definition and invocation. The corresponding examples are shown in Fig. 1.18.

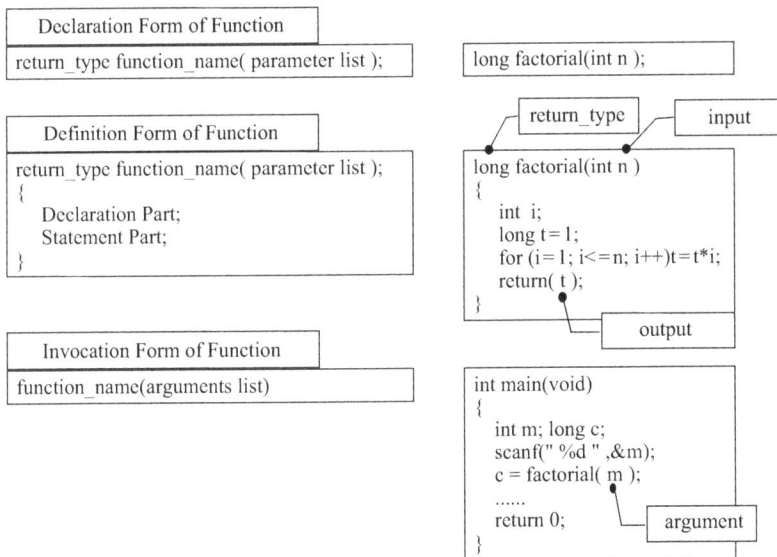

Fig. 1.18: Three forms of functions and concrete examples.

The declaration of function is similar to the declaration of variable. The parameters in function declaration are allowed to have types while ignoring names.

The definition of function includes three key elements of function design.

1. Functionality description: try the best to use one word to describe the functionality of the function, and use it as the name of the function.
2. Input: list qualitative descriptions of all the information to be provided to the function for processing. They determine the content of the parameter list. In the parameter list, the declaration form of the variable must be written.
3. Output: the type of output information decides the type of the function, that is, return type.

During the concrete execution of a function, corresponding operations can only be performed with the actual data to operate on. Therefore, when invoking functions the actual arguments must be listed in the reference form of variable. The forms for arguments and parameters in C language are shown in Fig. 1.19.

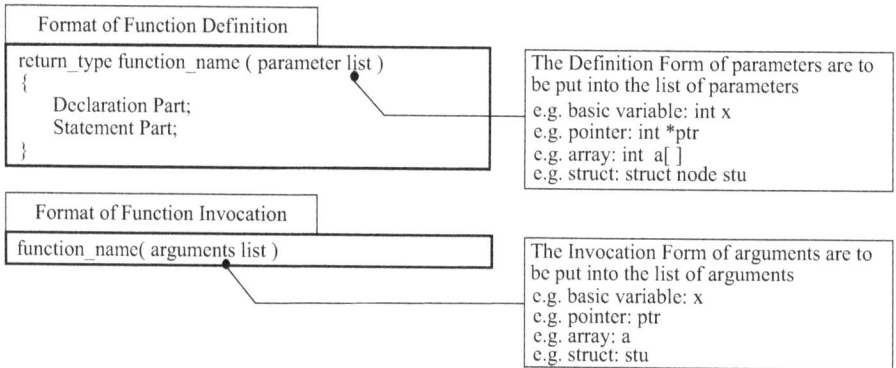

Format of Function Definition

return_type function_name (parameter list)
{
    Declaration Part;
    Statement Part;
}

The Definition Form of parameters are to be put into the list of parameters e.g. basic variable: int x e.g. pointer: int *ptr e.g. array: int a[ ] e.g. struct: struct node stu

Format of Function Invocation

function_name(arguments list)

The Invocation Form of arguments are to be put into the list of arguments e.g. basic variable: x e.g. pointer: ptr e.g. array: a e.g. struct: stu

Fig. 1.19: The forms of arguments and parameters in a C function.

1.5.2.2 The relation between algorithm design and function design

The implementation of algorithms is fulfilled through functions. Then which key elements of function are algorithms related to?

From the three key elements of functions we know that the function name should be the description of the functionality of the algorithm. The information to process for a function is received via its parameters, thus the types and contents of input information of the algorithm determine the number of types of parameters. The output of a function is achieved through return value. The type of the return value is the type of the function. Thus, the output information required by the algorithm determines the type of the function. Therefore, the name of the function and input/output interfaces are determined by the three key elements, namely functionality, input and output of the algorithm, as shown in Fig. 1.20. The function type, function name and parameters are also key elements constituting function header. They determine the framework structure of the function.

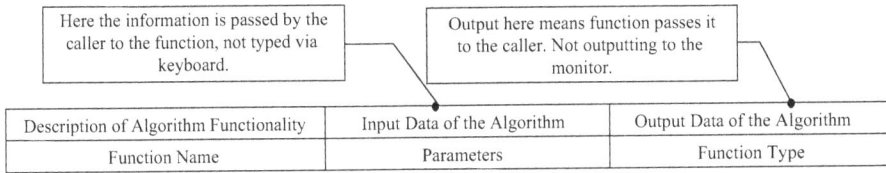

Here the information is passed by the caller to the function, not typed via keyboard.		Output here means function passes it to the caller. Not outputting to the monitor.	
Description of Algorithm Functionality	Input Data of the Algorithm	Output Data of the Algorithm
Function Name	Parameters	Function Type

Fig. 1.20: Key elements of algorithms and function structure.

1.5.3 Software design method

From the perspective of software engineering, to solve a problem using computer, besides the descriptions of problem-solving steps, related design and processing are also needed. The specific methods and their orders are as follows.

1.5.3.1 Test case design
According to the functionality requirement of the problem and according to the normal case, boundary case or exceptional/illegal case and others of the input data and design test cases.

1.5.3.2 Description of data structure
Design the storage structure, which includes the information and relations between information in the problem. We'll use data types in C language to describe them in this book.

1.5.3.3 Function interface and function structure design
According to the functionality, input and output of the problem, correspondingly establish the function type, parameters and return value of the function.

Note: In this book, when the input and output of the function refer to the same content, the return information of the function is expressed via reference passing, instead of return. When expressing this in the function framework, we'll add parentheses around such input parameter to indicate that the caller function will receive the calculation result of the callee function.

1.5.3.4 Pseudocode description of the algorithm
Using top-down, gradual refinement method, describe the steps to solving the problem.

1.5.3.5 Program implementation

Design code implementation according to the detailed pseudocode. Get the test results according to the test cases when necessary.

1.5.3.6 Algorithm efficiency analysis

Analyze the time complexity and space complexity of the algorithm. (Methods for algorithm efficiency analysis will be introduced in Section 1.7.)

1.5.4 General steps of algorithm design

To let computers do tasks designated by men, we have to first design an algorithm which specifies how to finish the designated task. The algorithm is a precise description of the process of problem solving. Different problems require different methods to solve. There might also be multiple algorithms to choose for the same problem. Although people have already designed a lot of classical algorithms which we can refer to, for example, iteration, exhaustive search, recurrence, recursion, greedy algorithms, backtracing algorithms, divide-and-conquer and dynamic programming, algorithm design is still a very difficult task. The difficulty lies in that algorithm design is different from normal mathematics/physics problems seen in introductory textbooks, which have formulas to be applied after establishing what the problem is. Then, is there any patterns in algorithm design? From the perspective that algorithm is steps for data processing, we can generalize the generic steps for algorithm design as follows:

- Set the initial conditions of the algorithm.
- Ascertain the conditions for the algorithm to end.
- Give the flow of algorithmic processing according to the common patterns of the problem.
- Consider the processing of boundary values or special values.
- Consider abnormal situations.

What are the common patterns of problems in algorithm design? The following are some examples.

Example 1.5: Practical example of algorithm design – get the value of n!

Solution: According to the normal steps of algorithm design, based on the mathematical definition of n!, for the general case of n!, we can first choose a not-so-large value which is also not a special value. For example, $n = 5$, to design the implementation of the algorithm.

For boundary values, special values, and abnormal cases, we can test those values after the general-case algorithm implementation in order to complete the algorithm.

1 Test case design

See Fig. 1.21.

Case	Test data	Expected result
Normal case of the problem	$n > 1$	Value obtained via the normal definition of $n!$
Boundary value or special value	$n = 0, n = 1$	Value obtained via the boundary definition of $n!$
Abnormal case	$n < 0$	Give error message

Fig. 1.21: Test case for $n!$ function.

2 Interface functionality descriptions

The interface functionality descriptions of the function are shown in Table 1.5.

Table 1.5: Interface and functionality description of $n!$ function.

Functionality description	Input information	Output information	
Obtain $n!$ factorial	int n	Long type	Abnormal: −1
			Normal: Result of $n!$

Please note that the "output" here refers to the function returning back to the caller, not to the monitor.

3 Algorithm description

Let S be the product of factorial, T be the number being operated upon, the pseudo-code is shown in Table 1.6.

Table 1.6: Pseudocode description of $n!$.

Top-level pseudocode description	First-level elaboration	Second-level elaboration
Input n	Input n	Input n
Obtain $n!$	Initialize product $S = 1$, multiplier $T = 1$	$S = 1, T = 1$
	Start putting result into the product S starting from 1 * 2. The multiplier is added by 1 each time.	Do $S = S*T$ Increase T by 1
	Stops when $T > n$	Until $(T > n)$
Output result	Output result S	Output: S

The pseudocode description should have the following two key features:

1. Concise and clear
   Describe the algorithm steps according to the structural features of the program (sequential, looping, branching). Pay attention to the indentation of the format. For example, in a while loop, the range of effect for while should be embodied by the indentation of the format.
2. Complete
   - Initial stage of the algorithm
   Initialization: if there's some initial value, then initialize it.
   Input: specify the input information at the beginning of the algorithm (can be omitted).
   - Algorithm processing stage
     If there are loops, then the three key elements of looping (initial condition, running condition, looping increment) should be complete.
   - Algorithm termination stage
     At the termination of the algorithm, specify the output information.

4 Code implementation

```
/*====================================
Functionality of function: Calculate n!
Function input: Integer n
Function output: Value of n!
=================================*/
long factorial(int n)
{
        int t;
        long s=1;
        if (n<0) return (-1);
        for ( t=1; t<=n; t++)
        {
            s=s*t;
        }
        return(s);
}
```

5 Test result

According to the various scenarios listed by the test cases, set up the corresponding data as input and record the results of the program execution to be compared with the preset results. If they are identical, the tests have passed. If they are different, then there are some problems with the program. We need to debug, find out the bug and finally obtain the correct results. The test results are given in Table 1.7.

Table 1.7: Test results.

		Normal case		Boundary value	Abnormal value
Test values	5	10	0	1	−1
Test results	120	3,628,800	1	1	−1

1.6 How to evaluate algorithms

There might be multiple algorithms to solve the same problem. Then there will be comparison and likely measures of good and bad. From which aspects should we analyze and evaluate algorithms? Is there any uniform evaluation standards and analysis methods? Only after the evaluation standard is unified can we have an objective ground to compare them with.

Let us first look at the design requirements for algorithms.

1.6.1 The design requirements of algorithms

One should consider the following several aspects when designing a good algorithm. They can also be said to be the evaluation standards for algorithms.

1.6.1.1 Correctness

Algorithms should satisfy the functionalities required by the concrete problem. This is the basic goal of algorithm design. The meaning of "correct" differs a lot in common usages. In general, the following are the four layers of correctness for a program:
1. The program contains no syntax errors.
2. The program can return results that satisfy the functionality requirement of the algorithm for several sets of inputs.
3. The program can return results that satisfy the functionality requirement of the algorithm for several sets of inputs that are carefully selected, representative and intentionally demanding.
4. The program can return results that satisfy the functionality requirement of the algorithm for all valid inputs.

Normally the correctness as described in layer 3 is used to judge whether a program is to be accepted.

1.6.1.2 Readability

Ensuring that the algorithm is correct, the readability of the algorithm should be put to the first place, that is, the programming efficiency is the most important. This is crucial nowadays, when many large-scale software need multiple persons to

collaborate on. Also, obscure and difficult-to-understand programs easily hide errors and are hard to debug.

1.6.1.3 Robustness

Robustness refers to the ability of the algorithm to react to and process unreasonable data inputs. It is also called error tolerance. A good algorithm should be able
to identify erroneous input data and adequately process and react to them.

Designing sensible and effective test cases so that program errors are discov-
ered as many as possible at the software testing stage is an effective method to ensure the robustness of the algorithm.

1.6.1.4 Efficiency

To be efficient means the algorithm runs at high efficiency. The following are the
two aspects to be inspected:

1. Efficient in time. The time efficiency of an algorithm refers to the execution
   time of the algorithm. An algorithm with relatively short execution time is
   called a time-efficiency algorithm.
2. Efficient storage space usage. The storage space of an algorithm refers to the
   maximum storage space needed by an algorithm during its execution. It mainly
   concerns the auxiliary storage space needed during execution. Algorithms that
   need fewer storage spaces are called memory-efficient algorithms.

Conventional researches and experiences have indicated that for most problems, it
is much easier to gain grounds on speed instead of space. Therefore, we focus the
discussions mainly on the time efficiency of algorithms.

There might be trade-offs between time and space efficiency in certain algorithms.

1.6.2 Measurement methods of algorithm efficiency

After we can ascertain that an algorithm is correct for a certain problem, we can then
look at its evaluation. What is the standard for algorithm evaluation? From a practical
perspective, if we have to run the algorithm for a few weeks in order to solve a problem, then this algorithm has hardly any practical use. Similarly, an algorithm that
needs 1 GB of memory will be hard to run in many machines nowadays. Both the time
and space usage are resources of the machine. Therefore, we can say that the evaluation of algorithm efficiency is based on how much resources of the machine it uses. We
can use the following methods to directly or indirectly analyze algorithm efficiency.

1.6.2.1 The after-execution analysis of algorithm performance

When we mention the execution efficiency of an algorithm, we'll naturally think of
using actual time units such as "seconds," "milliseconds," because they are directly

visible to the tester of the algorithm. The after-execution analysis of algorithm performance is also called afterward testing of the algorithm. It evaluates the efficiency of the algorithm using the actual time used to run the program.

In C language, the method of after-execution analysis can be realized by inserting timing functions time() or clock(), to measure the actual time spent by the algorithm to finish a certain functionality. The template is as follows:

```
#include <time.h>
//The unit of time for time() is normally seconds; the unit of time for clock()
is the timing unit of the CPU clock, which is normally 1 millisecond
clock_t start, stop;          // clock_t is defined as long type in time
header file
time (&start);                //Or start = clock();
/***************************************************
Here should be the functions to test the execution time
***************************************************/
time (&stop);                 // Or stop = clock();
long runTime = stop - start;
printf (" %ld\n ", runTime);
```

When an algorithm is converted into program and executed on the computer, the time needed for its execution is dependent on the following factors:

1. The speed of the hardware. The faster the speed of the CPU and read/write operations, the shorter the execution time of the program.
2. The programming language used. Normally, if the programming language is more high level, the execution efficiency will be lower. For example, assembly language usually has a higher execution efficiency than high-level programming languages.
3. The quality of the target code generated by the compiler. For compilers with better optimizations, the generated programs will be higher quality.
4. The scale of the problem. Apparently, a large-scale problem will normally take more time to solve than a small-scale problem.
5. The strategy selected by the algorithm. For the same problem, there might be different algorithms to solve.

Apparently, the first three elements are related to software/hardware environment and are unrelated to the design of the algorithm itself. The variations of these factors will make the execution time of the program under different execution environments incomparable. That is to say, the same program will have different execution times under different hardware/software environments. Therefore, it is usually inappropriate to use the absolute execution time of the program to determine the efficiency of the algorithm. It becomes very meaningful to find a generic, machine-independent method to describe algorithm efficiency.

1.6.2.2 The pre-execution analysis of algorithm efficiency

This refers to static theoretical analysis on the execution efficiency of the algorithm itself, which would provide feature functions about the time and space efficiency of the algorithm. It has no direct relation with the software/hardware of one particular computer.

The work involved in the pre-execution of algorithm efficiency analysis includes the following:

1. The time efficiency analysis of the algorithm – find out the factors related to the execution time of the algorithm and its feature function. Evaluate the algorithm from a time-efficiency perspective.
2. The space efficiency analysis of the algorithm – find out the feature function on the auxiliary memory space needed by the execution of the algorithm. Evaluate the algorithm from a space efficiency perspective.

1.7 The pre-execution analysis methods of algorithm efficiency

The pre-execution analysis refers to estimating the resources needed by an algorithm. The resources here refer to computation time of the machine, memory space and so on.

Since the computation time and memory space of the computer are limited resources, good algorithms must also pay attention to efficiency while ensuring correct results.

Think and Discuss

1. What are the key factors among the factors related to the execution time of the algorithm?
Discussion: The software/hardware-related factors notwithstanding, there are only two variables: the strategy employed by the algorithm and the size of the problem. We normally relate the size of the problem to the amount of data to be processed, represented with an integer. For example, solving the multiplication of matrices, the rank of the matrices is the size of the problem; searching within a list with n nodes, the number of nodes n is the size of the problem.

2. How to make the analysis of time efficiency independent of the software/hardware system?
Discussion: The time used by an algorithm is likely the sum of the execution time of each individual statement. The execution time of each statement is roughly the number of its execution (frequency) multiplied with the time needed for one execution. Therefore, the time needed by an algorithm is proportional to the number of execution of the statements within the algorithm. The time needed for one execution of a statement depends on the execution speed of the machine instruction and the code quality generated via compilation, which are hard-to-determine factors. We may thus suppose that each statement takes an equal amount of time to execute (unit time). Under such a supposition, we can then simply substitute the execution time of the algorithm with the number of executions (frequency) of basic operations.

In this way, our analysis of time can be independent of the software/hardware systems.

Term Explanation Statement frequency
If the size of the problem is n, the number of times the statements within an algorithm are executed is called statement frequency or time frequency, noted as $T(n)$.

What are the effects of the size of the problem and the problem-solving strategy on the efficiency of the algorithm? What are the relations between them? These are the issues mainly discussed below.

1.7.1 The size of the problem and the strategy of the algorithm

Example 1.6:
Example on the size of the problem and the strategy of the algorithm.

Write numbers 1–100 on cards. First, randomly shuffle them and then sort them in order again. What is the number of searches performed on all cards during the sorting process?

Solution: The size of the problem is $n = 100$. We can use the different strategies listed below for searching.

Strategy 1: Search for cards according to the ordering of the number.

First find 1, then find 2, then find 3 and so on. Then it takes at most 100 times to find 1, at most 99 times to find 2 among the remaining 99 cards and so on. When it reaches number 100 we only need one search.

The highest number of searches possible with this strategy: (100 + 1)*100/2.

When the size of the problem is n, the number of comparisons/searches will be: $T(n) = n^2/2 + n/2$

Strategy 2: Randomly pick cards for sorting.

This method is similar to poker-picking sorting; see Fig. 1.22. For example, 2 is picked, and then 5 is picked. Since 5 is smaller than 2, it is inserted after 2. Then 98 is picked, which is smaller than 5, so it is inserted after 5 and so on. Insert randomly picked cards into an already sorted array according to its value. Sort using this method of insertion, then we need to find each card only once, the total number of searches will be 100 times.

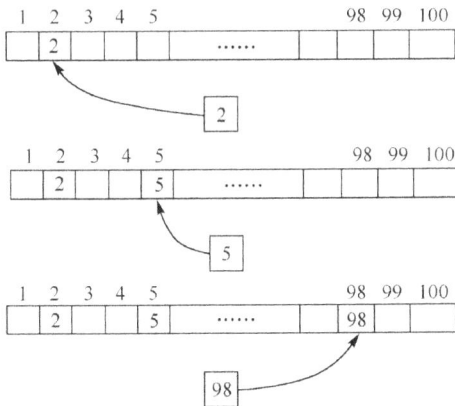

Fig. 1.22: Insertion sort.

When the problem size is n, the number of comparisons/searches: $T(n) = n$.

Think and Discuss

1. Comparing processing 10 numbers using strategy 1 with processing 100 numbers using strategy 2, which is faster?
Discussion: Then obviously method 1 is faster.

2. Can we then say method 1 is faster than method 2?
Discussion: When the size of data being processed is different, we can't reach an objective conclusion by comparing two algorithms.

From the above example, we can see that problem size is usually also an important factor for algorithm efficiency.

Conclusion

Normally, the time needed by an algorithm grows simultaneously with the input size n, as shown in Fig. 1.23.

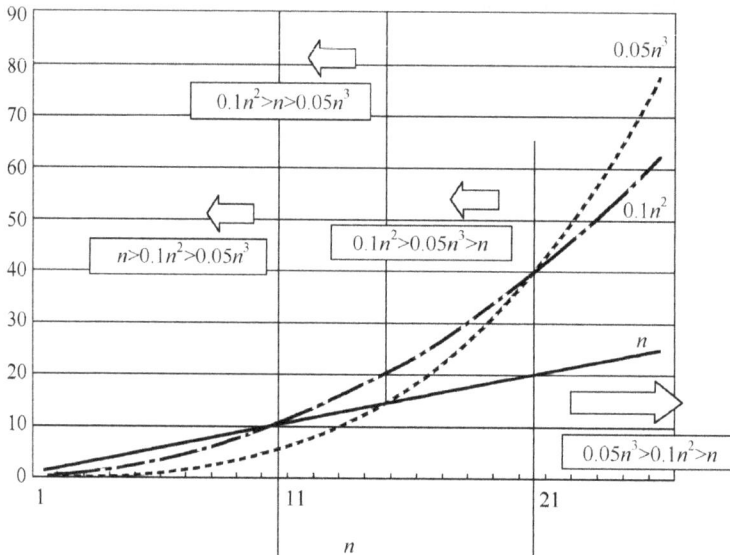

Fig. 1.23: Plot of algorithm efficiency.

1. For the same algorithm, when the amount of input is small, the execution time will be short; when the amount of input is huge, the execution time will be long.
2. For different algorithms, it is possible that in a particular interval of n, algorithm 1 is more efficient than algorithm 2, while the situation is reversed in another interval of n.
3. For different algorithms, when the input size is small, the algorithm efficiencies will be more similar. When the input size grows, the time needed by algorithms usually increases, and the time differences between algorithms will become much more obvious.

1.7.2 The upper and lower bounds of algorithm efficiency

In Example 1.6, the algorithm efficiency of method 1 has a probability component depending on "luck." The following are the three typical scenarios to consider (let the number of cards $n = 100$).

1.7.2.1 Best case
If the 100 cards are exactly sorted, then method 1 is the same as method 2, with the number of required lookups being:

$$T(n) = n = 100$$

1.7.2.2 Worst case
Each time it is needed to perform the most number of lookups in the remaining cards to find the needed card. Then, the most number of lookups would be:

$$T(n) = (n+1) \times n/2 = 5,050$$

1.7.2.3 Average case
First, consider the average number of lookups to find a designated card i among n cards, ASL_n (average search length). Let P_i be the possibility of finding the ith record in the list and C_i be the number of cards already compared before finding this record. Then, the average number of lookups:

$$ASL = \sum_{i=1}^{n} P_i C_i \tag{1.1}$$

where under equiprobable scenario, $P_i = 1/n (i = 1, 2, \ldots, n)$
From Fig. 1.24, we can get that $C_i + i = n + 1 \therefore C_i = n - i + 1$

Position where lookup begins	1	2	3	...	i	...	$n-1$	n
Number of remaining cards	n				C_i		2	1

Fig. 1.24: Correspondence table between lookup position and number of lookups.

Therefore,

$$ASL_n = \sum_{i=1}^{n} P_i \times (n - i + 1) = \frac{1}{n} \times \frac{(n+1) \times n}{2} = \frac{n+1}{2}$$

Then, the average search length to find a designated card i among $n-1$ cards $ASL_{n-1} = n/2$.

The average number of lookups of finding n designated cards among n cards:

$$ASL_n = \frac{n+1}{2} + \frac{n}{2} + \cdots + \frac{1+1}{2} = \frac{(n+3) \times n}{4}$$

Then, when $n = 100$, $T(n) = (100 + 3) \times 100/4 = 2{,}575$.

Normally, there are best-case scenario, average scenario and worst-case scenario for one algorithm. The worst efficiency refers to the efficiency of the algorithm under the worst conditions, when the input size is n. The best efficiency refers to the efficiency of the algorithm under the best conditions. The average efficiency refers to the efficiency of the algorithm under the "typical" or "random" input conditions. Normally, the analysis focuses on the worst situation.

The aim of algorithm analysis is to obtain the approximate execution time. Normally we want to get the upper and lower bounds of the time increment $T(n)$ when the size of the problem n increases, as shown in Fig. 1.25. The O, Ω, Θ, respectively, represent the upper bound, lower bound and exact bound of algorithm efficiency. Their exact definitions in mathematical terms are shown in Table 1.8, and the corresponding curves are shown in Fig. 1.26.

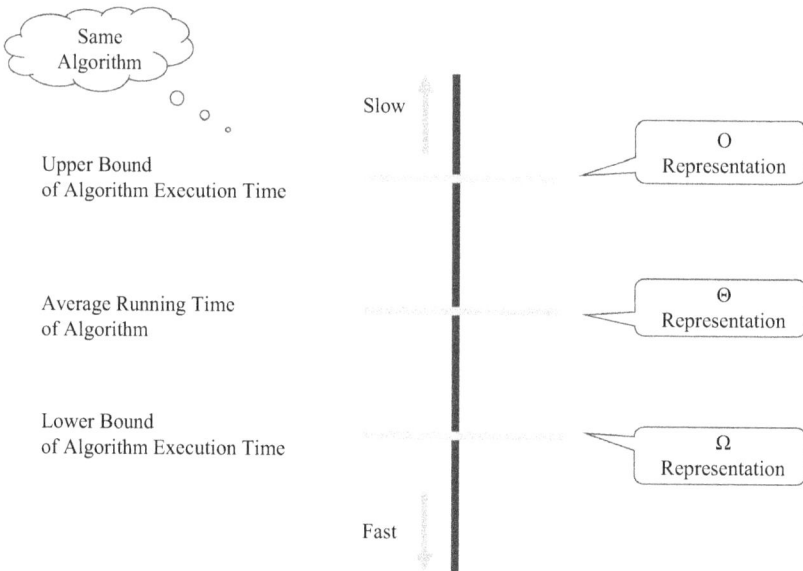

Fig. 1.25: Illustration of approximate representation of algorithm efficiency.

The difference between uppercase O and lowercase o: the condition for O is "there exists a positive constant c," while the condition for o is "for any positive constant c."

Table 1.8: The asymptotic time notation for algorithm execution.

Notation	Definition	Meaning
O	Definition: $f(n) = O(g(n))$, if there are two positive constants c and n_0, such that when $n \geq n_0$, $f(n) \leq c\, g(n)$	The asymptotic upper bound of $f(n)$ is $g(n)$
Ω	Definition: $f(n) = \Omega\,(g(n))$, if there are two positive constants c and n_0, such that when $n \geq n_0$, $f(n) \geq cg(n)$	The asymptotic lower bound of $f(n)$ is $g(n)$
Θ	Definition: $f(n) = \Theta\,(g(n))$ if there are two positive constants c_1, c_2 and n_0, such that when $n \geq n_0$, $c_1\, g(n) \leq f(n) \leq c_2\, g(n)$	The exact asymptotic bound of $f(n)$ is $g(n)$
o	Definition: $f(n) = o(g(n))$ if for any positive constant c, if there is an n_0, such that when $n \geq n_0$, $f(n) < cg(n)$	$g(n)$ dominates $f(n)$ asymptotically
ω	Definition: $f(n) = \omega(g(n))$ if for any positive constant c, if there is an n_0, such that when $n \geq n_0$, $f(n) > cg(n)$	$f(n)$ dominates $g(n)$ asymptotically

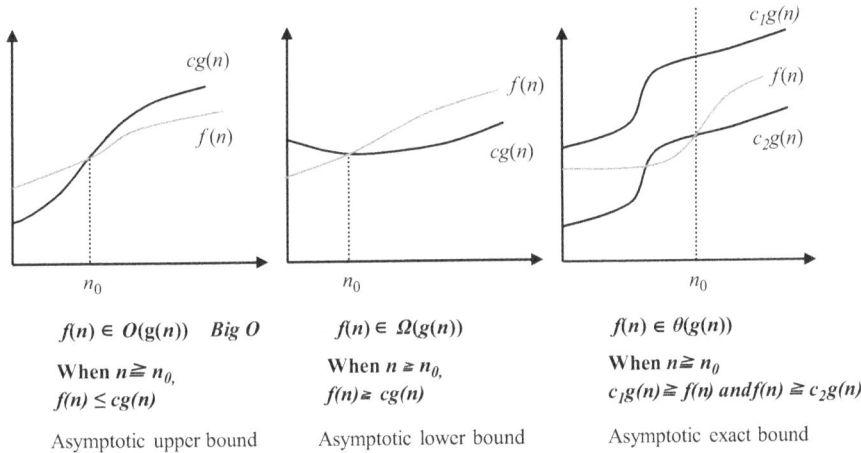

$f(n) \in O(g(n))$ Big O

When $n \geq n_0$,
$f(n) \leq cg(n)$

Asymptotic upper bound

$f(n) \in \Omega(g(n))$

When $n \geq n_0$,
$f(n) \geq cg(n)$

Asymptotic lower bound

$f(n) \in \Theta(g(n))$

When $n \geq n_0$
$c_1 g(n) \geq f(n)$ and $f(n) \geq c_2 g(n)$

Asymptotic exact bound

Fig. 1.26: Asymptotic representation method. Note: $f(n)$ and $g(n)$ are both nonnegative mathematical functions.

The difference between Ω and ω: the same as above.

$f(n) = O(g(n))$ means $g(n)$ is the asymptotic limit of $f(n)$. It can be interpreted as "when n is large enough, the speed of growth of $f(n)$ will be at most as fast as that of $g(n)$, but not greater."

$F(n) = o(g(n))$ means $g(n)$ is the nonexact asymptotic limit of $f(n)$. Nonexact means nontight. It can be interpreted as "when n is large enough, the speed of growth of $f(n)$ will not exceed that of $g(n)$, and will not be as fast as that of $g(n)$ either."

The relation between Ω and ω is the same as the relation between o and O.

$f(n) = \Theta(g(n))$ means $g(n)$ is the asymptotic exact limit of $f(n)$: when n is large enough, the speed of growth of $g(n)$ will be the same as that of $f(n)$, which corresponds to "the equivalent limit of algorithm" in Fig. 1.26. If the efficiency of an algorithm is both in $O(g(n))$ and in $\Omega(g(n))$, then it is in $\Theta(g(n))$.

Example 1.7:
Examples about Big-O notation 1.
(1) $f(n) = 3n + 2 = O(n)$
∵ We can find $c = 4$, $n_0 = 2$, to let $3n + 2 < 4n$
(2) $f(n) = 10n^2 + 5n + 1 = O(n^2)$
∵ We can find $c = 11$, $n_0 = 6$, to let $10n^2 + 5n + 1 < 11n^2$
(3) $f(n) = 7 \times 2^n + n^2 + n = O(2^n)$
∵ We can find $c = 8$, $n_0 = 5$, to let $7 \times 2^n + n^2 + n < 8 \times 2^n$

Beware that the asymptotic upper bound provided by the big-O notation can also be nonexact asymptotic. For example, $2n^2 = O(n^2)$ is exactly asymptotic, while $2n = O(n^2)$ is nonexact asymptotic. When we perform algorithm analysis, we want to obtain an upper bound as exact as possible.

Although the formal definitions of symbols O, Ω and Θ are indispensable for proving their abstract properties, we rarely use them to compare the scales of two specific functions. There is a relatively simple comparison method, that is, to calculate the ratio of the two functions in discussion at the limit.

Suppose $f(n)$, $g(n)$ are relative to the same variable n, then the limit of the ratio of the two is

$$\lim_{n->\infty} \frac{f(n)}{g(n)}$$

The relation between the result obtained at the limit and the gradual representation method is shown in Table 1.9.

Table 1.9: Comparison results of infinite amounts.

Limit value		Comparison result between f and g	Representation
Exists	$c = 0$	f is an infinity value smaller than g	$f(n) = o(g(n))$
	$0 \le c \le 1$	f is an infinity value the same as or smaller than g	$f(n) = O(g(n))$
	$c = 1$	f and g are infinity values of the same order	$f(n) = \Theta(g(n))$
	$1 \le c \le \infty$	f is an infinity value the same as or greater than g	$f(n) = \Omega(g(n))$
Doesn't exist	$c = \infty$	f is an infinity value greater than g	$f(n) = \omega(g(n))$
	Oscillates		

Note: c is a constant.

Example 1.8:
Example 2 of Big-O notation
(1) $f(n) = 3n + 2 = O(n)$

$$\because \lim_{n \to \infty} \frac{3n + 2}{n} = 3$$

When n is sufficiently large, the execution time of the program is proportional to n, expressed as $O(n)$: we say $f(n)$ and n are on the same order (has the same magnitude). Note that the frequency function that we pay attention to is on the denominator instead of the numerator, therefore the costant c is larger than 1, which is contrary to the definition shown in Table 1.9.
(2) $f(n) = 10n^2 + 5n + 1 = O(n^2)$

$$\because \lim_{n \to \infty} \frac{10n^2 + 5n + 1}{n^2} = 10$$

When n is sufficiently large, the execution time of the program is proportional to n^2, expressed as $O(n^2)$: we say $f(n)$ and n^2 are on the same order.
(3) $f(n) = 7*2^n + n^2 + n = O(2^n)$

$$\because \lim_{n \to \infty} \frac{7*2^n + n^2 + n}{2^n} = 7$$

When n is sufficiently large, the execution time of the program is proportional to 2^n, expressed as $O(2^n)$: we say $f(n)$ and 2^n are on the same order.

1.7.3 The asymptotic upper bound – the time complexity of the algorithm

Definition of time complexity
If $O(f(n))$ is the asymptotic upper bound of the number of executions of the statements in the algorithm $T(n)$, then we can say the asymptotic time complexity of this algorithm to be $O(f(n))$. The asymptotic time complexity is abbreviated as "time complexity."

Example 1.9: Example on time complexity 1
Time complexity analysis on multiplication algorithm on n-ranked matrices.
    The program statements on multiplication of n-ranked matrices are given in Table 1.10. The numbers of executions of the corresponding statements are given at "frequency" column, for example, the for loop in statement 1. When the i value goes from 1 to n, the statements inside of the loop body are executed for n times. When i is larger than n, since the program has to do another comparison on the loop condition $i \leq n$, the total number of executions of the statements is $n + 1$. The "number of executions of the statements" is the "frequency." In the same manner, we can get the frequency of statements 2–5.

The sum of the frequencies of statements on each line $f(n) = 2n^3 + 3n^2 + 2n + 1$.
    The time complexity of the matrices multiplication algorithm $T(n) = O(f(n)) = O(n^3)$.

Table 1.10: Time complexity analysis of algorithm for multiplication between n-rank matrices.

Index	Program statement	Frequency $T(n)$
1	for (i = 1; i≤n; i++)	$n + 1$
2	for (j = 1; j ≤ n; j++)	$n(n + 1)$
3	{ c[i][j] = 0;	n^2
4	for (k = 1; k ≤ n; k++)	$n^2(n + 1)$
5	c[i][j] + = a[i][k] * b[k][j] }	n^3

Conclusion

The asymptotic analysis of algorithms focuses on the growth pattern of the resource cost $T(n)$ when the data size n gradually increases. Specifically, it concerns itself with the comparison on the size of order of magnitudes. When n increases to a certain value, the term with the highest order in the expression for calculating resource cost will have the biggest influence. We can then ignore other constant terms and lower-order terms.

If the execution time of the worst-case scenario of an algorithm is faster than another algorithm, we normally consider the former algorithm to be more effective. When the size of the input is relatively small, the above conclusion might be wrong. For example, for two programs, respectively, $O(0.01*n^3)$ and $O(100*n^2)$, although the former is better than the latter when n is small, the time cost of the latter increases slower with regard to the data size. For input of a sufficiently large size, an algorithm with order $O(n^2)$ runs faster than an algorithm with order $O(n^3)$ under the worst-case scenario.

Example 1.10: Example 2 of time complexity
Analysis of time complexity of program statements
    The frequency and time complexity of program segments and the corresponding statements are shown in Table 1.11.

For the first program segment, if the execution time of the algorithm is a constant irrelevant to the size of the problem n, then the time complexity of the program is constant order, noted as $T(n) = O(1)$.

    The analysis of the fourth program segment $f(n)$ is shown in Table 1.12, where $f(n)$ is the number of executions for the statement i = i*2. The condition for the last execution of the program is i = n, that is, $2^{f(n)-1} = n$.

Table 1.11: Table of time complexity analysis for Example 1.10.

Index	Program segment	The relation between frequency $f(n)$ and size n	Time complexity $O(f(n))$
1	x = x + 1; y = x + 2;	$f(n) = 2$	$O(1)$
2	for(i = 0;i < n;i++) x++;	$f(n) = 2n + 1$	$O(n)$
3	for(i = 0;i < n;i++) for(j = 0; j < n; j++) x++;	$f(n) = (n + 1) + n(n + 1) + n^2$	$O(n^2)$
4	i = 1; while(i ≤ n) i = i*2;	$2^{f(n)-1} = n$	$O(\log_2 n)$

Table 1.12: Analysis table for the time complexity of multiplication statements.

$f(n)$	1	2	3	...	k	...	$f(n)$
i	1	2	2^2		2^{k-1}		$2^{f(n)-1}$
$i = i*2$ value	2	2^2	2^3		2^k		$2^{f(n)}$

1.7.4 The comprehensive discussion on the time complexity of algorithms

1.7.4.1 The practical implications of the time complexity of algorithms

The time complexity doesn't represent how much time it costs a program to solve a concrete problem, but represents the rate of growth of execution time when the problem size increases. For computers that process data at high speed, we can't evaluate a program solely based on the efficiency on processing a certain set of data, but should see whether after the data size increases hundredfold, the execution time of the program is still the same, also increases hundredfold or even increases tens of thousands of times.

Why do we emphasize the growth rate of the number of executions of the statements for large-size input? This is because the difference in execution time for small-size input is usually insufficient to separate efficient and nonefficient algorithms. Following is the comparison of algorithm efficiencies on processing the same set of data with different methods.

Example 1.11: The efficiency of search
How to search an ordered sequence of numbers with high efficiency?

Solution:
Method 1: Sequential search
    In the discussion at Section 1.7.2 about the upper bound and lower bound of algorithm efficiency, we already have a calculation about the average number of successful searches for a node:

$$ASL_{sequential} = \sum_{i=1}^{n} p_i c_i = \frac{1}{n} \times \frac{(1+n) \times n}{2} = \frac{n+1}{2} \tag{1.2}$$

Then the average time complexity of sequential search would be

$$T(n) = O\left(\frac{n+1}{2}\right) = O(n).$$

Method 2: Binary search

Previously we have already introduced this search method. For the array given in this example, the lookup order and number of lookups in each node are shown in Fig. 1.27. Suppose the number to lookup is x, then we start the search process from the middle of the array. First, we compare it with 56. If it is smaller than that, then we continue the binary search at the left half of 56. If it is bigger, then we continue the binary search at the right half of 56. If it is equal, then we have found it and the number of lookups is 1. Recursively searching the whole array with the above method, the average number of lookup for the successful search of a node is the product of the lookup numbers for all the nodes and the lookup probability, see eq. (1.3):

$$ASL_{binary} = \sum_{i=1}^{h} p_i c_i = \frac{1}{n} \times (1 \times 2^0 + 2 \times 2^1 + 3 \times 2^2 + \cdots + i \times 2^{i-1}) = \frac{(h-1) \times 2^h + 1}{n} \tag{1.3}$$

Suppose on each level the nodes are full, then the relation between the level h and the number of nodes n is: $n = 2^0 + 2^1 + \cdots + 2^{h-1} = 2^h - 1$.

Thus we have $h = [\lg(n+1)]$.

Therefore, the time complexity of binary search is

$$T(n) = O\left(\frac{(h-1) \times 2^h + 1}{n}\right) = O\left(\frac{(\log n) \times n}{n}\right) = O(\log n)$$

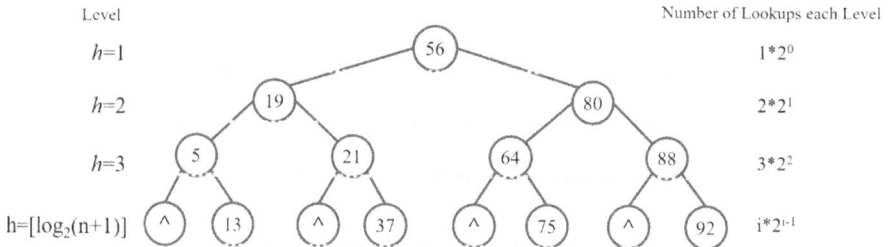

Data	5	13	19	21	37	56	64	75	80	88	92
Number of Sequential Lookups	1	2	3	4	5	6	7	8	9	10	11
Number of Binary Lookups	3	4	2	3	4	1	3	4	2	3	4
Possibility of match p_i						$1/n$					

Fig. 1.27: Illustration of binary search.

From the above analysis, sequential search is much less efficient than the binary search.

1.7.4.2 Function values with significant meanings to algorithm analysis

The common time complexities and their related values are given in Table 1.13 and the corresponding curves are shown in Fig. 1.28.

Table 1.13: Common time complexities and related values.

Classification		Polynomial order						Nonpolynomial order	
		Constant order	Logarithmic order	Linear order	Linear logarithmic order	C-power order		Exponential order	Factorial order
Form		$O(1)$	$O(\log n)$	$O(n)$	$O(n \log(n))$	$O(n^c)$		$O(C^n)$	$O(n!)$
Example		c	$\log_2 n$	n	$n \log_2 n$	n^2	n^3	2^n	$n!$
Problem size n	10	10	3.3	10	$3.3*10^1$	10^2	10^3	10^3	$3.6*10^6$
	10^2	10^2	6.6	10^2	$6.6*10^2$	10^4	10^6	$1.3*10^{30}$	$9.3*10^{157}$
	10^3	10^3	10	10^3	$1.0*10^4$	10^6	10^9		
	10^4	10^4	13	10^4	$1.3*10^5$	10^8	10^{12}		
	10^5	10^5	17	10^5	$1.7*10^6$	10^{10}	10^{15}		
	10^6	10^6	20	10^6	$2.0*10^7$	10^{12}	10^{18}		

Note: The c in the table is a constant.

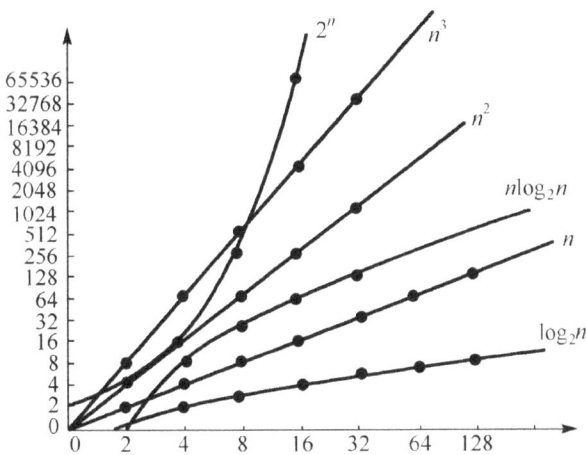

Fig. 1.28: Curves for the common time complexities.

In an ascending order, the common time complexities are, respectively:

Constant order < logarithmic order < linear order < linear logarithmic order < polynomial order < exponential order.

If we suppose the computer can perform 1 million operations per second, the time to complete computation of each order (the units are seconds if unspecified) is shown approximately in Fig. 1.29.

n	$\log n$	n	$n\log n$	n^2	n^3	2^n	3^n	$n!$
10	10^{-6}	10^{-5}	10^{-5}	10^{-4}	10^{-3}	10^{-3}	0.059	3.62
20	10^{-6}	10^{-5}	10^{-5}	10^{-4}	10^{-2}	1	58 minutes	8×10^4 years
50	10^{-6}	10^{-4}	10^{-4}	0.0025	0.125	36 years	2×10^{10} years	10^{51} years
1000	10^{-6}	10^{-3}	10^{-3}	1	0.28 hours	10^{333} years	very huge	very huge
10^6	10^{-5}	1	6	11.6 days	3×10^4 years	very huge	very huge	very huge
10^9	10^{-5}	0.28 hours	2.5 hours	3×10^4 years	very huge	very huge	very huge	very huge

Fig. 1.29: Time complexity and machine time.

If no matter the size of the data, the program always processes the data in constant time, then this program is really good, with $O(1)$ time complexity (also called constant time complexity). If the time cost increases linearly with the increase in data size, the time complexity of the program is $O(n)$, for example, finding the biggest value among n unordered numbers. Algorithms such as bubble sort and insertion sort will have $O(n^2)$ time complexity. And then some algorithms that rely on iteration might have exponential growth on execution time, this is $O(c^n)$, exponential complexity. Some even have $O(n!)$, power complexity.

As we can observe, there are two classes of time complexities mentioned above. The first are ones such as $O(1)$, $O(\log(n))$, $O(n^c)$, we call them polynomial complexity, since the input size n appears as a base number. Another class is ones such as $O(c^n)$ and $O(n!)$, which are nonpolynomial.

If an algorithm has a logarithmic number of basic operations, it can finish almost instantly on any input of practical size. An algorithm with an exponential number of operations can only be used to solve problems of really small sizes. Normally it is considered that algorithms with exponential complexity are practically incomputable, while algorithms with complexity better than $O(n^2)$ are efficient.

When the value of n is very large, the time needed between exponential algorithms and polynomial algorithms is very huge. Therefore, if one can simplify a certain classical algorithm with exponential time complexity to polynomial time complexity, it would be a magnificent breakthrough.

1.7.4.3 Computation rules for time complexity
Previously, the program examples we performed on algorithm analysis were all program segments with single functionality. When the program is relatively complicated, how should we perform efficiency analysis? We can divide them into the following several cases. Suppose the time for program segment 1 and program segment 2 are, respectively, $T_1(n)$ and $T_2(n)$, then the total running time is $T(n)$.

1. Addition rule (program juxtaposition)

For an algorithm composed of two continuous execution parts, its overall efficiency is determined by the part with higher growth, that is, determined by the part with lower efficiency:

$$T(n) = T_1(n) + T_2(n)$$
$$= O(f_1(n)) + O(f_2(n))$$
$$= O(\max(f_1(n), f_2(n)))$$

2. Multiplication rule (program embedding)

For looping structures, the execution time of the looping statement is mainly spent in executing the looping body in multi-iteration and checking looping conditions. We can use the "multiplication rule" under big-O notation:

$$T(n) = T_1(n) \times T_2(n) = O(f_1(n)) \times O(f_2(n)) = O(f_1(n) \times f_2(n))$$

3. Special case

When the time complexity for the number of executions of the basic operations does not only depend on the problem size n, but also on the input data of the problem, we can consider the following complexities to measure the algorithm complexity:
- Average time complexity of the algorithm
- Time complexity of the algorithm under the worst case

For complex algorithms, we can divide them into several easy-to-estimate parts, and use addition rule and multiplication rule to obtain the time complexity of the whole algorithm.

When analyzing the time complexity of algorithms, we need to check whether the number of executions of the basic operations depends only on the input size. If it also depends on other factors, then the worst-case efficiency, average efficiency and best-case efficiency (if necessary) need to be studied separately. See Example 1.12.

Example 1.12:
Study on the effect of input data of the problem on the algorithm efficiency
    The algorithm to find the given value k in the array $A[N]$ is as follows:

```
int search(int k)
{
    int i = N-1; // i is the subscript to be searched for
    while ( i >= 0 && A[i] != k )  i--;
    return i;
}
```

Question: Is the number of executions of basic statements only related to the problem size?

Discussion: The frequency of the statement i– is not only related to n, but also to the values of the elements in the array A and the value k.

Worst-case scenario: it is found in the last element of the array A, or not found. The time frequency $f(n) = n$, then $O(f(n)) = O(n)$.

Average case: Suppose the possibility of each element in array A being found is the same, $1/n$, then the average number of lookups to find one element is $(1 + n)*n/2$. The time frequency $f(n) = (1/n)*(1 + n)*n/2 = (1 + n)/2$, then $O(f(n)) = O(n)$.

! **Think and Discuss** We mainly consider the execution time under the worst-case scenario, that is, the longest execution time under the worst scenario with input size n. What are the reasons for this?

Discussion: The worst-case execution time scenario of an algorithm is the upper bound for the execution time under any input. This ensures that the execution time of the algorithm can't be longer than this.

For certain algorithms, the worst-case scenario frequently occurs. For example, when searching a database, if the data item being searched is not in it, the worst-case scenario of the search algorithm occurs.

The time cost of "average case scenario" is frequently similar to that under the worst-case scenario.

If the complexity of an algorithm reaches the lower bound of the complexity for this problem, then this algorithm is called the best algorithm.

1.7.4.4 General methods for algorithm efficiency analysis
1.   Analysis methods for the efficiency of nonrecursive algorithms
    –   Decide which parameter(s) to use as the measure for input size.
    –   Find out the basic operations of the algorithm (normally, they are in the inner loop of the algorithm).

- Check whether the number of executions of the basic inputs only depends on input size. If it also relies on some other characteristics, such as input order, then we need to study worst-case efficiency, average efficiency and best-case efficiency separately.
- Establish an expression to calculate the number of executions for the basic operations of the algorithm.
2. Analysis methods for the efficiency of recursive algorithms
   - Find out the basic operations of the algorithm. Express the number of basic operations in the form of inductive equations.
   - Decide which parameters to use as the measurement of input size.
   - Check whether the numbers of executions of basic operations are different for different inputs of the same size. If they are different, then individual studies on the worst-case efficiency, average efficiency and best-case efficiency must be carried out.

1.7.5 The analysis methods on the space efficiency of the algorithm

The analysis on the space efficiency of the algorithm is similar to the analysis on the time efficiency of the algorithm. It tries to find the influence of the problem size on the space needed to run the algorithm. Specifically, we try to find the function relation between them after setting aside irrelevant factors.

There are two aspects involved for the memory space of an algorithm: the memory space for the algorithm itself and the memory space needed during the execution of the algorithm.

The memory space occupied by the algorithm itself is related to the length of the code implementing the algorithm. It is hard to ascertain its function relation with the problem size. Also, once an algorithm is decided, its space usage will not change according to the changes of problem size.

The memory space needed by the algorithm during execution is mainly the memory space allocated for local variables. It includes two parts: space allocation for the parameters and space allocation for local variables defined with the function body.

The memory space needed by the input/output data of the algorithm is decided by the problem to be solved. It is passed by the parameter table via function invocations. If the space occupied by the input data only depends on the problem itself, and doesn't change with the change of algorithms, then we don't need to consider its size. If the space needed depends on specific inputs, then the worst-case scenario is normally considered.

The memory space temporarily occupied by the local variables during an algorithm's execution changes with the changes of algorithms. Some algorithms only need to occupy limited temporary working units, and the space doesn't change with the change of problem size. The temporary working units needed by some algorithms are related to the problem size n, and increases with the increase of n. When n is relatively large, relatively many memory units will be needed. Please see the example below on memory space analysis of algorithms.

Example 1.13:
Example of analysis on memory usage of algorithm
   Calculate the value of the polynomial function $f(x)$, $f(x) = a_0 + a_1x + a_2x^2 + \cdots + a_{n-1}x^{n-1}$.

Solution: Function structure design is shown in Table 1.14.

Table 1.14: Function design of polynomial calculation.

Functionality description	Input	Output
Calculate the value of the polynomial evaluate	Coefficient float coef[]	float f(x)
	Variable float x	
	size int n	
Function name	Parameters	Function type

Algorithm 1: pseudocode is shown in Table 1.15.

Table 1.15: Pseudocode for polynomial calculation 1.

Top-level pseudocode description	First-level elaboration	Second-level elaboration
Compute the value of the function	Set two arrays to store the power of x and polynomial a_n	int A[N] stores the power of x, float coef[N] stores the coefficients
	Compute the power of x and store it in the array	A[0]=1, i=1 if i<n A[i] = x*A[i-1]; i++;

	Multiply the power of x by the corresponding coefficient respectively	f=0,i=0;
		if i<n
		f = f + coef[i]*A[i]; i++;

Program implementation:

```
# define N 100
float evaluate (float coef[ ], float x, int n )
{
    float f; int A[N], i;
    for (A[0]=1, i=1; i<n; i++ )
        A[i] = x*A[i-1];
    for (f = 0, i=0; i<n; i ++)
        f = f + coef[i]*A[i];
    return(f);
}
```

The space analysis of the execution of algorithm 1 is as follows.

The size of this problem, n, is the number of items in the polynomial expression. coef[] belongs to input/output, and requires memory space. In the local variables, $A[N]$ occupies the most memory and grows with the problem size n. The other local variables x, f, i are unrelated to the growth of n. Therefore, according to the analysis method for time complexity, the space complexity of algorithm 1 is $O(n)$.

Algorithm 2: the pseudocode is given in Table 1.16.

Table 1.16: Pseudocode for polynomial calculation 2.

Top-level pseudocode description	First-level elaboration	Second-level elaboration
Compute the value of the function	Multiply x starting from the last item of f(), start from the reverse direction	float coef[] stores the coefficients, n is the number of items
		f = coef[n],i=n-2; if i≥0 { f = f*x + coef[i]; i-; }

Program implementation:

```
# define N 100
float evaluate (float coef[ ], float x, int n )
{   float f; int i;
    for (f = coef[n], i= n-2; i>=0; i --)
        f = f*x + coef[i];
    return(f);
}
```

The space analysis of algorithm 2 is as follows.

Similar to the analysis method of algorithm 1, the temporary memory occupied by the local variables of this algorithm, x, n, f, i, won't change with regard to the increase in the value of n. Therefore, the space complexity of algorithm 2 is $O(1)$.

$O(1)$ represents that the temporary space needed by the algorithm won't change together with the size of the problem and is irrelevant to the input amount. This kind of algorithm is called in-place algorithm.

From the above examples, we can give the definition of space complexity.

> **Definition**
>
> Space complexity is the measure of the temporary memory space occupied by an algorithm during its execution. It is also a function of problem size n, noted as
>
> $$S(n) = O(g(n))$$
>
> where $g(n)$ refers to the temporary memory space needed by the execution of the algorithm, also called auxiliary space.

The computational method of space complexity is the same as that for time complexity in a mathematical sense. It is just that space complexity calculates the same-order upper bound of the sum of auxiliary memory units, while time complexity calculates the same-order upper bound of the execution frequency of statements.

Normally, the complexity of an algorithm is an umbrella term for both its time complexity and its space complexity. We use "time complexity" to refer to the requirement on execution time and "space complexity" to refer to the space requirement. When we use the term "complexity" without any quantifier, we normally refer to the time complexity. Research experience indicates that for most problems, the speed gain will be far bigger than the space gain. Therefore, we focus our attention mainly on the time efficiency of the algorithms.

For an algorithm, the time complexity and space complexity frequently influence each other. When we pursue a better time complexity, the space complexity might become worse. On the contrary, when we pursue a better space complexity, the time complexity might become worse, that is, the algorithm needs more execution time.

Example 1.14:
Comprehensive example of algorithm analysis

There is a recursive algorithm which computes the nth item of a Fibonacci sequence. Analyze its complexity.

Solution: The definition of Fibonacci sequence is

$$f_0 = 0, \quad f_1 = 1;$$

$$f_n = f_{n-1} + f_{n-2} (n > = 2)$$

The code is as follows:

```
/*=================================================================
Functionality of the function: Recursively compute the nth item of the
Fibonacci sequence
Function input: n value
Function output: The nth item of Fibonacci sequence
=============================================================*/
long Fib(long n)
{   if (n <= 1) return n;              // Base case of recursion
    else return Fib(n-1)+Fib(n-2);    // Recursive conditions
}
```

The execution process of recursive algorithms is divided into two stages: induction and returning. In the induction stage, it transforms the solution of a relatively complex problem (with size n) to the solution of problems that are simpler than the original problem (with size smaller than n), as shown in Fig. 1.30.

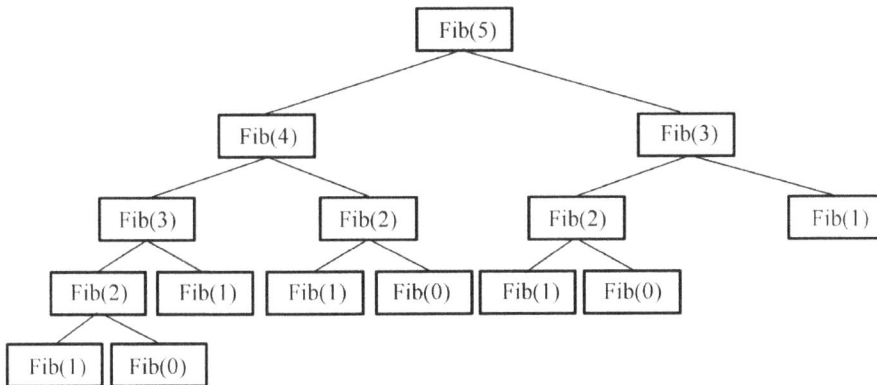

Fig. 1.30: The recursion invocation tree of the Fibonacci function.

For example, to solve Fib(n), we need to transform it into solving Fib(n–1) and Fib (n–2). That is to say, to calculate Fib(n), we must first compute Fib(n–1) and Fib(n–2). Then, to compute Fib(n–1) and Fib(n–2), we must first compute Fib(n–3) and Fib(n–4), and so forth, until we calculate Fib(1) and Fib(0), which should immediately return the results 1 and 0. In the induction stage, there must be a condition which ends the recursion. In the function Fib, such conditions are the cases where n is 1 and n is 0.

In the returning stage, after obtaining the solution to the simplest case, the algorithm returns level by level, and obtain the solutions to the relatively more complex problems, respectively. For example, after obtaining Fib(1) and Fib(0), it returns to obtain the result of Fib(2). Returning level by level, after it obtains the results of Fib(n–1) and Fib(n–2), it returns to obtain the result of Fib(n).

According to Fig. 1.30, we can obtain the relation between n and the number of executions of Fib(n); see Fig. 1.31.

If $n = 0$, Fib(0) only needs to perform one calculation, $T(0) = 1$;

If $n = 1$, Fib(1) also only needs to perform one calculation, $T(1) = 1$;

If $n = 2$, since Fib(2) is composed from Fib(1) and Fib(0), $T(2) = T(0) + T(1) + 1$.

The last plus 1 is the calculation that adds Fib(1) and Fib(0) together.

variable	0	1	2	3	4	5	6	7	...	n
T(n)	1	1	3	5	9	15	25	41		$T(n–1)+T(n–2)+1$

Fig. 1.31: The number of calculations for recursion.

According to the frequency relation in Fig. 1.31, we can perform the following deduction:

$T(n) = T(n-1) + T(n-2) + 1$

$\because T(n-1) > T(n-2)$

$\therefore T(n) < 2 \star T(n-1) < 2 \star 2 \star T(n-2) < 2 \star 2 \star 2 \star T(n-3) \ldots < 2^{n-1} T(n-n+1)$

$\qquad = 2^{n-1} T(1) = 2^{n-1}$

$\therefore T(n) \in O(2^n)$

And $\because T(n-1) > T(n-2)$

$\therefore T(n) > 2 \star T(n-2) > 2 \star 2 \star T(n-4) > 2 \star 2 \star 2 \star T(n-6) > \cdots > 2^{n/2} \star T(n-n) = 2^{n/2}$

$\therefore T(n) \in \Omega(2^{n/2})$

Therefore, the asymptotic upper bound and asymptotic lower bound of the Fibonacci recursive functions are $O(2^n)$ and $\Omega(2^{n/2})$.

To obtain the exact asymptotic bound of the Fibonacci recursive function, we need the deduction from the general formula for Fibonacci sequence.

The general form of second-order linear inductive sequence is

$$af(n+2) + bf(n+1) + cf(n) = 0 \tag{1.4}$$

The general formula for second-order linear inductive sequence is

$$f(n) = \alpha x_1^n + \beta x_2^n \tag{1.5}$$

The characteristic equation for second-order linear inductive sequence is

$$ax^2 + bx + c = 0 \tag{1.6}$$

From expression (1.4) we know that Fibonacci sequence is a second-order linear inductive sequence. Thus we can obtain:

$$a = 1; \ b = -1; \ c = -1$$

The characteristic equation of Fibonacci equation is $x^2 = x + 1$.

Solving the equation: $x_1 = \left(1 - \sqrt{5}\right)/2$ and $x_2 = \left(1 + \sqrt{5}\right)/2$

From eqs. (1.4) and (1.5), we obtain

$$\begin{cases} f(n) = \alpha \times \left[(1 - \sqrt{5})/2\right]^n + \beta \times \left[(1 + \sqrt{5})/2\right]^n \\ f(n+2) - f(n+1) - f(n) = 0 \end{cases}$$

We get

$$\alpha = 1/\sqrt{5} \beta = -1/\sqrt{5}$$

Therefore,

$$f(n) = \frac{1}{\sqrt{5}} \left[\left(\frac{1 + \sqrt{5}}{2}\right)^n - \left(\frac{1 - \sqrt{5}}{2}\right)^n \right]$$

Asymptotic values

$$f(n) = \frac{1}{\sqrt{5}} \left(\frac{1 + \sqrt{5}}{2}\right)^{n+1}$$

$$\because T(n) = T(n-1) + T(n-2) + 1 \ \therefore T(n) \in \Theta\left(\frac{1 + \sqrt{5}}{2}\right)^n = \Theta(1.618^n)$$

Final results:

$$T(n) \in O(2^n) - \text{asymptotic upper bound}$$

$$T(n) \in \Omega(2^{n/2}) = \Omega(1.414^n) - \text{asymptotic lower bound}$$

$$T(n) \in \Theta\left(\left(1 + \sqrt{5}\right)/-2\right)^n = \Theta(1.618^n) - \text{asympototic exact bound}$$

The curves for the corresponding upper bound, lower bound and exact bound for the time complexity of recursive computation of the nth item of the Fibonacci sequence are shown in Fig. 1.32.

1.8 Comprehensive evaluation of algorithm performance

The evaluation of an algorithm should consider its time complexity, space complexity and logical complexity (the logical complexity of a program impacts its developmental period and maintenance).

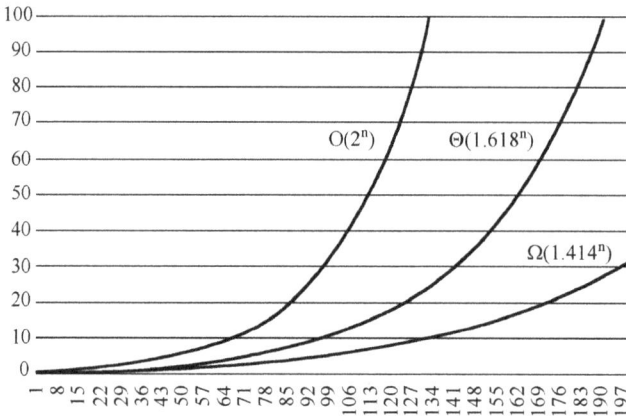

Fig. 1.32: Time complexity curves.

It's hard to get an algorithm with low memory space requirement, short running time and excellent all-round capacities. The reason is that sometimes these requirements contradict each other. Savings on execution time is frequently achieved via sacrificing more memory space. Savings on memory space probably costs more computation time. Therefore, we usually have particular focuses depending on the actual problem.

- If the program is used relatively few times, then ease of understanding can be put as the highest concern.
- For a program frequently used for multiple times, then the speed of the algorithm is the highest concern.
- If the data size of the problem to be solved is very big, and the storage space of the machine is relatively limited, then space efficiency should be the highest concern.

There's also a constraint relation between the efficiency and the ease-of-understanding and ease-of-programming of algorithms. These two requirements sometimes contradict each other. Therefore, for an algorithm repeatedly run, efficiency is the highest concern, while for an algorithm seldom run, the understandability and ease-of-programming are emphasized.

There are usually multiple algorithms to solve the same problem. The evaluation of these algorithms usually displays the property of "trade-off between time and space." To improve the time cost of an algorithm, one can usually increase the space cost as the price to come up with a new algorithm. To reduce the space cost of an algorithm, one can increase the time cost in exchange for the savings on memory space.

1.9 Chapter summary

The connections between main contents of this chapter are shown in Fig. 1.33.

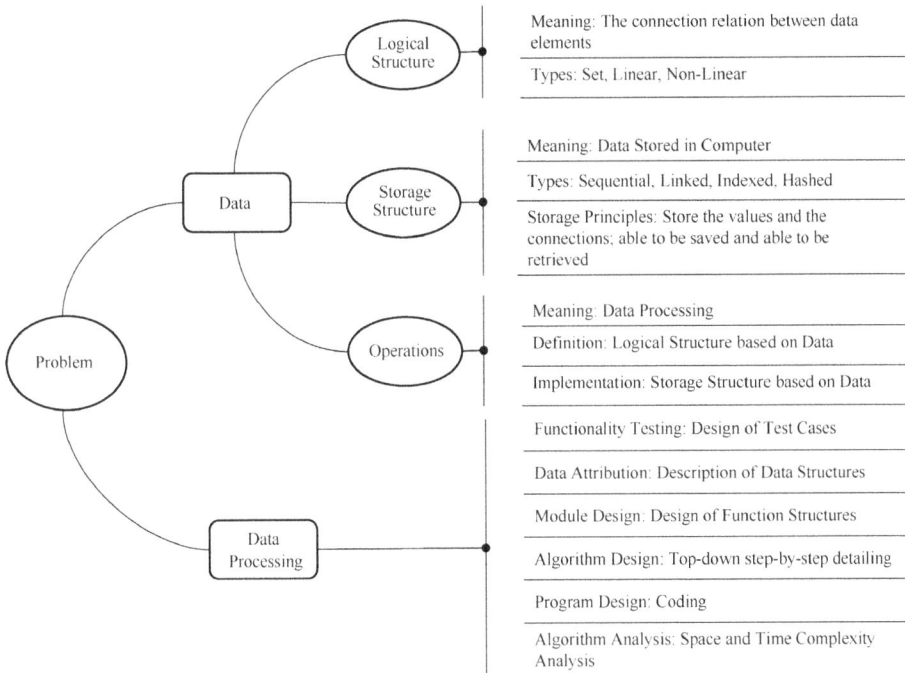

Fig. 1.33: The connections between the basic concepts in data structures.

The three key elements of data structures are logic, storage and operations.
Logical structure refers to how the data element in the problems are related.
Storage structure stores the data values and logical relations into memory units.
Operations refer to plans that describe data processing with algorithms.
One logical relation can be stored in multiple ways.
"Store the value and store the relations," "Be able to be stored and be able to be retrieved."
These two rules for storage are to be followed when designing storage structures.
When the storage structures are different, the algorithm efficiencies differ as well.
The algorithm efficiency is viewed in two aspects: time and space.
The time complexity is approximated in "Big-O" notation.
It refers to asymptotic upper bound and is related to the computation size n.

1.10 Exercises

1.10.1 Multiple-choice questions

1. In data structures, the data structure that is irrelevant to the computer used is ( ).
   (A) Logical   (B) Storage   (C) Logical and Storage   (D) Physical

2. The characteristic of an algorithm to correctly realize expected functionality is the ( ) of the algorithm.
   (A) Correctness   (B) Readability   (C) Robustness   (D) Effectiveness

3. The indivisible basic unit of data is ( ).
   (A) Element   (B) Node   (C) Data type   (D) Data item

4. The data structure is logically divided into ( ) in discussions about data structure.
   (A) Inside structure and outside structure
   (B) Static structure and dynamic structure
   (C) Linear structure and nonlinear structure
   (D) Tight structure and nontight structure

5. The logical relation between data refers to ( ) of data elements.
   (A) Correlation   (B) Structure   (C) Data item   (D) Storage method

6. Among the following statements about the logical relations of data, ( ) is correct.
   (A) The logical structure of data is the description of relations between data
   (B) The logical structure of data reflects the storage method of data in computer
   (C) The logical structure of data is divided into sequential structure and chain-like structure
   (D) The logical structure of data is divided into static structure and dynamic structure

7. The computer algorithm refers to ( ).
   (A) Method of computation
   (B) Method of ordering
   (C) The finite calculation sequence used to solve problems
   (D) Method of arrangement

8. A computer algorithm must have five characteristics including input, output and ( ).
   (A) Feasibility, portability and extensibility
   (B) Feasibility, certainty and finiteness
   (C) Certainty, finiteness and stability
   (D) Readability, stability and security

9.   The aim of algorithm analysis is ( ).
     (A) Find out the sensibleness of data structures
     (B) Study the input–output relation in algorithms
     (C) Analyze the efficiency of algorithms to search for improvements
     (D) Analyze the readability and documentation of algorithms

10. The two main aspects of algorithm analysis are ( ).
     (A) Space complexity and time complexity
     (B) Correctness and simplicity
     (C) Readability and level of documentation
     (D) Complexity of data and program

1.10.2 Practical problems

1.   Get the time complexities of the program segments described by the pseudoco-
     des below.

```
(a)
i=1, j=0;
while (i+j<=n)
{
  if (i>j)  j=j+1;
  else  i=i+1;
}
(b)
for i=1 to n
  for j=1 to n
    for k=1 to j
    x=x+1
    end for
  end for
end for
(c)
for i=1 to n
  for j=1 to i
    for k=1 to j
    x=x+1
    endfor
  endfor
endfor
```

2. The execution time of one algorithm is $1,000n$, and that of another algorithm is approximately 2^n. What are the time complexities of these two algorithms? Which has a higher complexity? When the problem size $n \leq 13$, which algorithm is more appropriate?

3. It is known that there are two algorithms solving the same problem. The time complexities are, respectively, $O(2^n)$ and $O(n^{10})$. Suppose the computer can continuously run for approximately 100 days and can realize 10^5 basic operations per second. Under this condition, what are the sizes (i.e., the range of n) of problems that can be solved by these two algorithms, respectively? Which algorithm is more appropriate? Try to explain your reasons.

4. Give the algorithms for computing the first n items in a Fibonacci sequence both recursively and nonrecursively, and compare their time complexity. Try to use time or clock function to test the actual execution time of the machine when $n = 100$, and analyze the results.

2 The data structure whose nodes share a linear logical relation – linear list

Main Contents
- The logical structural definition of linear list
- The description methods of various storage structures
- Realizing basic operations on the two types of storage structures of linear list

Learning Goals
- Get familiar with the two types of storage structures of linear list, and the basic operations on it
- Get familiar with the different characteristics and suitable application scenarios of the two types of storage structures of linear list

2.1 Viewing the linear list from the perspective of logical structure

2.1.1 The sequential relations that exist in practical problems

2.1.1.1 The one-to-one correspondence relation that exists in queuing

When traveling abroad in groups, the group members usually do not know each other. One of the major concerns of the tour guide is to ensure that nobody gets lost. When performing the head count, there is one simple method: line everybody up in one queue, and everybody only needs to remember the person in front of him (we might call that person in front "the forward"). Whenever somebody gets lost, the tour guide only needs to ask "whose 'forward' is missing," in order to figure out that person in the shortest time possible.

In this queue, except for the person in the beginning and the end, everybody is bordered in front and at the back by exactly one person. We can view one person as a node, and we may call such a relation between nodes as "one-to-one," that is to say, except for the first and the last data elements, every other data element is connected both in front and at the back (Fig. 2.1).

2.1.1.2 The representation method of alphabetical table

"Caesar Code" is fabled to be an encryption method invented by Emperor Caesar of ancient Rome to prevent the enemy from intercepting intelligence information. The encryption can be realized with the cipher table shown in Fig. 2.2. For example, if the overt information is the word "CAESAR," then the cipher phrase translated via

https://doi.org/10.1515/9783110595581-002

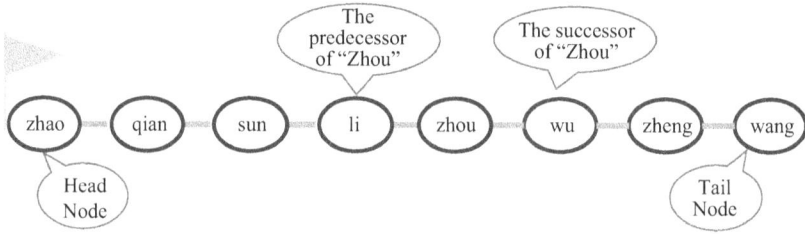

Fig. 2.1: The one-to-one correspondence in queuing.

Plain text	A	B	C	D	E	F	G	H	I	J	K	L	M	N	O	P	Q	R	S	T	U	V	W	X	Y	Z
Cipher	B	A	E	F	K	I	L	C	J	G	D	M	Q	Z	H	Y	O	P	T	X	V	R	N	W	U	S

Fig. 2.2: Cipher table.

the cipher table is "EBKTBP." Even if the enemy intercepts this password, they supposedly won't be able to figure out its actual meaning without the cipher table.

To realize this encoding and decoding process, one has to first store the cipher table on the computer. In C language we can store the table using an array. The data type of the elements in the table is char.

char code[27] = "baefkilcjgdmqzhyoptxvrnwus";

We can view one char in the cipher table as a node. Then the elements of each array also have a one-to-one sequential correspondence relation between each other.

2.1.1.3 The structure of phone number tables

To manage user information, the telephone company has set up a phone number table, as shown in Fig. 2.3. In the table, every row is a node, and the type of the data element in the table is the type of the data structure.

Client name	Telephone	ID Number	Address
Zhang 1	138*****	6101131980***	***
Li 2	152*****	6101131981***	***
Wang 1	139*****	6101131990***	***
Zhang 2	139*****	6101131972***	***
Li 1	188*****	6101131976***	***
...	......		

Fig. 2.3: Table of phone numbers.

In data structures, we call this kind of structure with one-to-one correspondence relation between data elements as linear list. In a linear list, except for the first and the last data elements, every other data element is connected both in the front and at the back.

2.1.2 The logical structure of linear lists

Linear list is one of the most basic, simplest and most frequently used data structures. Its logical structure is simple and it is easy to implement and operate upon.

2.1.2.1 The definition of linear list
A linear list is a finite list composed of n ($n > 0$) nodes of the same type.
Annotated as ($a_1 a_2 \ldots a_i \ldots a_n$)
where a_i represents a node, whose concrete meaning differs under different scenarios $(1 \le i \le n)$; n represents the length of the linear list. The list is empty when $n = 0$.

2.1.2.2 The logical features of the linear list
The logical structure of a linear list is shown in Fig. 2.4: among the nodes of the linear list, there is an ordered, linear and one-dimensional relation.

Fig. 2.4: The logical relation in linear lists.

1. There exists only one node called "the first" node, that is, the beginning node a_1.
2. There exists only one node called "the last" node, that is, the terminal node a_n.
3. Except for the first node, every node in the collection has only one predecessor.
4. Except for the last node, every node in the collection has only one successor.

Note: All the nodes in the same linear list must be of the same data type.

2.1.2.3 Major operations on the linear list
In the management of a phone number book, we will usually have operations such as setting initial values, getting the length of the list, querying for information of a client, inserting or deleting client information and printing the whole list. Abstracting them into operations on a linear list, they can be summarized as follows.
1. Initialization – giving initial values to the relevant parameters in the linear list
2. Getting the length – getting the number of elements in the linear list
3. Getting an element – getting the value of the element at the given location

4. Lookup – querying the location of the element that has the given value
5. Insertion – inserting the given value at the given location
6. Deletion – deleting the value at the given location or the element with the given value
7. Iteration – scanning the linear list from beginning to end, performing designated operations

2.2 One of the storage structures of linear lists – sequential list

Putting every element of the linear list one by one in a continuous storage space is called sequential list.

2.2.1 The design of storage structure of a sequential list

The logical feature of linear lists is that the ordering relation between each node is one-to-one. In the computer, a one-dimensional array is a group of storage unit with continuous addresses which sequentially stores data of the same type, in which all elements also have a sequential one-to-one correspondence with each other. Therefore, we can use one-dimensional array to store each node of the linear list. According to the storage principle of "store the connections when storing the nodes," although the storage method of sequential list does not directly store the logical relation between the nodes, the nodes still manifest the logical relation of adjacency via the adjacency of physical addresses, that is, storage addresses.

2.2.1.1 The definition of sequential list
To store linear lists using arrays is called the sequential storage structure or sequential image of linear lists. Linear lists stored in this way are called sequential lists, as shown in Fig. 2.5. The index of elements of the linear list i starts from 1 in the figure. However, since in C language array index starts from 0, when we express operation algorithms on linear lists below, when expressing the array index stored by the linear list, we specifically use k for representation, $0 \le k \le n - 1$.

Index	0	1	...	k−1	k	k+1	...	n−1
Element	a_1	a_2	...	a_{i-1}	a_i	a_{i+1}	...	a_n

Fig. 2.5: Storing linear list with one-dimensional array.

2.2.1.2 The storage characteristics of sequential list

The storage of sequential list has the following characteristics:
- Logical adjacency corresponds to the adjacency of physical addresses
- Any element can be randomly accessed

Keyword Explanation Random access
Requiring the same constant time to visit any element in its storage, such a storage structure is random access structure. For example, for an array structure, as long as a subscript is chosen, we can visit the corresponding element, no matter where the subscript is within the array. The so-called constant visit time is, to say the time needed to get to any element within the array, the same with the time complexity of $O(1)$.

The way to calculate the address of the element a_i: $LOC(a_i) = LOC(a_1) + (i-1) \times L$, $(1 \leq i \leq n)$

where $LOC(a_i)$ represents the address of the data element a_i and L is the length of an individual element.

2.2.1.3 The design of the sequential list storage structure

Think and Discuss How to design the structure of the sequential list so that it completely describes the whole information of the sequential list?
Discussion: When we are defining the array in which we put the sequential list, the first problem we encounter is how long the array should be.
  To push this problem one step further is to ask how long the sequential list should be. Should it be exactly the same as the number of elements within the sequential list, or should it be more than the number of elements? If they are the same, then we cannot realize the insertion operation of the linear list. Therefore, it should be reasonable to set the length of the sequential list to be a bit longer than the number of current elements. Then, to facilitate computation, we must know the position of the last element within the sequential list. This can be indicated by setting a "last" pointer, and can also be indirectly indicated by a counter recording the number of elements, as shown in Fig. 2.6. To set aside backup space is for the purpose of having additional space for the insertion of new nodes.

Considering array index starts from 0 in C language, for the convenience of processing, in later applications, we specify that when last = –1, the sequential list is empty.

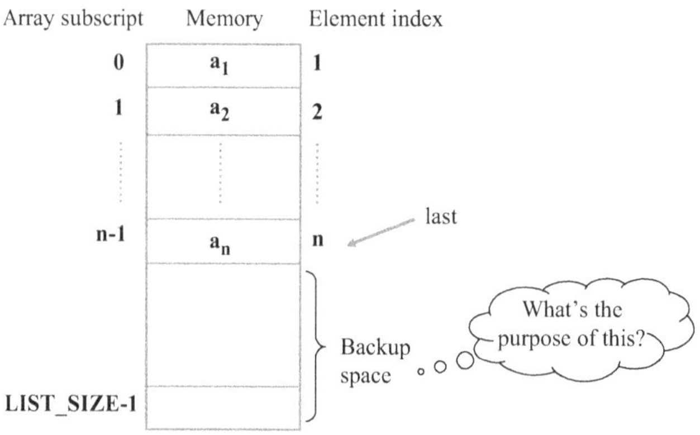

Array subscript　　Memory　　Element index

$$\begin{array}{c|c|c}
0 & a_1 & 1 \\
1 & a_2 & 2 \\
\vdots & \vdots & \vdots \\
n\text{-}1 & a_n & n \\
\end{array}$$

last

What's the purpose of this?

Backup space

LIST_SIZE-1

Fig. 2.6: Storage space of sequential list.

After the above discussion, we can give the type description of the sequential list as follows (Fig. 2.7).

Data structure description

typedef int ElemType;　　// Suppose the type of elements in the sequential list is integer

\# define LIST_SIZE 1024　　// Suppose the maximum length of the sequential list is 1024

typedef struct

{　ElemType data[LIST_SIZE];

　　int last;　　　　// Points to the location of the last node

} SequenList;

SequenList *LPtr;　　// Points to the pointer of SequenList struct

Note: In subsequent operations on sequential list we'll all use pointers of this name

Fig. 2.7: Structure definition of sequential list.

i　**Knowledge ABC** typedef – Giving a new name to a type

typedef is a keyword of C language. It is used to let the user define new type names on the basis of original data types (including basic types, struct types and pointers). Its syntax is:

typedef type_name type_identifier;

typedef is a system-reserved keyword. "type_name" is the name of a known data type, including basic data types and user-defined data types. "type_identifier" is the new type name. For example:

```
typedef int INT16; // Whenever INT16 appears in the program, it represents type int.
typedef long INT32; // Whenever INT32 appears in the program, it represents type long.
```

The advantage of using typedef in programming is to simplify some complicated type declarations. It can also improve the readability of programs.

Think and Discuss

Question 1: Why specifically set ElemType as the type of the node.

Question 2: What is the advantage of putting data array and last in the same structure?

Question 1 Discussion: Make the algorithm more generic. The node type can have different meanings in different questions, but the processing method will remain the same.

Question 2 Discussion: Make it easier to pass data between functions. All the information of the sequential list can be passed as a whole.

2.2.1.4 Think and discuss on the application of "struct"

Since the data in data structures are frequently composite types, we need to familiarize ourselves with the concept of struct. The following revises the concepts about struct via discussing problems in the storage of sequential list.

Question 1 Will the system allocate memory for the struct described below?

```
typedef struct
{ ElemType data[LIST_SIZE];
  int last;
} SequenList;
```

Question 2 What is the difference between the below two definitions of struct? How will the system allocate memory?

```
SequenList *L;
SequenList  L;
```

Question 3 How will the nodes be represented after we have defined the struct variable L?

```
SequenList L;
```

Question 4 How do we represent a node from the pointer p after p pointed to the memory used by L?

```
SequenList  L;
Sequenlist *p=&L;
```

Question 5 As shown in Fig. 2.8, what should we do when the node contains multiple data items, instead of the primitive type int?

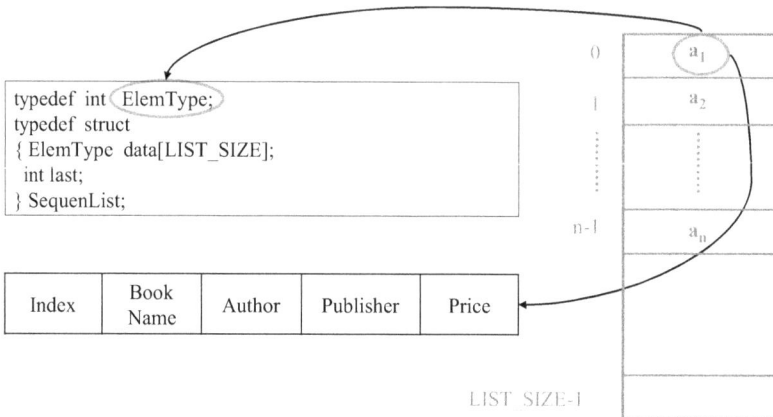

Fig. 2.8: The generic definition of node type.

Question 1 Discussion
Here, typedef gives an alternative name "SequenList" to the struct type, for the purpose of convenience instead of defining a variable. This describes the size of the memory space needed, and would not actually allocate memory space since no variable has been initialized.

Question 2 Discussion
SequenList *L; // Defines struct variable
defines a pointer to struct. A pointer to struct points to the data that is contained in the struct. The pointer variable itself only occupies the memory space of an int. The space allocated is sizeof(int);

SequenList L; // Defines struct variable

defines a struct variable. For such a variable, memory space is allocated according to the size of the type. Thus, the memory allocated is sizeof(SequenList).

Question 3 Discussion
First way of referring to a member of a struct: struct variable.struct member

```
L.data[0]=a1; // Assign value a1 to the position with subscript 0 in the
sequential list
X=L.last; // Get the value of last
```

Question 4 Discussion
Second way of referring to a member of struct: `struct pointer -> struct member`;

?

```
p-> data[0]=a1;
X=p->last
```

Question 5 Discussion We can just change the type definition of `ElemType`:

?

```
typedef struct card
{  int num;
   char name[20];
   char author[10];
   char publisher[30];
   float price;
} ElemType;
```

2.2.2 The operations on sequential list

According to the definition of sequential list, the following are the operations on it:
1. Initialization – giving initial values to the relevant parameters in the linear list
2. Getting the length – getting the number of elements in the linear list
3. Getting an element – getting the value of the element at the given location
4. Lookup – querying the location of the element that has the given value
5. Insertion – inserting the given value at the given location
6. Deletion – deleting the value at the given location or the element with the given value
7. Iteration – scanning the linear list from beginning to end, performing designated operations

2.2.2.1 The insertion operation of ordered list
Insert a node x in the position i of the sequential list, so that a sequential list of length n:

$$(a_1, \ldots, a_{i-1}, a_i, \ldots, a_n)$$

becomes a sequential list of length $n + 1$:

$$(a_1, \ldots, a_{i-1}, x, a_i, \ldots, a_n)$$

The demonstration of the insertion operation of sequential list is shown in Fig. 2.9. Normally, when we insert a new element before the ith ($1 \le i \le n$) element, we need to start from the last element a_n, move the $n - i + 1$ elements between a_n and the ith element to one position later. After the moving ends, the ith position will be empty. Then we can insert the new element. After the insertion ends, the length of the sequential list increases by 1.

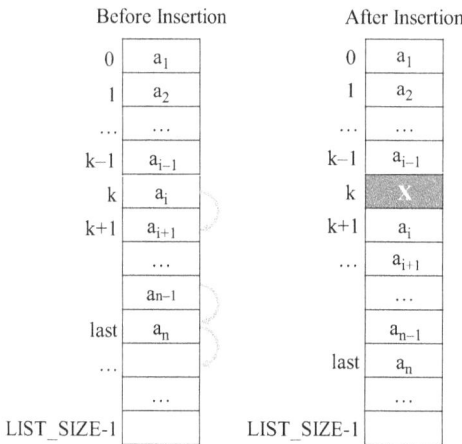

Fig. 2.9: Illustration of insertion operation on sequential list.

1. Design of test cases

The position of the insertion can be at the designated index or before the designated value. We design the algorithm according to the former case here.

The design table of test cases is given in Table 2.1.

Table 2.1: Test cases for insertion operation on sequential list.

	Normal cases	Boundary values	Abnormal cases
Insertion index k	$0 \le k \le n$	$K = 0, n$	$!(0 \le k \le n)$
Sequential list	Not full	Not full	Full or not full
Expected outcome	Successful insertion	Successful insertion	Failed insertion

Case 1: *k* is an illegal position, that is, the value of *k* is outside of 0 to *n*.

Case 2: The sequential list is already full.

Note: The various situations in case 1 and case 2 are not directly related. For example, when *k* is a normal value, the sequential list can either be in the illegal situation of "full" or in the normal situation of "not full."

2. Design of function structure

According to the table of test cases (Table 2.1), we can design the return values of the function to be: 1 – successful insertion; 0 – abnormalities have occurred.

The design of the function structure is given in Table 2.2.

Table 2.2: Function structure for insertion operation on sequential list.

Functionality description	Input	Output
Insertion of element in the sequential list `Insert_SqList`	Address of the sequential list `SequenList *`	Completion flag `int` 0: Abnormal 1: Normal
	Value to insert `ElemType`	
	Position to insert `int`	
Function name	Parameters	Function type

3. The pseudocode description of the algorithm

Intended behavior: Insert the new element *x* at a position with index *k* in the sequential list

Pseudocode description is given in Tables 2.3 and 2.4.

Table 2.3: Pseudocode for insertion in sequential list 1.

Description of the pseudocode in general	First level of elaboration
Insert new element *x* in position *k* of the sequential list	Dealing with abnormalities: return "unsuccessful" flag
	Move elements within the sequential list, empty the position indexed *k*
	Insert new element *x*
	Modify the pointer to the last element
	Return "successful" flag

Table 2.4: Pseudocode for insertion in sequential list 2.

Second level of elaboration	Third level of elaboration
If k is an illegal position, return 0; If the sequential list overflows, return 0;	if (k<0 || k>(LPtr->last+1)) return 0; if (LPtr->last ≥ LIST_SIZE−1) return 0;
Starting from the last element of the sequential list, move (last − k + 1) elements by one position	j=LPtr->last; when j≥k LPtr->data[j+1]=LPtr->data[j]; j--;
Insert x to the position k of the list	LPtr-> data[k]=x;
Last + 1	LPtr-> last=LPtr-> last+1;
return 1	return 1

4. Program implementation

```
/*====================================================================
Function functionality: Operation in sequential list - insertion of element
Function input: Address of the sequential list, value to insert, position to
insert
Function output: Completion flag - 0: Abnormal 1: Normal
====================================================================*/
int Insert_SqList(SeqList *LPtr, ElemType x, int k)
{ int j;
   if (LPtr->last>=LIST_SIZE-1) return FALSE; //Overflow
   else if (k<0 || k > (LPtr->last+1)) return FALSE;
   //Illegal Position
       else
       {
           for(j=LPtr->last; j>=k; j--)
           //Starting from the last element of the sequential list
           {
               LPtr->data[j+1]=LPtr->data[j];
               //Move the element (last- ) positions
           }
           LPtr-> data[k]=x;
           // Put x into the position k of the list
```

```
        LPtr-> last= LPtr-> last+1;
        // Modify the pointer to the last position
     }
  return TRUE;
}
```

5.   Analysis on the algorithm efficiency
The problematic factor here is the number of nodes. Let it be n, then after inserting new elements, it becomes $n + 1$. The time cost of this algorithm is mainly on the instruction which recursively moves elements. The number of times this instruction is executed (i.e., the number of times the nodes are moved) is last $- k + 1 = n - k$. From this we can see that the number of moves of nodes does not only depend on the length of the list but is also related to the insertion position k. See Table 2.5.

Table 2.5: Analysis of insertion position and number of moves.

Index of insertion k	0	1	2	...	k	...	$n-1$	n
Number of moves	n	$n-1$	$n-2$	...	$n-k$	...	1	0
Possibility p_k	$1/(n + 1)$	$1/(n + 1)$	$1/(n + 1)$	...	$1/(n + 1)$	...	$1/(n + 1)$	$1/(n + 1)$

Without loss of generality, suppose the probability of inserting a node into the list in any position ($0 \le k \le n$) is the same.
   Best-case scenario: When $k = n$, the instruction to move nodes will not be executed. The time complexity will be $O(1)$.
   Worst-case scenario: When $k = 0$, the instruction to move nodes will be executed repeatedly n times, we will need to move all nodes originally in the list.
   Average scenario: Inserting a node into kth position of a sequential list with length $n + 1$, there will be $n - k$ moves. Expressing the average number of moves with $E_{is}(n)$:

$$E_{is}(n) = \sum_{k=0}^{n} p_k(n - k) = \frac{1}{n+1} \times \frac{n(n+1)}{2} = \frac{n}{2}$$

From this we can see that the insertion operation on sequential list moves half of the elements in the list. The average time complexity is $O(n)$.

2.2.2.2 Deletion operation on sequential list
Deleting the ith ($1 \le i \le n$) node of the linear list, so that the linear list with length n is

$$(a_1, \ldots, a_{i-1}, a_i, a_{i+1}, \ldots, a_n)$$

becomes a linear list of size $n - 1$:

$$(a_1, \ldots, a_{i-1}, a_{i+1}, \ldots, a_n)$$

The demonstration of the deletion operation on sequential list is shown in Fig. 2.10. We will also have to move the nodes in order to fill the void caused by the deletion operation, so that even after the deletion the elements are still adjacent to each other in terms of physical addresses, maintaining the logical adjacency. If $i = n$, then we can simply delete the terminal node and there is no need to move the nodes; if $1 \le i \le n-1$, then we must move the nodes at positions $i + 1, i + 2, \ldots, n$ to positions $i, i + 1, \ldots, n - 1$ one by one. In total, we need to move forward the $(i + 1)$th to the nth nodes, that is, $(n - i)$ elements.

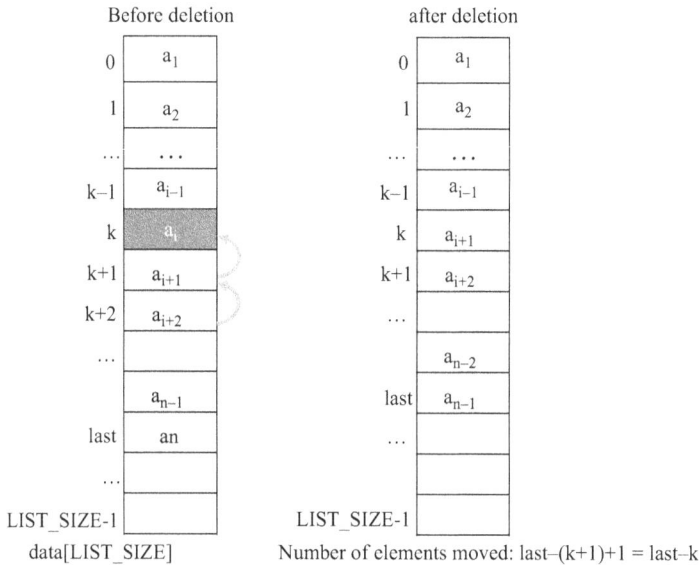

Fig. 2.10: Demonstration of deletion operation on sequential list.

Let the index of the ith node be k, then we need to move forward the $(k + 1)$th node to the last node, that is, (last $- k$) elements.

1. Design of test cases

Input: the address of the sequential list, the index of the node to delete, k.

Output: flag indicating whether the operation succeeded.

Test cases are given in Table 2.6.

According to the table of test cases, output information is designed as: 1 – deletion successful; 0 – abnormalities occurred.

2. Description of the data structure: same as insertion operation.
3. Design of function structure: see Table 2.7.

Table 2.6: Test cases for deletion operation on sequential list.

	Normal cases	Boundary values	Abnormal cases
Index of element to delete	$0 \leq k \leq n-1$	$K = 0, n-1$	$!(0 \leq k \leq n-1)$
Sequential list	Not empty	Not empty	Empty
Expected result	Deletion successful	Deletion successful	Deletion failed

Table 2.7: Function structure design of deletion operation on the sequential list.

Function description	Input	Output
Deleting element from sequential list Delete_SqList	Address of sequential list: SequenList * Position of deletion: int	Completion flag int 0: Abnormal 1: Normal
Function name	Parameters	Function type

4. Pseudocode description of the algorithm

Delete the node with index k inside the sequential list. Pseudocode is given in Tables 2.8 and 2.9.

Table 2.8: Pseudocode for deletion operation on sequential list 1.

Top-level description of pseudocode	First-level elaboration
Delete the node at index k in the sequential list	Abnormalities occurred, return
	Move the elements in order, cover the deleted units Modify the pointer to the last position of the elements Return normally

Table 2.9: Pseudocode for deletion operation on sequential list 2.

Second-level elaboration	Third-level elaboration
k is out of range of the list is empty, return 0	if !(0≤ k ≤ LPtr->last) return 0; if LPtr->last==-1 return 0;

Starting from the $(k + 1)$th element of the sequential
list, move forward (last – k) elements
	int j=k;
	While (j ≤ LPtr-> last)
	    LPtr-> data[j] = LPtr-> data [j+1];
	    j++;

Last – 1 Return 1	LPtr-> last –; return 1

5. Program implementation

From the three-level detailing of the pseudocode, we arrive at the corresponding program implementation:

```
/*=================================================================
Functionality of the Function: Operation on Sequential List - Deletion of
Element
Input of Function: Address of Sequential List, Index of the node to delete
Output of function: completion flag: 0: abnormal 1: normal
===============================================================*/
int Delete_SqList(SeqList *LPtr, int k)
{
    if (( k >= 0 && k<= LPtr->last) &&( LPtr->last!=-1))
    {
       for ( int j = k;  j <= LPtr->last;  j++ )
       {
            LPtr->data[j] = LPtr-> data[j+1];
       }
       LPtr->last --;
       return TRUE;      //Successful Deletion
    }
    return FALSE;     //Abnormalities
}
```

6. Analysis of the efficiency of the algorithm

Let the number of nodes be n. As insertion operation, the time cost of deletion operation is mainly on instructions that move the nodes forward. The number of execution of this instruction is last $-$ $k = n - 1 - k$; therefore, the number of moves performed on the nodes does not only depend on the length of the list, but also on the position of deletion; see Table 2.10.

Table 2.10: Analysis on the relation between deletion index and number of moves.

Deletion index k	0	1	2	...	i	...	$n - 2$	$n - 1$
Number of moves	$n - 1$	$n - 2$	$n - 3$	...	$n - i - 1$	...	1	0
Probability p_k	$1/n$	$1/n$	$1/n$	...	$1/n$	...	$1/n$	$1/n$

Best-case scenario: when $k = n - 1$, no moves will occur. The time complexity is $O(1)$. Worst-case scenario: when $k = 0$, the instruction will be executed repeatedly $n - 1$ times, as we need to move all the original nodes in the list.

Average scenario: suppose that the possibility of deleting a node is the same at any position of the list, then the average number of moves E_{dl} is

$$E_{\mathrm{dl}}(n) = p_k \sum_{k=0}^{n-1} (n-k) = \frac{1}{n} \times \frac{(n-1) \times n}{2} = \frac{n-1}{2}$$

From this we can see that performing the deletion operation on the sequential list will move half of the elements in the list on average. The average time complexity of the algorithm is $O(n)$. Both the deletion and insertion operations on sequential list belong to the same category.

2.2.2.3 Lookup operation of elements in sequential list

Find the given value in the sequential list (when there exist multiple values that are the same, only find the first one).

Line of thought: starting from the first element, compare the element with the given value. If those two are equal, then the lookup succeeds; otherwise, if after looking through n elements there is no match, then there is no element matching the search condition, and the search fails.

1. Test cases are given in Table 2.11.

Table 2.11: Test cases for lookup of elements.

	Normal cases	Abnormal cases
Sequential list	There is the given value in the sequential list	The given value does not exist in the sequential list
Predicted result	Found	Not found

2. Function structure is given in Table 2.12.

Table 2.12: Function structure for element lookup.

Description of functionality	Input	Output
Look up the given value in the sequential list Locate_SqList	Address of sequential list: SequenList * Value of the node: ElemType	Normal: index: int Abnormal: −1
Function name	Parameters	Function type

3. Function implementation

```
/*=================================================================
Functionality of the function: Operation on sequential list - locate the given
value
Input of the function: Address of the sequential list, value of the node
Output of the function: Normal: index of the element; Abnormal: -1
=================================================================*/
int Locate_SqList(SeqList *LPtr, ElemType key)
{
    for(int i=0; i<= LPtr->last; i++)
        if(LPtr->data[i]== key) return i;
    return -1;
}
```

Average time complexity: $f(n) = (1/n) * (1 + n) * n/2 = (1 + n)/2$

$$O(f(n)) = O(n)$$

2.2.2.4 Accessing data element from sequential list

Obtain the value of the element at the given index.

Line of thought: Since the sequential list uses the array data structure, it is a random access structure; thus, we can directly get the value of the element in the corresponding array. We only need to pay attention to whether the given index is out of bounds.

1. Test cases are given in Table 2.13.

Table 2.13: Test cases for accessing data elements.

Test scenario	Normal cases	Boundary cases	Abnormal cases
	The index is between 0 and $n - 1$	The index is 0; The index is $n - 1$	The index is out of bounds
Predicted results	Element obtained	Element obtained	Operation failure

2. Function structure is given in Table 2.14.

Table 2.14: Function structure for accessing data elements.

Functionality description	Input	Output
Get the value of the element at the given index in the sequential list Get_SqList	Address of the sequential list SequenList *	Return Normal: 1
	Index int	Abnormal: 0
	(Node value: ElemType)	Node value: ElemType
Function name	Parameters	Function type

Note: Both input and output in Table 2.14 have "node value" item, which means we pass the parameter by its address.

3. Program implementation

```
/*==============================================================
Functionality of the function: Operation on the sequential list - obtain the
value of the element at the given index
Function input: Address of the sequential list, index
Function output: Normal: 1, Abnormal: 0
==============================================================*/
int Get_SqList( SeqList *LPtr, int i, ElemType *e)
{
    if( i<0 || i>LPtr->last) return FALSE;
    if( LPtr->last <0) return FALSE;
    *e= LPtr->data[i];
    return TRUE;
}
```

4. Analysis on the efficiency of the algorithm: time complexity $O(1)$.

2.2.3 Discussion on the sequential storage structure

The characteristic of the sequential list is that the elements that are adjacent logically are also adjacent in their physical storage locations. Also, the memory space of the sequential list needs to be preallocated.

Advantages:

1. Various high-level languages have arrays; thus, it is easy to implement.
2. Compact usage of memory space.
3. Random access using the index of the element.

Disadvantages:
1. When realizing insertion and deletion operations in the sequential list, half of the elements are moved on average; thus, the operation efficiency is low on sequential lists where n is big.
2. We need to preallocate the memory space according to the biggest space usage estimation. If the estimate is too high, the later parts of the sequential list will be largely idle; if the estimate is too low, there will be overflow.
3. It is hard to expand the size of the list.

2.3 The second storage method for linear list – linked list

Think like an amateur; execute as an expert [2]   Takeo Kanade

2.3.1 Introduction 1 – the story of word

Microsoft has decided to develop a worldwide-applicable word-processing software, Word. The design goal was to possess stronger functionalities than any other similar software that already existed. The development team met a challenging issue when designing the software – as a generic software, how much space should be allocated for each document to satisfy the needs of different users? Specifically:

Issue 1: as the designers of the software, how do they know how much information the users enter, that is, how many pages of documents do the users need?

Issue 2: what to do under the circumstance where even the users themselves cannot preestimate how many pages the document will contain?

How to solve the above issues?

According to our existing knowledge about arrays and data structures to satisfy the needs of all users, it is only possible to allocate an array structure as large as possible. The drawbacks of such an approach are obvious: once Word is run, then a lot of memory will be occupied by the software, and the performance of the machine will suffer. However, most users do not need so many pages in their documents, so such an approach is not reasonable.

The most practical line of thought is, no matter how many pages are requested by the users, they always start from the first page. Therefore, when Word is first launched and initialized, the system allocates the memory space of one page for the users. If the page is full and the user still needs a new page, then allocate a new page from memory for the users to use. This is the method of allocation according to the needs.

Such a method sounds good on paper. But if we need to dynamically allocate space when the program is running, does the programming language provide such mechanisms? Fortunately, at least now there are library functions in C language that implement such functionalities.

Following up on the functionalities of dynamic memory allocation, we can see that the location of each new page is randomly assigned by the system, and cannot follow the need of the programmer, who might want each page to be stored contiguously in the memory space. Then, the new question is, how to connect such dynamically allocated pages with each other in the memory space based on page numbers? That is to say, there has to be a certain kind of correspondence between the logical connection among pages and their storage locations, so that we will be able to find them after they are stored. According to the experience from the sequential lists discussed above, we can view one page as one node, and store them in order, that is, the logical relations between the nodes will be embodied via the adjacency in storage spaces. Now the question can be summarized as: the logical relation among the nodes is orderly, while the storage is discrete and unorderly. How do we store the logical relation among the nodes under such circumstances?

Continuing our line of thought, can we record the address of the next node on some data field of the first node? In this way, we can find the second node after knowing the first node, and so on. As shown in Fig. 2.11, only in this way do we finish the storage of both data and the relations among data. This illustrates the two basic principles of data storage mentioned in the introduction.

(a) Data storage principle A: store both the value and the relations.
(b) Data storage principle B: data should be able to get both stored and retrieved.

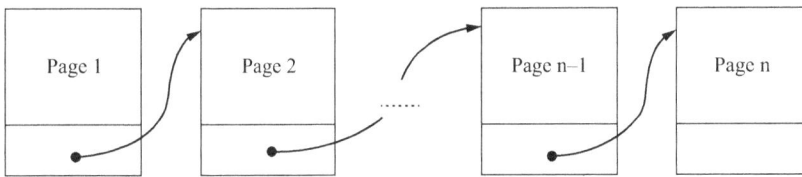

Fig. 2.11: The discrete storage form of linear logical relation.

Since the form of Fig. 2.11 is similar to "links" in our daily life, we call it "linked list."

Knowledge ABC Dynamic memory management
The basic problem in dynamic memory management is: how does the system: 1. allocate memory according to the requests; 2. recycle memory for reuse?
Idle blocks: unallocated memory blocks with contiguous addresses are called "idle blocks."
Occupied blocks: memory blocks with contiguous addresses that are already allocated to users are called "idle blocks."
When the system has just started, the whole memory can be seen as a huge "idle block." As user requests come in, system distributes the corresponding memory in order, as shown in Fig. 2.12(a).

U1	U2	U3	U4	U5	

(a) Initial period of system operation

U1		U3		U5	

(b) After a period of time of system operation

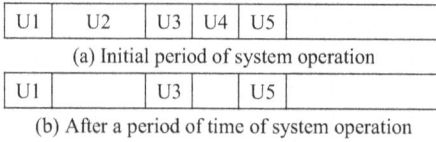

Fig. 2.12: Memory status: (a) initial period of system operation and (b) after a period of system operation.

While the system is running, memory is divided into two sections: lower address section (left, some of which occupied) and higher address section (right, idle). After a period of time, some programs finish running and release the memory occupied by them, making it idle block again. This will cause an interlacing between the idle blocks and occupied blocks, as shown in Fig. 2.12(b).

When the system is in the status shown in Fig. 2.12(b), and a new user comes in to request memory, how should the system respond?

Method 1: the system continues allocating from higher address section, until it can no longer do so. Only when the remaining idle blocks cannot satisfy the allocation request, the system recycles all the unused memory blocks, and reorganizes the memory, compacting all the idle blocks into a huge idle block in order to prepare for reallocation.

Method 2: idleness linked list. Idleness linked list contains all the information about idle blocks, with each node corresponding to one idle block. When the user requests allocation, the system searches the idleness linked list, finds a suitable idle block according to a certain strategy to perform the allocation and deletes the corresponding node. When the user releases the occupied memory, the system recycles it and inserts it into the idleness linked list, as shown in Fig. 2.13. Common operating systems frequently use linked lists to manage memory.

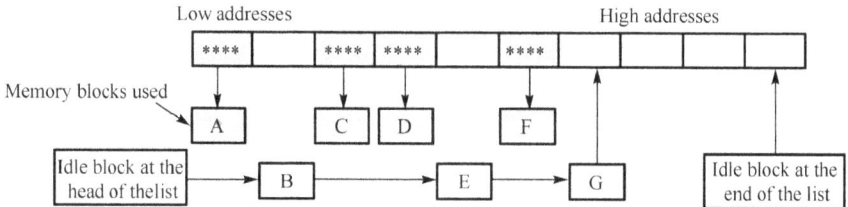

Fig. 2.13: Memory management.

2.3.2 Introduction 2 – linked lists in mobile phones

The previous "story about Word" was actually fabricated in order to illustrate the principles and applications of linked lists. The following is a real example of the usage of linked list in mobile phones.

Nowadays, a lot of places provide free WiFi for mobile phones and notebooks to connect to the Internet wirelessly. In a lot of cases, one has to enter username and password to connect to the Internet. This is an identity verification mechanism for legal and safe communication. Usually, the verification is performed between the mobile phone and the wireless access point (shortened as AP, is the connection point for wireless devices such as mobile phone and notebooks to enter into wired network). Identity verification is quite time-costly, and the position of the mobile phone user constantly changes. To ensure the real-timeness of communications, that is, prevent temporary disconnection during conversations or freezing of video streaming, now a frequently employed technology is preverification of identity between the mobile phone user and AP, in order to realize swift switching of APs and ensure the real-timeness of the communication operations. See Fig. 2.14.

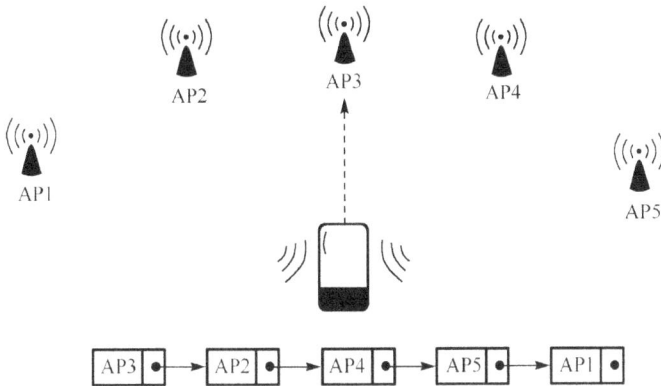

Fig. 2.14: WiFi authentication.

Here is how preverification of identity is realized in detail: when the mobile phone user logs in via AP3, he does not only complete the identity verification with AP3, but also finish those with other APs around to which he is possible to switch, for example, AP1, AP2, AP4 and AP5. All those APs were already detected by AP3 and stored in it. AP3 will transfer the information about the other APs (e.g., the result of verification and preshared key for verification) to the mobile phone. As the user moves, the AP will also dynamically change, for example, leaving AP3 and arriving near AP5. In this way, the number of APs in the mobile phone will also constantly change. Since it is impossible to preestimate the number of APs, according to the number of currently available APs, the mobile phone will dynamically create nodes to store AP information, using linked list as the storage structure. In this way, the storage space in an embedded system such as mobile phone is saved, making it a reasonable storage plan. The preverification process involves the creation of linked lists and the insertion of new nodes, and the switching process involves the iteration of nodes in the linked list. After the mobile phone has left the corresponding AP for some period of time, if the information stored in this node is no longer used, the deletion operation on this node will be performed.

In other practical problems, there are many examples of the application of linked list. For example, when a computer receives input information, and it is impossible to forecast the input length, equal-length data structure will be used as nodes to store received information; if they are not enough, then more storage nodes will be dynamically requested. On the Internet, the sending and receiving of information is also realized via segmentation (grouping) of data.

Linked storage structure is widely applied. After we know its principles, we can "execute as an expert" to design the data structure of linked lists.

2.3.3 The storage of singly linked lists

2.3.3.1 The structural design of nodes of linked lists

First, we need to consider the structure of linked nodes and follow the storage principles. We should include the two types of information below:
- The information in the storage node a_i itself
- The addresses of the nodes adjacent to the storage node a_i

The structure of the node is shown in Fig. 2.15, in which:

Information stored in the node	Address of adjacent node
data	next

Fig. 2.15: Structure of the linked node.

data – stores the value of the node; it is usually called "data field."

next – stores the address of the immediate successor of the node; it is usually called "pointer field" or "link field."

Note: 1. The linked list links the n nodes of the linear list together according to their logical sequences, using the link field of each node.
2. The linked list in which every node has only one link field is called singly linked list.

2.3.3.2 How are the nodes in the linked list linked together in the storage space?

Example 2.1: Example demonstrating the linked storage structure.
How to store the linear list (bat, cat, fat, hat, mat, rat, sat, vat) into the linked list?
Solution: The address of every node in the linear list is obtained via dynamic allocation (for knowledge on dynamic allocation in C language, see Knowledge ABC below Fig. 2.23) and ordered according to the storage address. During a certain computation, the situation in the linked list is shown in Table 2.15. We can fill out the pointer fields in Table 2.15 according to the logical order of the data field of each node.

After filling Table 2.15, we will discover two problems:

Table 2.15: Storage Information for Linked List.

Storage address	Data field	Pointer field
1	hat	43
7	cat	14
13	fat	1
19	vat	
25	rat	37
31	bat	7
37	sat	19
43	mat	25

Problem 1: How should we fill in the pointer field of the last node "vat"?
Problem 2: Is it inconvenient to find which one is the first node just from the table?

To solve the above problems, we can set a "head" pointer to record the position of the first node. The storage address of each node in a singly linked list is stored in the next field of its preceding node, but the starting node does not have a predecessor; thus, we should point the header pointer "head" to the starting node. The last node does not have a successor, so we should set the pointer field of the last node to empty, marking it with the empty pointer NULL, as shown in Fig. 2.16. The logical structure of the linked list is demonstrated in Fig. 2.17.

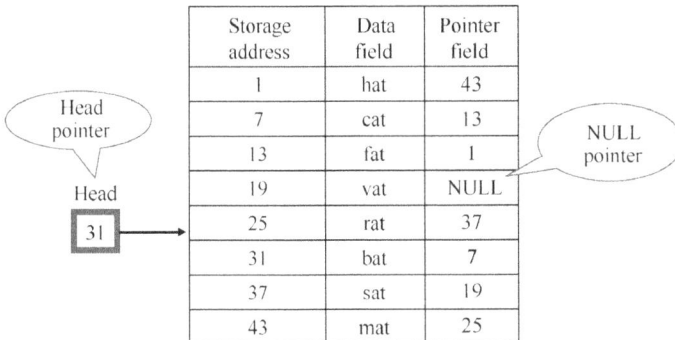

Fig. 2.16: The storage information of the linked list.

The linked list is determined uniquely by the head pointer. Singly linked list can be named by the name of the head pointer, for example, a linked list with head pointer named head can be called list head.

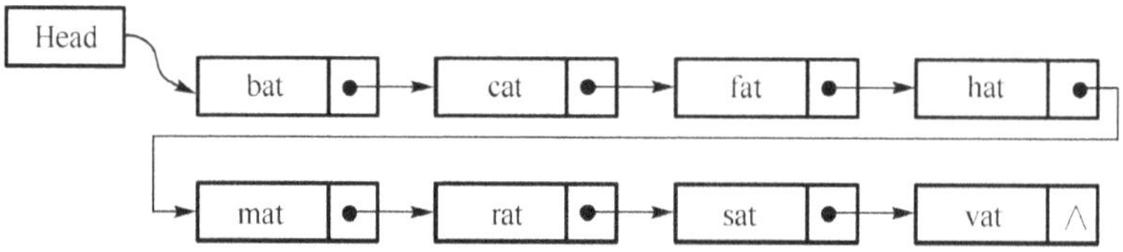

Fig. 2.17: The logical structure of the linked list.

 Term Explanation Linearly linked list
A linked list with only one pointer field in a node is also called singly linked list. In a singly linked list, except for the first and the last nodes, every node has one predecessor and one successor. Thus, we call singly linked list as linearly linked list.

The structure and type descriptions of a node in a singly linked list are shown in Fig. 2.18. In this structure, member "next" is a bit special, that is, it is a pointer to the same type as the node. It means:
1. next is a pointer;
2. next is of type struct node;
3. the value of next is an address of a node of type struct node;
4. the storage space pointed to by next stores value of type struct node.

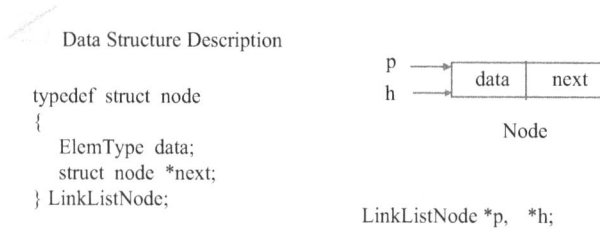

Data Structure Description

```
typedef struct node
{
    ElemType data;
    struct node *next;
} LinkListNode;
```

LinkListNode *p, *h;

Fig. 2.18: Structural description of singly linked lists.

Example 2.2: Analysis of node structure via tracing.
Program implementation of the linkage between two nodes in shown in Fig. 2.19.

 Fig. 2.19: Two nodes linking with each other.

Solution:

1. Line of thought for the algorithm

To realize the linkage between two nodes as shown in Fig. 2.19, the steps are as follows:

(1) Construct two nodes x, y

(2) Fill the address of node y into the pointer field of node x.

2. Program implementation

```
typedef struct node
{
  int data;
  struct node *next;
} LinkListNode;
int main( )
{
  LinkListNode x,y,*p; // Define space for nodes x,y
  x.data=6;                    // Give value to the data field of node x
  x.next=NULL;                 // Set the pointer field of node x to NULL
  y.data=8;
  y.next=NULL;
  p=&y;
  x.next=p;        // Write the address of node y into the pointer field of node x
  return 0;
}
```

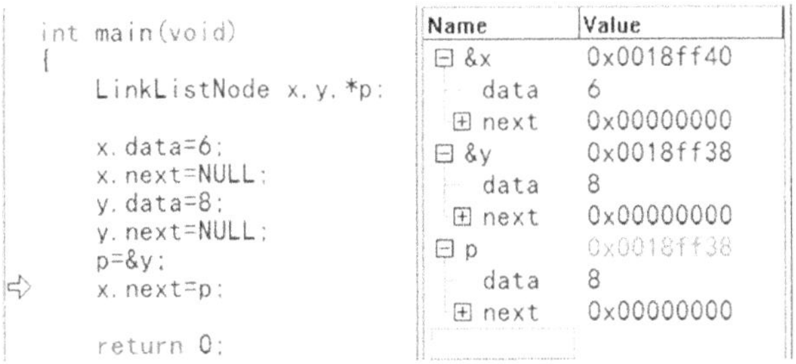

Name	Value
⊟ &x	0x0018ff40
data	6
⊞ next	0x00000000
⊟ &y	0x0018ff38
data	8
⊞ next	0x00000000
⊟ p	0x0018ff38
data	8
⊞ next	0x00000000

```
int main(void)
{
    LinkListNode x, y, *p;

    x.data=6;
    x.next=NULL;
    y.data=8;
    y.next=NULL;
    p=&y;
⇨   x.next=p;

    return 0;
```

Fig. 2.20: Step 1 of tracing of node structure.

Figure 2.20 shows the memory form of struct variables x,y and the values they contain. The struct pointer p records the address of y.

Figure 2.21 shows the situation when we put the address of y into x.next.

Figure 2.22 shows we can find the address of node y via x.next.

From the results of the tracing, we can map the relation between the addresses of nodes x and y, shown in Fig. 2.23.

```
int main(void)
{
    LinkListNode x, y, *p;

    x.data=6;
    x.next=NULL;
    y.data=8;
    y.next=NULL;
    p=&y;
    x.next=p;

    return 0;
```

Name	Value
⊟ &x	0x0018ff40
data	6
⊞ next	0x0018ff38
⊟ &y	0x0018ff38
data	8
⊞ next	0x00000000
⊟ p	0x0018ff38
data	8
⊞ next	0x00000000

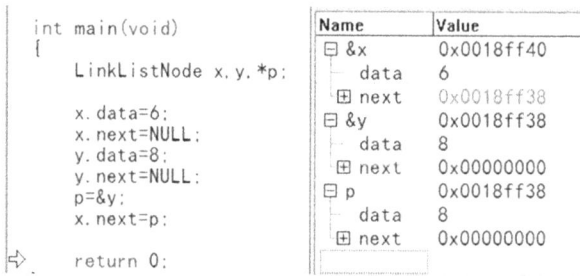

Fig. 2.21: Step 2 of tracing of node structure.

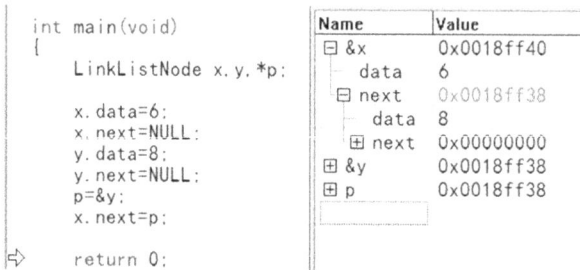

```
int main(void)
{
    LinkListNode x, y, *p;

    x.data=6;
    x.next=NULL;
    y.data=8;
    y.next=NULL;
    p=&y;
    x.next=p;

    return 0;
```

Name	Value
⊟ &x	0x0018ff40
data	6
⊟ next	0x0018ff38
data	8
⊞ next	0x00000000
⊞ &y	0x0018ff38
⊞ p	0x0018ff38

Fig. 2.22: Tracing of node structure step 3.

Fig. 2.23: Relation between nodes.

The memory space for the linked list in this example is allocated statically. Another method is to request for space when the program is running, that is, dynamic requesting.

Knowledge ABC Dynamic memory allocation
In C language, there is an allocation method for memory spaces called "dynamic memory allocation": when the program needs memory space during runtime, it gets allocated designated memory spaces via "requests"; when the memory requested becomes idle, it can be released at any time so that the system can reallocate it. The related library functions include malloc( ), calloc( ), free( ), realloc( ). When using these functions, you should include headers stdlib.h or malloc.h or alloc.h at the beginning of the program.

Memory Allocation Function malloc()
Function format: void* malloc(unsigned size);
Function functionality: allocate a block of size bytes from the memory.

Parameters: Size is an unsigned integer, which is used to designate the number of bytes of the memory space needed.

Return value: The address of the newly allocated memory. If there is not enough memory to be allocated, NULL is returned.

Note: (1) When size is 0, NULL is returned.

(2) void* is a pointer to void type. It can point to data storage unit of any type. Void type pointers need explicit type conversions in order to be used as pointers to other types.

Function to Free Memory free( )   **!**
Function format: void free(void*block);
   Function functionality: release the memory allocated via calloc( ), malloc( ) and realloc( ) as free memory space.

Parameters: block is a pointer to void type, which points to the memory space to be released.

Return value: None

Example: void free(void *p); frees the memory space pointed to by p from dynamic memory area. p is the return value from calling malloc. Function free does not have a return value.

1. The request for node: p=(LinkListNode *)malloc(sizeof(LinkListNode));
    Function malloc allocates memory space sized LinkListNode, and puts its beginning address to pointer variable p.
2. The release of the node: free(p);
    Release the memory space used by the node variable, pointed to by p.
3. Visiting data items in the node.
    Use the node pointer p to visit variables stored in the node
    Method one: (*p). data and (*p).next
    Method two: p->data and p->next

Think and Discuss   **!**
Question 1: Do the two frames mean the same thing in Fig. 2.24 linked list discussion question 1.

```
p=(LinkListNode *)malloc(sizeof(LinkListNode));
h=(LinkListNode *)malloc(sizeof(LinkListNode));
```
```
p=h=(LinkListNode *)malloc(sizeof( LinkListNode ));
```

Fig. 2.24: Linked list discussion question 1.

Question 2: What are the values of the expressions in Fig. 2.25

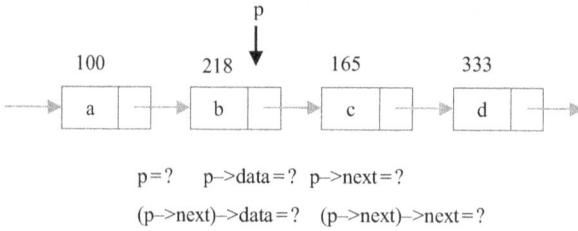

Fig. 2.25: Linked list discussion question 2.

Discussion on question 1: Not the same. In the first box, two nodes are requested. In the second box, only one node is requested.
  Discussion on question 2:

```
p=218    p->data=b   p->next=165
(p->next)->data=c   (p->next)->next=333
```

Think and Discuss What are the advantages of storing the nodes discretely?
Discussion: The characteristic of linked list is to store logically adjacent elements using nonadjacent storage units. In terms of memory management, we do not need to use a whole block of contiguous memory to store data that is logically adjacent.

2.3.4 Operations on the singly linked list

Normally, we draw singly linked lists as sequences of nodes connected by arrows. The arrow between nodes represents the pointer (address) in the pointer field. Two common forms of singly linked lists are shown in Fig. 2.26. headA is called singly linked list without head node; headB is singly linked list with head node, where the head node is positioned in the first place in the list. The head node has the same structure as other nodes, but does not contain values itself, and only signifies the

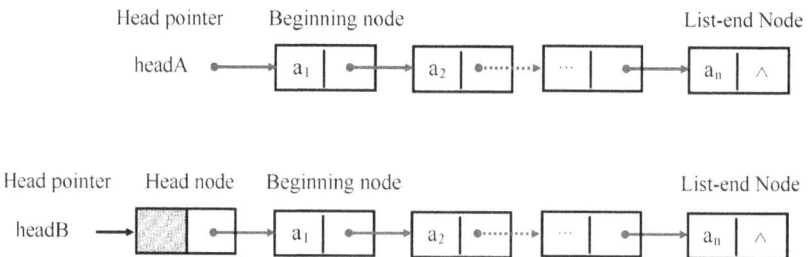

Fig. 2.26: Two common forms of singly linked list.

beginning of the list. In some applications, it can be used to store additional information such as the length of the list.

In singly linked lists without head nodes, the head pointer directly points to the first node in the singly linked list.

Think and Discuss What is the purpose of setting the head pointer?
Discussion: Head pointer is not mandatory in a linked list. It is just for the convenience of operation. It has the following two advantages.
1. Since the position of the beginning node is stored in the pointer field of the head pointer, we can operate on the first position of the linked list in the same manner as we operate on other positions, and there is no need for special processing.
2. No matter whether the linked list is empty, the head pointer will point to a non-NULL pointer, which is the head node (in an empty list, the head node will contain NULL in the pointer field); thus, the processing of both empty and nonempty lists is unified.

According to the characteristics of the linked list, in this section we will discuss operations on linked list, including initialization, construction, lookup, insertion and deletion.

2.3.4.1 Initialization of singly linked lists

Construct an empty singly linked list with only one head pointer. An example of the empty list is shown in Fig. 2.27.

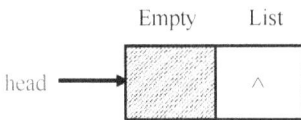

Empty List

head ──────▶

Fig. 2.27: Empty linked list.

Function design is given in Table 2.16.

Table 2.16: The design of the function for initialization of linked list.

Functionality description	Input	Output
Initialization of singly linked list initialize_LkList	None	Pointer to the head of the linked list: LinkListNode *
Function name	Parameters	Function type

Program implementation

```
/*=================================================================
Functionality of the function: Operation on the singly linked list -
Initialization
Function input: None
Function output: Head pointer of the linked list
=============================================================*/
LinkListNode *initialize_LkList(void)
{
    LinkListNode *head;
    head=(LinkListNode *)malloc(sizeof(LinkListNode)); //Request one node
    if(head ==NULL)  exit(1); //The allocation of memory failed
    head->next=NULL; //Set the pointer field to NULL
    return head;
}
```

Note: Normally for a program that requests very little memory, there would not be problems when dynamically requesting new node spaces. But in real applications, especially programs that require a lot of memory, whenever there is dynamic request of memory, you must check whether the request is successful, in order to prevent the situation where the system does not have any more memory to allocate.

Example 2.3: Using the method of dynamically requesting nodes, implement the linkage of the two nodes in Example 2.2.

Solution:
To implement the linkage between the two nodes in Fig. 2.28, the steps are as follows:
1. Dynamically request for two nodes 3 and y (the results of dynamic request are the addresses of the nodes xPtr and yPtr).
2. Fill the address of node y, yPtr, into the pointer field of node x.

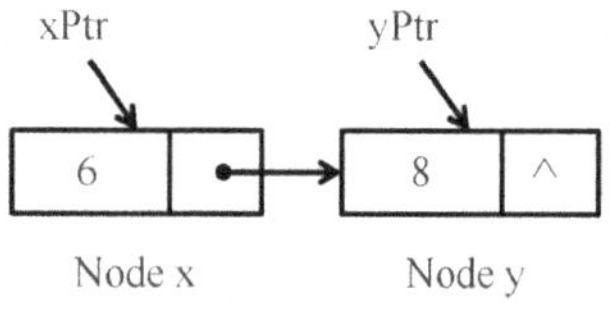

Fig. 2.28: Connection between two nodes 2.

Program implementation

```
typedef struct node
{
    int data;
    struct node *next;
} LinkListNode;
int main(void )
{
    LinkListNode *xPtr,*yPtr;// Define pointers to nodes
    xPtr =(LinkListNode *)malloc(sizeof(LinkListNode)); // Request node x
    xPtr->next=NULL; // Set the pointer field of node x to NULL
    yPtr =(LinkListNode *)malloc(sizeof(LinkListNode)); // Request node y
    yPtr->next=NULL; // Set the pointer field of node y to NULL
    xPtr->data=6; // Give value to the data field of node x
    yPtr->data=8; // Give value to the data field of node y
    xPtr->next=yPtr; // Write the address of node y to the pointer field of node x
    return 0;
}
```

Step-by-step tracing
1.   Request node x, whose address is 0x004317a0. See Fig. 2.29.

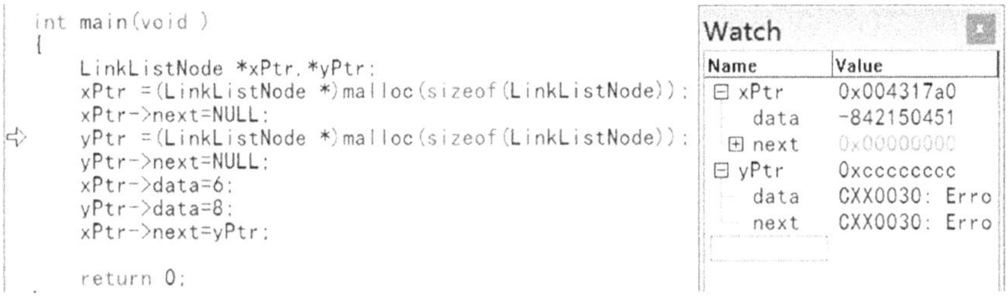

Fig. 2.29: Step 1 in dynamic request for node.

2.   Request node y, whose address is 0x00431760; see Fig. 2.30. Fill the data fields of nodes x and y with 6 and 8, respectively.

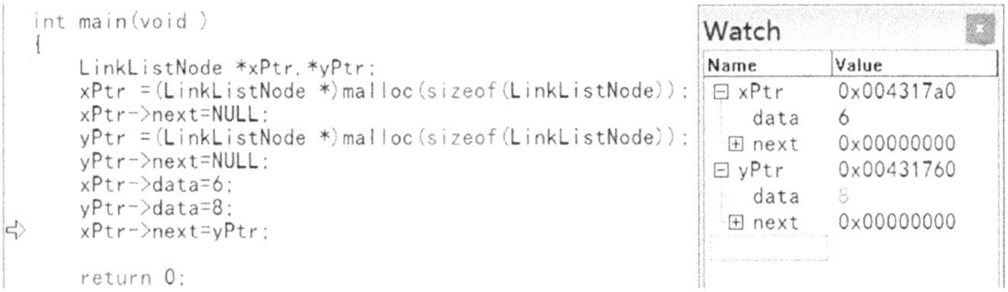

Fig. 2.30: Step 2 in dynamic request for node.

3. Fill the address of node y, 0x00431760, into the pointer field of x; see Fig. 2.31.

```
int main(void )
{
    LinkListNode *xPtr, *yPtr;
    xPtr =(LinkListNode *)malloc(sizeof(LinkListNode));
    xPtr->next=NULL;
    yPtr =(LinkListNode *)malloc(sizeof(LinkListNode));
    yPtr->next=NULL;
    xPtr->data=6;
    yPtr->data=8;
    xPtr->next=yPtr;

    return 0;
```

Watch	
Name	Value
⊟ xPtr	0x004317a0
data	6
⊟ next	0x00431760
data	8
⊞ next	0x00000000
⊟ yPtr	0x00431760
data	8
⊞ next	0x00000000

Fig. 2.31: Step 3 in dynamic request for node.

2.3.4.2 Construction of singly linked lists

To store the n elements of a linear list into one singly linked list, head is the head pointer. There are various methods to construct singly linked lists; we will introduce them separately.

1. Constructing the singly linked link by inserting to the end

Construct the linked list by continuously inserting nodes into the end of singly linked lists. The steps are shown in Fig. 2.32. The description can be seen at the first-level elaboration of the pseudocode (Table 2.17).

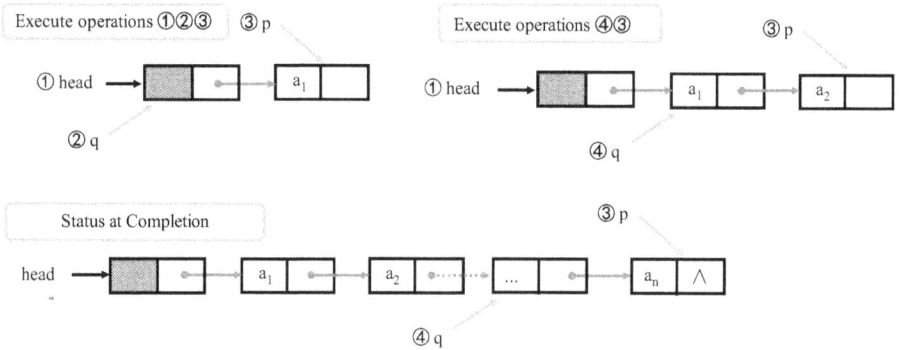

Fig. 2.32: Steps of constructing a linked list by inserting to the rear.

Table 2.17: The data structure for constructing linked list by inserting to the rear.

Functionality description	Input	Output
Construct linked list by inserting to the rear Create_Rear_LkList	Node value ElemType	Head pointer to the linked list LinkListNode *
	Number of nodes int	
Function name	Parameters	Function type

- Description of the data structure: see Fig. 2.33.
- Design of function structure: see Table 2.19.
- Pseudocode description of the algorithm: see Table 2.18.
- Program implementation

```
/*=====================================================================
Functionality of the function: Operation on singly linked list - Construct
linked list by insertion to the end
Function input: Array of node values, number of nodes
Function output: Head pointer of the linked list
=====================================================================*/
LinkListNode *Create_Rear_LkList(ElemType a[],int n )
{
    LinkListNode *head,*p, *q;
    int i;
    head=(LinkListNode *)malloc(sizeof(LinkListNode));
    q=head;
    for(i=0;i<n;i++)
    {
        p=(LinkListNode *)malloc(sizeof(LinkListNode));
        p->data=a[i];
        q->next=p;
        q=p;
    }
    p->next=NULL;
    return head;
}
```

Data structure description

head	data	next
Head pointer	node	

Head pointer of the linked list: LinkListNode *head
node values :   ElemType a[]
number of nodes :   int n

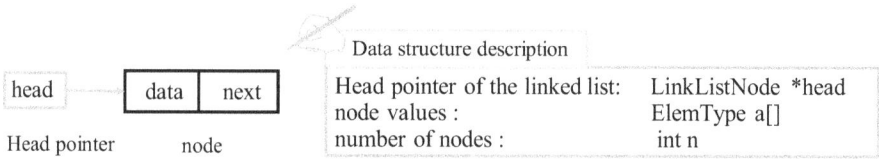

Fig. 2.33: Description of the data structure.
Note: A group of node values will be used to construct the linked list. So the parameters are designed to be in the form of array.

Table 2.18: Steps of constructing a linked list by inserting toward the end.

Top-level pseudocode	First-level elaboration	Second-level elaboration
Insert the node to the end of the linked list, until the number of nodes satisfies the requirement.	(1) Request head pointer head	head=malloc(sizeof (LinkListNode));
	(2) Precursor pointer q=head	q=head;
	(3) Request current node p; add the value to the node p; add the address of p to the pointer field of the precursor pointer q	p=malloc(sizeof(LinkListNode)); p->data=a[i];q->next=p;
	(4) q=p	q=p;
	(5) Set the pointer field of the last pointer to NULL	p->next=NULL;
	Repeat steps 3–4 until the number of nodes satisfies the requirement	

2. Construction of singly linked list by inserting to the head
Starting from an empty list, construct a linked list by continuously inserting nodes to the head of the list. The steps are shown in Fig. 2.34. The description can be seen at the first-level elaboration of the pseudocode.
Method 1:
- Description of data structure: same as the construction of singly linked lists by inserting to the end.
- Design of function structure: same as the construction of singly linked lists by inserting to the end.
- Description of the algorithm in pseudocode: see Table 2.19.
- Program implementation

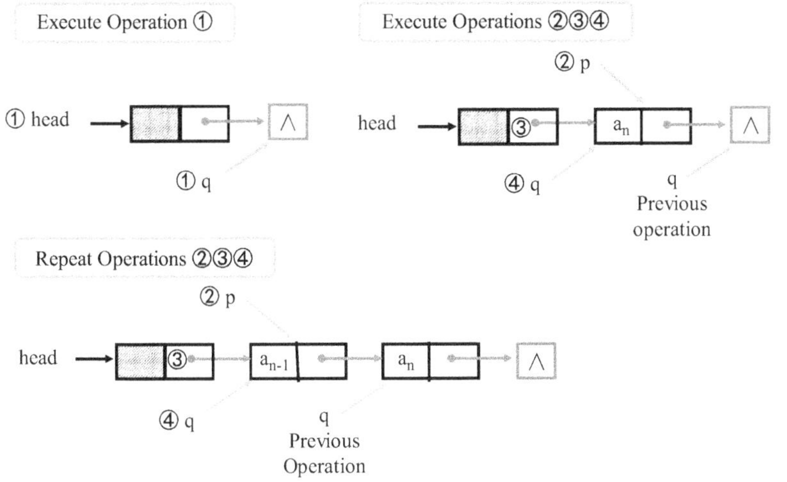

Fig. 2.34: Method 1 of constructing linked lists by inserting to head.

Table 2.19: Steps of constructing singly linked list by inserting to the head.

Description of top-level pseudocode	First-level elaboration	Second-level elaboration

Insert nodes to the head of the linked list, until the number of nodes satisfies the requirement	① Construct new node head
	Set the pointer field to NULL
	Record the successor address of head into q
		head=malloc(sizeof (LinkListNode));
		head->next=NULL;
		q=head->next;

	② Construct new node p
	Fill in value to the data field of node p
	Connect node p with node q
		p=malloc(sizeof (LinkListNode));
		p->data=a[i];
		p->next=q;

	③ Connect head node with node p	head->next=p;
	④ Record the successor of head in q	q=head->next;
	⑤ Repeat ②~④ until the linked list is constructed	

```
/*========================================================================
Functionality of the function: Operation on singly linked list - Method 1 of
constructing linked list by inserting to head
Function input: Array of node values, number of nodes
Function output: Head pointer of the linked list
========================================================================*/
```

```
LinkListNode *Create_Front1_LkList(ElemType a[], int n )
{
    LinkListNode *head, *p, *q;
    int i;
    head=(LinkListNode *)malloc(sizeof(LinkListNode));
    head->next=NULL;
    q=head->next;
    for(i=n-1; i>=0; i--)
    {
        p=(LinkListNode *)malloc(sizeof(LinkListNode));
        p->data=a[i];
        p->next=q;
        head->next=p;
        q=head->next;
    }
    return head;
}
```

Method 2: Demonstration is shown in Fig. 2.35. Description is shown as pseudocode.

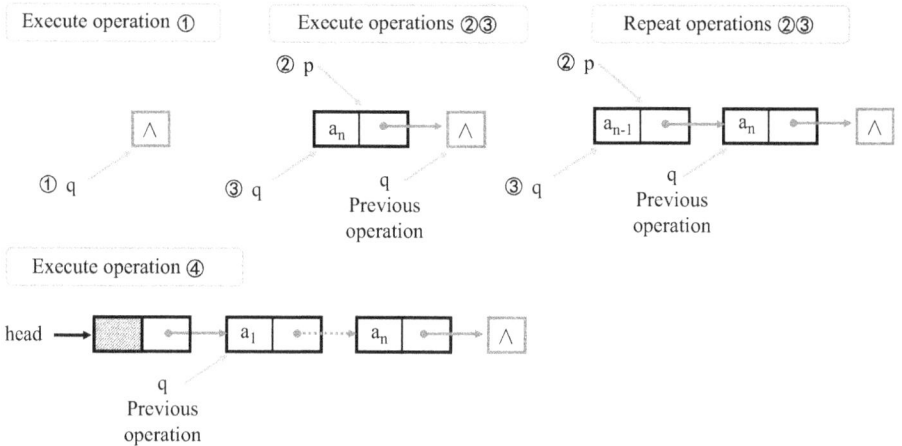

Fig. 2.35: Method 2 of constructing linked lists by inserting to head.

Pseudocode description of the algorithm is given in Table 2.20.

Table 2.20: Method 2 of constructing linked list by inserting to head.

Top-level pseudocode description	First-level elaboration	Second-level elaboration
Continuously insert nodes to the head of the existing linked list, until the number of nodes satisfies the requirement. Link in the head node as the last step.	① q=NULL	q=NULL

	② Construct new node p
	Insert value in the data field of node p
	Connect node p with node q
		p=malloc(sizeof (LinkListNode));
		p->data=a[i];
		p->next=q;

	③ q=p	q=p
	Repeat ②–③ until *n* nodes are all linked	
	④ Construct head node head Connect head with q	head=malloc(sizeof (LinkListNode)); head->next=q;

Program implementation

```
/*========================================================================
Functionality of the function: Operation on singly linked list - Method 1 of
constructing linked list by inserting to head
Function input: Array of node values, number of nodes
Function output: Head pointer of the linked list
========================================================================*/
LinkListNode *Create_Front2_LkList(ElemType a[],int n )
{
    LinkListNode *head, *p, *q;
    int i;
    q=NULL;
    for(i=n-1; i>=0; i--)
    {
        p=(LinkListNode *)malloc(sizeof(LinkListNode));
        p->data=a[i];
        p->next=q;
        q=p;
    }
```

```
head=(LinkListNode *)malloc(sizeof(LinkListNode));
head->next=q;
return head;
}
```

Method 3: Demonstration is shown in Fig. 2.36. Description is seen at pseudocode.

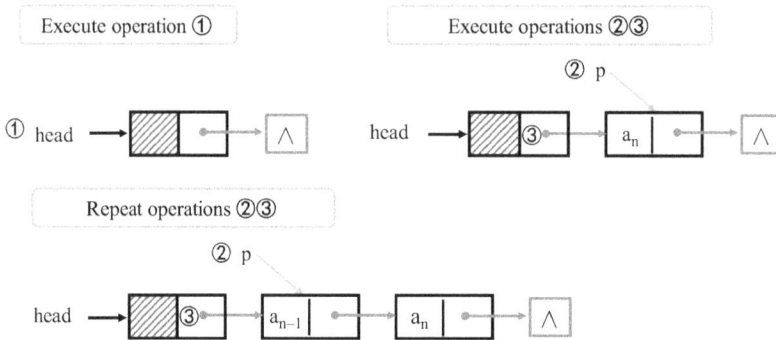

Fig. 2.36: Method 3 of constructing linked lists by inserting to head.

Pseudocode description of the algorithm is shown in Table 2.21.

Table 2.21: Method 3 of constructing linked list by inserting to head.

Top-level pseudocode description	First-level elaboration	Second-level elaboration
Insert nodes to the head of the linked list, until the number of nodes satisfies the requirement	① Construct head node head, Set pointer field to NULL	head=malloc(sizeof (LinkListNode)); head->next=NULL;
	② Construct new node p Insert value in the data field of node p Set the successor of p to the successor of head	p=malloc(sizeof (LinkListNode)); p->data=a[i]; p->next=head->next;
	③ Linked the head pointer with p	head->next=p;
	Repeat ②–③ until the linked list is finished constructing	

```
/*======================================================================
Functionality of the function: Operation on singly linked list - Method 3 of
constructing linked list by inserting to head
Function input: Array of node values, number of nodes
Function output: Head pointer of the linked list
=====================================================================*/
LinkListNode *Create_Front3_LkList( ElemType a[],int n )
{
    LinkListNode *head,*p;
    int i;
    head=(LinkListNode *)malloc(sizeof(LinkListNode));
    head->next=NULL; // There is no initial value in the data field of head
    for(i=n-1; i>=0; i--)
    {
        p=(LinkListNode *)malloc(sizeof(LinkListNode));
        p->data=a[i];
        p->next=head->next;
        head->next=p;
    }
    return head;
}
```

2.3.4.3 Lookup operation on singly linked list
There are two methods of lookup on a singly linked list: by value or by index.

1.   Lookup of node by value on a singly linked list
Find the keyword in a singly linked list.

(1) Design of test cases
Input: head pointer to the singly linked list, the keyword to look up
   Output: the address of the node that stores the keyword
   The range of test cases is given in Table 2.22.

Table 2.22: Test cases for lookup by value on singly linked lists.

	Normal cases	Boundary values	Abnormal cases
Head pointer to the list head	Head is not NULL	There is only one beginning node in the linked list	Head is empty
Expected results		Keyword found: Return the address of the node Keyword not found: Return NULL	Return NULL

! **Think and Discuss** When the keyword is not found, is it appropriate to return NULL?
Discussion: When the keyword is not found, we still have to return the pointer which has the same type as pointer to node address. In order to differentiate with normal address, returning NULL is appropriate.

(2) Description of data structure: omitted
(3) Design of function structure: see Table 2.23.

Table 2.23: Structure of function for lookup of node by value in a singly linked list.

Functionality description	Input		Output	
Lookup by value on a singly linked list `Locate_LkList`	Head pointer of the linked list: `LinkListNode *`		Found	Node address: `LinkListNode *`
	Keyword value: `ElemType`		Not found	NULL
Function name	Parameters			Function type

(4) Pseudocode description of the algorithm
Starting from the beginning node, compare the value of each node with the given value key one by one. If there is some node that has a value the same as the key, then return the address of the node that was first found to have the value key. Otherwise return NULL. The steps are given in Table 2.24.

Table 2.24: The steps of lookup by value on singly linked lists.

Top-level pseudocode description	First-level elaboration	Second-level elaboration
Search for the keyword key in the singly linked list	Skip the head pointer	p=head->next;
	If the current node p is not NULL Compare the value of p to the keyword Not equal: p points to the next node Equal: End	When p != NULL if (p->data != key) p=p->next; else break;
	Return the address of node p	return p;

Think and Discuss Does the pseudocode take care of abnormal situations?
Discussion: The list is not empty but the value is not found – p=NULL.
Empty list, head ->next=NULL – p=NULL

(5) Program implementation

```
/*=================================================================
Functionality of the Function: Operation on singly linked list - Find node
based on value
Function input: Head pointer to the linked list, value of the node
Function output: Found: Return the pointer to the node; Not found: Return NULL
=================================================================*/
LinkListNode * Locate_LkList( LinkListNode *head, ElemType key)
{
    LinkListNode *p;
    p=head->next; //Skip the head pointer
    while(p != NULL && p->data != key )
    //Node is not NULL and the value of the node is not key
    {
        p=p->next; //p points to the next node
    }
    return p;
}
```

(6) Analysis of the algorithm
The execution time of this algorithm is related to the value of key in the input. See Table 2.25.

Table 2.25: The analysis on the efficiency of lookup by value on singly linked lists.

Node position	1	2	3	...	i	...	n
Times of lookup	1	2	3		i		
Probability of match	$1/n$	$1/n$	$1/n$		$1/n$		$1/n$

The average time complexity is

$$T(n) = \frac{1}{n}\sum_{i=1}^{n} i = \frac{1}{n} \times \frac{(1+n)n}{2} = \frac{1+n}{2} = O(n)$$

2. Lookup of node by index in singly linked lists
(1) Design of test cases
   Input: Head pointer to the singly linked list, the index of the node to look up, *i*.
   Output: The address of the *i*th node.
   The range of test cases is given in Table 2.26.

Table 2.26: Test cases on lookup of value by index.

	Normal cases	Boundary values	Abnormal cases
Value of *i*	0 < *i* ≤ length of list	*i* = 0, 1, length of list	*i* > length of list
Linked list	Not null	N/A	Empty

> **!**
>
> **Think and Discuss** How to determine the abnormal cases and output values?
> **Discussion:** Based on Table 2.26, we can consider the following abnormal cases mainly:
> ①The list is not empty, *i* is out of range; ② empty list

(2) Description of data structure: omitted
(3) Design of function structure: see Table 2.27.

Table 2.27: Function structure for lookup by index in singly linked list.

Functionality description	Input	Output
Lookup in singly linked list by index Get_LkList	Head pointer to the linked list (LinkListNode *)	Node address LinkListNode *
	Node index int	
Function name	Parameters	Function type

(4) Pseudocode description of the algorithm
Method of lookup:
-   The situation where it is found: see Fig. 2.37.
    After the counter j is set to 0, the pointer p starts scanning along the linked list from the head node. When p finishes scanning the next node, j is increased by 1.
    Condition for continuing the scan: (1) j<I (2) p->next is not NULL
    Condition for found: (1) j = i(2)p is not NULL

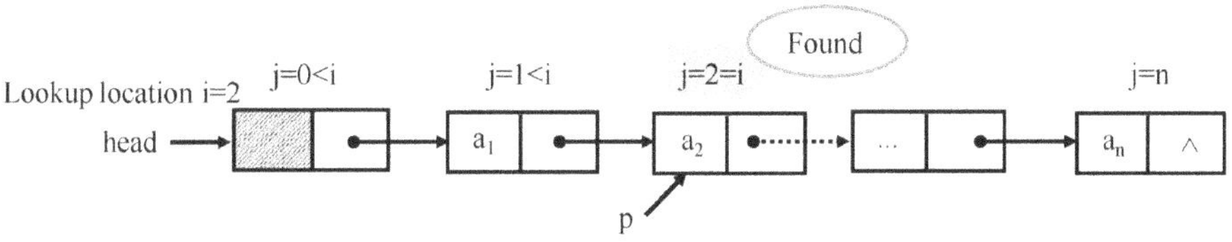

Fig. 2.37: "Found" scenario in sequential lookup on singly linked list.

-   Case of not found: see Fig. 2.38.
    When the successor of p is NULL and j ≠ i, it indicates we cannot find the ith node. Attention: head node is the 0th node. i = 0 should also be classified as abnormality.

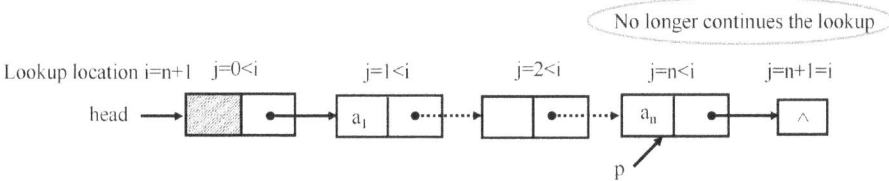

Fig. 2.38: "Not found" scenario when performing sequential lookup on singly linked lists.

Pseudocode is given in Table 2.28.

Table 2.28: Steps for lookup by index in singly linked list.

Top-level pseudocode description	First-level elaboration	Second-level elaboration
Find the ith node in the singly linked list (for head node, i = 0)	Address of current node p = head, Set counter j = 0	p = head; j = 0;
	When the ith node is not reached and the next node is not NULL Set conditions for a new search	if (j<i && p->next != NULL) p = p->next; j++;
	If the ith node is found, return its address. Otherwise, return NULL	if (i==j) return p; else return NULL;

Think and Discuss Is linked list random access data structure?   !
Discussion: In the linked list, even if you know the index of the node to visit, *i*, you cannot visit it directly as in the sequential list. You can only start from the head pointer of the linked list, search one by one using the link field next, until you reach the ith node. Therefore, linked list is not random access data structure.

(5) Program implementation

```
/*=======================================================================
Functionality of the Function: Operation on singly linked list - Find node
based on index
Function input: Head pointer to the linked list, index of the node to search
for
Function output: Found: Return the pointer to the node; Not found: Return NULL
=======================================================================*/
LinkListNode *Get_LkList(LinkListNode *head, int i )
{
    int j;
    LinkListNode *p;
    p=head;j=0;
    if (i==0) return NULL;
    while( j<i && p->next != NULL)
    // Has not reached the ith node and the next node is not NULL
    {
        p=p->next;
        j++;
    }
    if (i==j) return p; // Found the ith node
    else return NULL;
}
```

(6) Analysis of algorithm
In the algorithm, the condition for the while statement to end is to reach the end of the list or satisfy j≥i, the frequency of which at most will be i and is related to the searched index. Under the assumption of equal possibility, the average time complexity is

$$T(n) = \sum_{i=0}^{n-1} \frac{1}{n} \times i = \frac{1}{n} \frac{(n-1) \times n}{2} = \frac{n-1}{2} = O(n)$$

2.3.4.4 The insertion operation on singly linked lists
1.   Insert x after the node a_i of the singly linked list; it is known that the address of a_i is Ptr.

(1) Design of test cases
Input: Address of the point of insertion Ptr

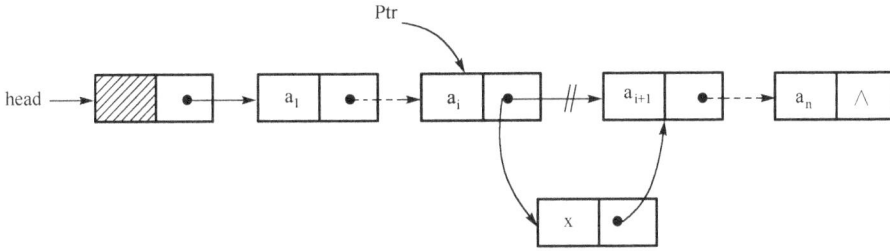

Fig. 2.39: Demonstration of insertion in singly linked list 1.

Value of the node to insert x
Output: None
Range of test case values is given in Table 2.29.

Table 2.29: Test cases for insertion in singly linked list.

	Normal cases	Boundary value	Abnormal cases
Linked list	Not empty	Head node and end node	Empty list

(2) Design of function structure (Table 2.30)

Table 2.30: The function structure of insertion at the designated position on singly linked lists.

Functionality description	Input	Output
Insertion at designated position on singly linked lists: Insert_After_LkList	Address of the point of insertion LinkListNode*	None
	Node Value ElemType	
Function name	Parameters	Function type

(3) Pseudocode description of the algorithm
The insertion operation on singly linked lists is demonstrated in Fig. 2.40. The pseudocode description is in Table 2.31.

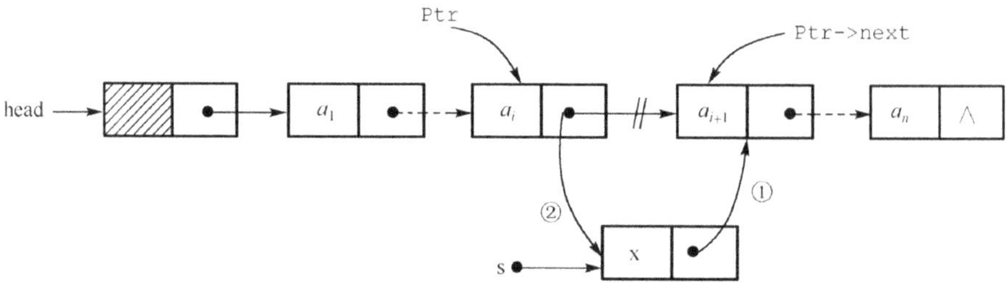

Fig. 2.40: Demonstration of insertion in singly linked list 2.

Table 2.31: Steps of insertion at the designated position on singly linked lists.

Top-level pseudocode description	First-level elaboration
Insert a node with value x after the designated node	① Construct new node s, fill in value x
	② Link node s with the successor node of Ptr
	③ Change the successor node of Ptr to s

(4) Program implementation

```
/*========================================================================
Functionality of the Function: Operation on singly linked list - Insert node
after the designated index
Function Input: Address of the position to insert, node value
Function Output: None
=======================================================================*/
void Insert_After_LkList(LinkListNode *Ptr,ElemType x )
{
    LinkListNode *s;
    s=(LinkListNode*)malloc(sizeof(LinkListNode));
    s->data=x;
    s->next=Ptr->next;
    Ptr->next=s;
}
```

2. Insert x before the node a_i in the singly linked list; we have already known the address of a_i as Ptr. See Figure. 2.41.

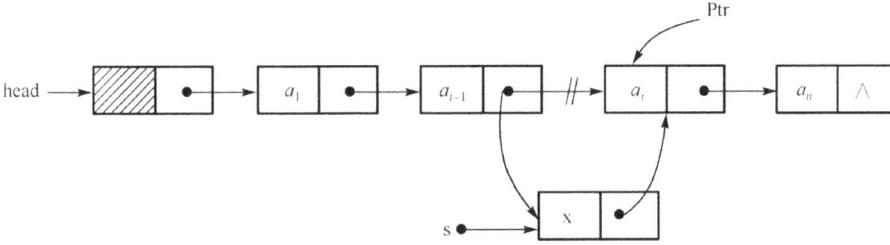

Fig. 2.41: Demonstration of insertion in singly linked list 3.

(1) Design of test cases
Input: (1) Head pointer to the linked list (2) Address of node a_i (3) Node value x
Output: None
    Range of values for test cases is given in Table 2.32.

Table 2.32: Test cases for insertion in singly linked list.

	Normal cases	Boundary values	Abnormal cases
Linked list	Not empty	Head node/read node	Empty list

(2) Design of function structure: see Table 2.33.

Table 2.33: Function structure for inserting before the designated index in singly linked lists.

Functionality description	Input	Output
Insert node before the designated position in the singly linked list Insert_Before_LkList	Head pointer of the linked list: LinkListNode * Address of node a_i: LinkListNode * Node value: ElemType	None
Function name	Parameters	Function type

(3) Pseudocode description of the algorithm
Demonstration of the operation is shown in Fig. 2.42, and pseudocode is given in Table 2.34.

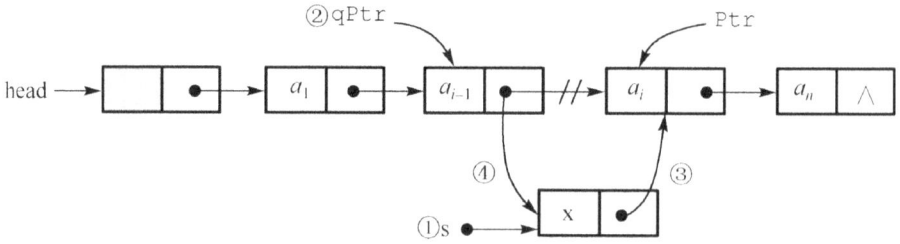

Fig. 2.42: Demonstration of insertion operation on singly linked lists 4.

Table 2.34: Steps for insertion before the designated position in singly linked lists.

Top-level pseudocode description	First-level elaboration	Second-level elaboration
Insert node with value x before the designated node Ptr	① Construct new node s and fill in the data	s = malloc(sizeof (LinkListNode)); s->data = x;
	② Starting from the head node, find the predecessor of Ptr, qPtr	qPtr =head; while (qPtr ->next != Ptr) qPtr=qPtr->next;
	③ Link the new node into the linked list	s->next=Ptr;
	④ Change the pointer field of the predecessor of node s	qPtr->next=s;

(4) Program implementation

```
/*==============================================================================
Functionality of the Function: Operation on Singly Linked List - Insert Node
Before the Designated Position
Function Input: Head pointer to the linked list, address of the point of
insertion, node value
Function Output: None
==============================================================================*/
void Insert_Before_LkList(LinkListNode *head, LinkListNode *Ptr, ElemType x)
{
    LinkListNode *s, *qPtr;
    s=(LinkListNode *)malloc(sizeof(LinkListNode));
    s->data=x;
    qPtr=head;
    while ( qPtr->next != Ptr )    qPtr=qPtr->next;
```

```
    s->next=Ptr;
    qPtr->next=s;
}
```

2.3.4.5 Deletion operation on singly linked lists

The method of deletion on singly linked list differs based on the given information. This section discusses the following two scenarios:
- Scenario 1: delete the successor node of the given node, the given node is Ptr.
- Scenario 2: delete the ith node in the singly linked list (for head node, $i = 0$).

Although for the deletion operation we need to know the address of the node, for the deletion function in scenario 1, it is hard to check whether that address has some abnormalities. To facilitate the processing of abnormal cases, we can give the index of the node to delete, i; via "lookup by index" function, find the address of node i. If it is normal, then we perform the deletion; if it is abnormal we do not perform the deletion. In this way, we ensure the address parameter received by the deletion function in scenario 1 is normal. Abnormal situations will not be checked again inside the function.

1. Delete the successor node of the designated node in the singly linked list

(1) Design of function interface and function structure
Input: Address of the node Ptr
Output: The address of the deleted node fPtr
Note:
- Check for abnormality should be done before calling this function.
- The function returns the address of the deleted node, without releasing the memory occupied by this node. Given that the caller might need to continue using this node, and thus the timing of freeing this node will be decided by the caller. Sometimes this is more convenient, but we need to remember that once the node is not used anymore, it needs to be released; otherwise memory leakage will ensue (Table 2.35).

Table 2.35: Function structure of deletion on singly linked lists.

Functionality description	Input	Output
Delete the successor of the designated node in the singly linked list Delete_After_LkList	Address of the node: LinkListNode *	Address of the node to be deleted: LinkListNode *
Function name	Parameters	Function type

(2) Pseudocode description of the algorithm

The demonstration of deletion on singly linked lists is shown in Fig. 2.43. The pseudocode description is given in Table 2.36.

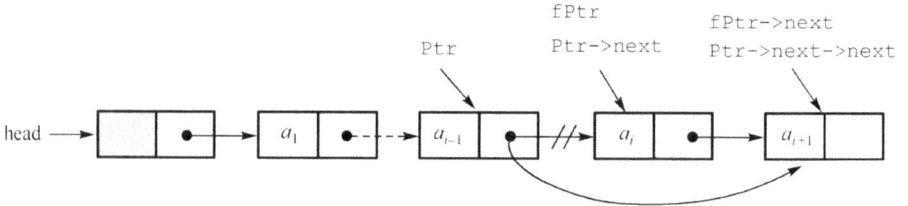

Fig. 2.43: Demonstration of deletion of the successor of the designated node on singly linked list.

Table 2.36: Steps of deletion operation on singly linked lists.

Top-level pseudocode description	First-level elaboration	Second-level elaboration
Delete the successor node of the designated node	Find the successor address, fPtr, of the designated node Ptr	fPtr= Ptr->next
	Link Ptr with the successor node of fPtr	Ptr->next= fPtr->next

(3) Program implementation

```
/*=================================================================
Functionality of the Function: Operation on Singly Linked Lists - Delete the
Successor node of the Designated Node
Function Input: Address of the Designated Node
Function Output: Address of the Deleted Node
=================================================================*/
LinkListNode * Delete_After_LkList( LinkListNode *Ptr)
{ LinkListNode *fPtr;
  fPtr=Ptr->next;
  Ptr->next=fPtr->next;
  return fPtr;
}
```

2. Deleting the designated node *i* of the singly linked list

(1) Design of test cases
Input: head pointer to the list, index of the node
Output: address of the deleted node
    Range of values of the test cases is given in Table 2.37.

Table 2.37: Test cases for deletion operation on singly linked lists.

	Normal cases	Boundary values	Abnormal cases
Linked list	Not empty		Empty
Address of the node	Inside of the linked list	Head node Read node	

(2) Design of function structure: see Table 2.38.

Table 2.38: Function structure of deletion of designated node on singly linked lists.

Functionality description	Input	Output	
Delete the *i*th node in the singly linked list: `Delete_i_LkList`	Head pointer to the linked list: `LinkListNode *`	Normal	Address of the deleted node: `LinkListNode *`
	Index of the node: `int`	Abnormal	NULL
Function name	Parameters	Function type	

(3) Pseudocode description of the algorithm (Fig. 2.44)

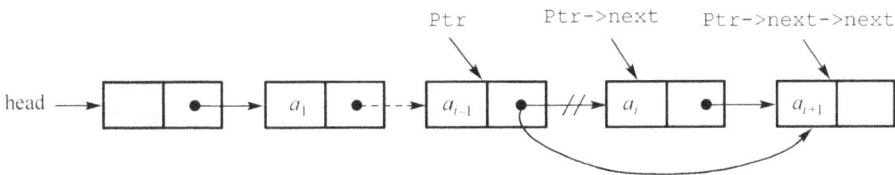

Fig. 2.44: Deletion of the designated node *i*: (a) nonempty list and (b) empty list.

Table 2.39: Deletion of the designated node *i* on singly linked lists.

Top-level pseudocode description	First-level elaboration	Second-level elaboration
Deletion of the *i*th node	Find the address of the predecessor of *i*, Ptr	Ptr=GetElem(head,i-1);
	If Ptr is normal	if((Ptr!=NULL)&&(Ptr->next!=NULL))
	Delete the successor node of Ptr	qPtr=DeleteAfter (Ptr);
	Return the address of the deleted node	return qPtr

! **Think and Discuss** In the deletion of the designated node in Table 2.38, are all abnormal cases taken care of?
Discussion: function GetElem will return NULL when it cannot find the node *i*. In this case function DeleteAfter to delete the successor of *i* will not be executed, but qPtr will still be returned. So qPtr should have an initial value of NULL; in this way, we do not need to check whether DeleteAfter is executed or not.

(4) Program implementation

```
/*=========================================================================
Functionality of the Function: Operation on the Singly Linked List - Delete
the ith Node
Function Input: Head pointer to the linked list, index of the node
Function Output: Normal: The address of the deleted node Abnormal: NULL
=========================================================================*/
LinkListNode *Delete_i_LkList( LinkListNode *head, int i)
{ LinkListNode *Ptr,*qPtr=NULL;
  Ptr=Get_LkList(head,i-1); // Find the address of the predecessor of i
  if( Ptr!=NULL && Ptr->next!=NULL )
      qPtr=Delete_After_LkList(Ptr);
  return qPtr;
}
```

(5) Analysis of the algorithm
Most of the time cost is spent on the search operation Get_LkList, so the time complexity is also $O(n)$.

2.3.5 Discussion of singly linked lists

The elements in the linked list are also ordered linearly. But different from arrays, the linear order of arrays is determined by the indices, while the order in linked lists is instead determined by the pointers in each element. Compared with sequential structure, its operation is more complicated.

1. Dynamic structure, no need to preallocate space: using the linked list structure, we can overcome a shortcoming of sequential list which is the need to know the size of the data beforehand. Linked lists can sufficiently use the memory space of the computer and realize flexible dynamic memory management.
2. Pointer occupies additional storage space: as linked lists have additional pointer fields, they occupy additional spaces.
3. Does not allow for random access, slow to query: linked lists lose the advantage of being able to be accessed randomly of arrays. And it is only possible to query toward one direction in singly linked lists.
4. For insertion and deletion operations on linked lists, there is no need to move the node, only the pointer needs to be moved.

2.3.6 Circular linked lists

2.3.6.1 Structural design of circular linked lists

For a singly linked list, since each node only stores the address of the successor node, the search can only go forward and not backward. The problem is, if we do not start from the head pointer, we would not be able to visit all nodes.

To solve this issue, we only need to change the pointer field of the end node from NULL to the head node, and thus make the whole singly linked list form a circle. In this way, starting from any node in the middle, we can still visit the whole linked list structure, as shown in Fig. 2.45. Empty list is a special case, in which the pointer field of the head pointer points to itself. This is its difference with single-direction linked lists. It is not mandatory for circular linked lists to have head nodes, but they will make the expression more convenient and uniform, for example, as in the case of empty list.

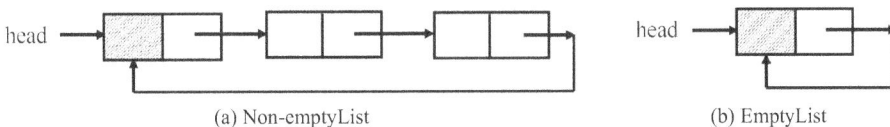

(a) Non-emptyList   (b) EmptyList

Fig. 2.45: Circular linked lists.

2.3.6.2 Operations on circular linked lists

The operations on circular linked lists are basically the same as those on singly linked lists. The differences are as follows:

1. When establishing a circular linked list, one must let the pointer of its last node point to the head node, instead of setting it to NULL as in singly linked lists.
2. When checking whether the end of the list has been reached, one should see whether the value of the link field of the current node is the head node. If the value stored is the head node, then the end of the list has been reached. It is not like in singly linked lists, where link field is compared with NULL.

On circular linked lists, sometimes the head pointer will not be given, in its place the rear pointer will be given, as shown in Fig. 2.46.

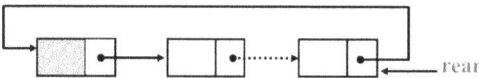

Fig. 2.46: Circularly linked list with only rear pointer.

Example 2.4:
Constructing a singly linked circular list
    Use the insert-to-the-end method to construct function Create_Rear_LkList; it suffices to change the statement p->next=NULL before returning to p->next= head.

The program is as follows:

```
/*================================================================
Functionality of the Function: Operation on singly linked list - Construct
circular linked list
Function input: The array of node values, number of nodes
Function output: The address of the rear pointer to the circular linked list.
=================================================================*/
LinkListNode *Create_Circle_LkList(ElemType a[],int n )
{
    LinkListNode *head,*p, *q;
    int i;

    head=(LinkListNode *)malloc(sizeof(LinkListNode));
    q=head;
    for(i=0;i<n;i++)
    {
        p=(LinkListNode *)malloc(sizeof(LinkListNode));
        p->data=a[i];
```

```
        q->next=p;
        q=p;
    }
        p->next=head;
        return p;
}
```

Example 2.5:
Link two singly linked circular lists into one singly linked circular list.
Interface information:
Input: Two rear pointers ra, rb
Output: None

The steps for the merge are shown in Fig. 2.47. The steps from (a) to (d), respectively, correspond to steps ①–④ in the first-level elaboration of pseudocode described in Table 2.40. The "memory pool" in the figure indicates an idle and available area in the memory.

Program implementation:

```
/*====================================================================
Functionality of the Function: Link two singly linked circular lists a and b
into one
Function Input: Rear pointer of list a, rear pointer of list b
Function Output: None
====================================================================*/
void Connect_L(LinkListNode *ra, LinkListNode *rb)
{
    LinkListNode *p;
    p=ra->next;
    ra->next=rb->next->next;
    free(rb->next);
    rb->next=p;
}
```

If we perform such linking operation in a singly linked list with or without head pointer, we need to traverse the first list, find node a_n, then link b_1 after a_n, which takes $O(n)$ time to execute. The implementation on a singly linked circular list with rear pointer only requires modifying the pointer without needing to traverse the whole list; thus, the time complexity is $O(1)$.

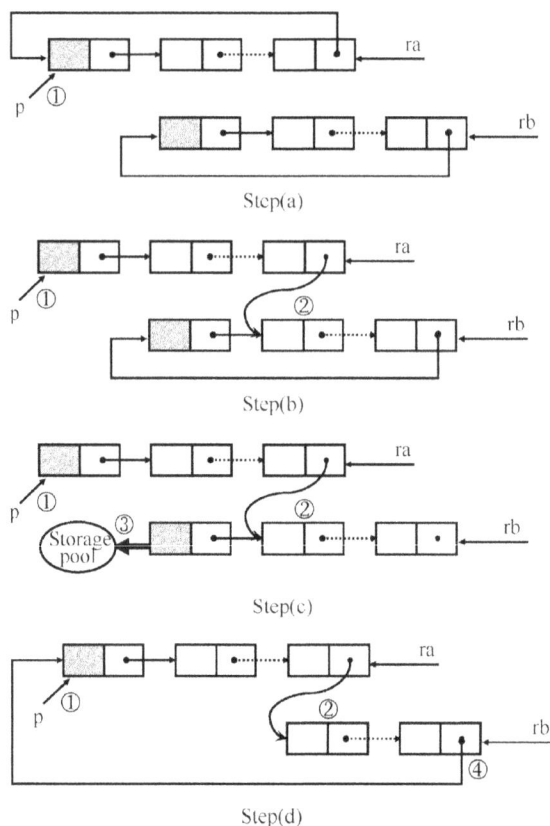

Fig. 2.47: Steps of merging two singly linked circular lists.

Table 2.40: Steps of merging two singly linked circular lists.

First-level elaboration	Second-level elaboration
① Record the address of the head node of list a	p=ra->next; ①
② Link the head node of b to the rear node of a	ra->next=rb->next->next; ②
③ Free the memory for head node of b	free(rb->next); ③
④ Link the rear node of b to the head node of a	rb->next=p; ④

The test program is shown below:

```
int main()
{
    ElemType a[]={2,4,6,8,10};
    ElemType b[]={1,3,5,7,9};
    LinkListNode *ra,*rb;
    LinkListNode *head;
    ra=Create_Circle_LkList(a,N);
    rb=Create_Circle_LkList(b,N);
    head=ra->next;
    Connect_L(ra,rb);
    return 0;
}
```

The results are shown in Fig. 2.48.

2.3.7 Doubly linked list

2.3.7.1 Structural design of doubly linked lists

In the sequential list, we can easily find both the predecessor and successor of an element. But in a singly linked list we can only find the successor. If we want to operate on the immediate predecessor of a node, we will have to start the search from the head node again, since there is only position record of the successor node, and no information on the predecessor node. Then, can we add a data item recording the address of the immediate predecessor node? This is straightforward in structural implementation. See Fig. 2.49.

In C language, a node in doubly linked list can be defined as follows:

```
typedef struct Dnode
{ ElemType data;
    struct Dnode *prior,*next;
} DLinkListNode;
```

If Ptr is a pointer pointing to a certain node in the doubly linked node, as shown in Fig. 2.50, then there is the following relation between the node pointers (Fig. 2.51):

```
Ptr->prior->next = Ptr = Ptr->next->prior
```

```
void Connect_L(LinkListNode *ra,
{
    LinkListNode *p;
    p=ra->next;
    ra->next=rb->next->next;
    free(rb->next);
    rb->next=p;
}

int main()
{
    ElemType a[]={2, 4, 6, 8, 10};
    ElemType b[]={1, 3, 5, 7, 9};

    LinkListNode *ra, *rb;
    LinkListNode *head;

    ra=Create_Circle_LkList(a, N);
    rb=Create_Circle_LkList(b, N);
    head=ra->next;

    Connect_L(ra, rb);
    return 0;
}
```

Name	Value
⊟ head	0x020b1750
data	−842150451
⊟ next	0x020b1710
data	2
⊟ next	0x020b16d0
data	4
⊟ next	0x020b1690
data	6
⊟ next	0x020b1650
data	8
⊟ next	0x020b1610
data	10
⊟ next	0x020b1590
data	1
⊟ next	0x020b1550
data	3
⊟ next	0x020b1510
data	5
⊟ next	0x020b14d0
data	7
⊟ next	0x020b1490
data	9
⊟ next	0x020b1750
data	−842150451
⊞ next	0x020b1710

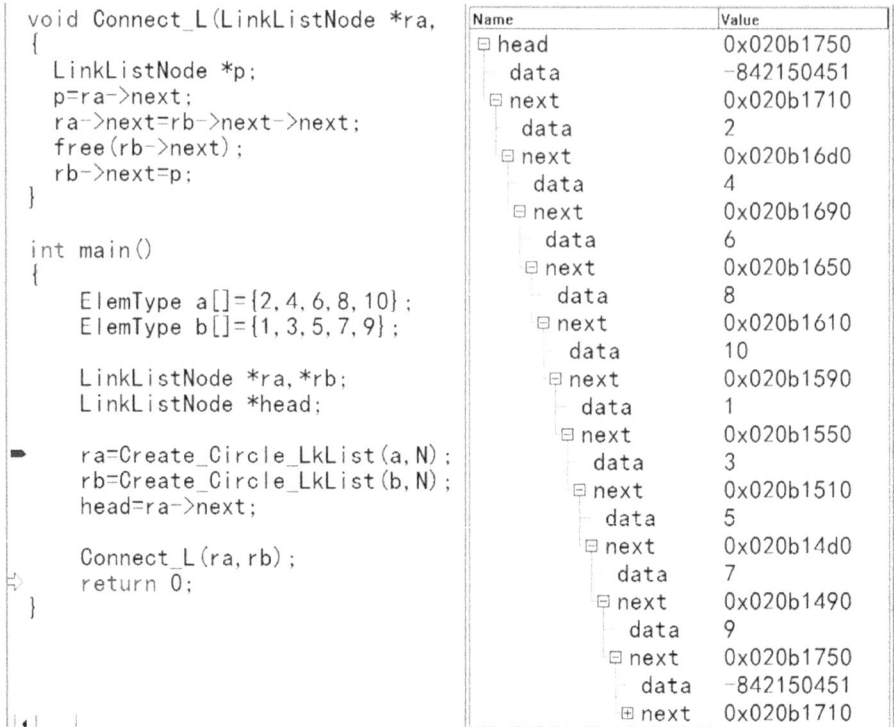

Fig. 2.48: Two circular lists linked with each other.

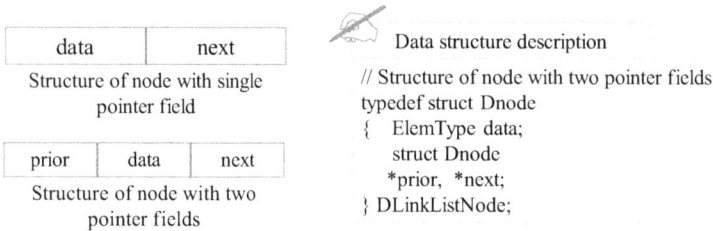

data	next

Structure of node with single
pointer field

prior	data	next

Structure of node with two
pointer fields

Data structure description

```
// Structure of node with two pointer fields
typedef struct Dnode
{   ElemType data;
    struct Dnode
    *prior, *next;
} DLinkListNode;
```

Fig. 2.49: Singly linked and doubly linked list node structure.

Double-direction circular linked list

Empty double-direction circular linked list

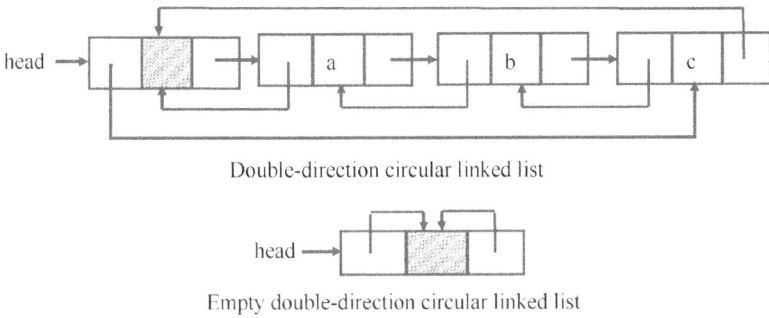

Fig. 2.50: Doubly linked circular lists.

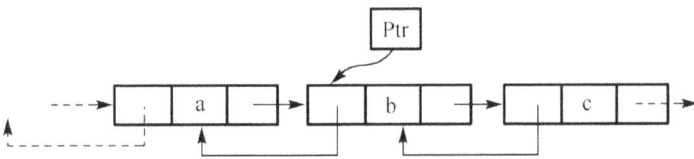

Fig. 2.51: Pointers in doubly linked lists.

2.3.7.2 Operations on doubly linked lists

Compared with singly linked lists, the operations on doubly linked lists are basically the same, when they only involve going in one direction in order, for example, finding the length of the linked list or finding the designated value. If the operations involve seeking the predecessor node, then they will be simpler than the corresponding operations in singly linked lists. Such operations include insertion and deletion of nodes. If you are interested, you may implement the specific algorithms by yourselves.

2.3.8 Summary on linked lists

Linked list is a dynamic data structure, which requests memory once it adds a new node; on the contrary, arrays get their memory allocated at once. Therefore, linked lists are not like arrays, which always occupy continuous memory. However, linked lists do not have idle memory; thus, they have higher spatial efficiency compared with arrays.

When we pass a linked list, we normally pass its head pointer.

Singly linked lists: must always find a node from the beginning till the end. Can only be traversed forward and not backward.

Doubly linked lists: both forward and backward traversals are possible. It can improve the time performance of algorithms effectively. However, since each node needs to record two pointers, it occupies slightly more space. This is what we call "trade space for time."

2.4 Examples of the application of linear lists

Output the node values in a singly linked list in reverse order. The question requires traversing the singly linked list, and output its node values in reverse order.

Method 1

2.4.1 Algorithm design

Starting from the head node of the singly linked list, store the node values in the external array from the rear to the front one by one. Then output the content of the external array in the end.

2.4.2 Program implementation

```
#include<stdio.h>
#include<malloc.h>
#define N 6 //Number of nodes in the linked list
typedef int ElemType

typedef struct node
{
  ElemType data;
   struct node *next;
} LinkListNode;

LinkListNode *Create_Rear_LkList(ElemType a[], int n);
// Construct the linked list
void PrintList(LinkListNode *L); //Output the linked list

int main()
{
  LinkListNode *L;
  ElemType list[N] = { 1, 2, 3, 4, 5, 6 };//Node values of linked list

  L = Create_Rear_LkList(list, N);
```

```
  PrintList(L);
  return 0;
}

void PrintList(LinkListNode *L)
{
  LinkListNode *p;
  int array[N];
  int i = N - 1;
  p = L->next;//Skip the head node
  while (p) //Linked list is not empty
    {
      array[i--] = p->data;
      //Store the node value from the rear of the array to the front one-by-one
      p = p->next;
    }
  while (++i<N) printf("%d ", array[i]);//Output the values in the array
  return;
}
```

Method 2
Realize the reversal using recursion.

The recursion will find the rear node, and when it returns it will output the value of the node.

```
void PrintList(LinkListNode *L)
{
  if(L->next!=NULL) PrintList(L->next);
  printf("%d",L->data);
}
```

The call to the function within the main function should be "PrintList(L->next);".

2.5 Comparisons between sequential list and linked list

This chapter introduces the logical structure of linear lists and its two storage structures: sequential storage structure and linked storage structure. Through previous
discussions, we know they have their respective advantages, as given in Table 2.41.
Advantages of sequential storage:

Table 2.41: Comparison of features between sequential list and singly linked list.

			Sequential list	Linked list
Space		Allocation method	Static allocation	Dynamic allocation
		Storage density	Is 1	Smaller than 1
Time		Access method	Random access	Sequential access
	Operations	Insertion/deletion	$O(n)$	$O(1)$
		Sequential access	$O(1)$	$O(n)$

Note: Storage density refers to the ratio between the number of storage units occupied by the data element within a node and the storage units occupied by the whole node.

- Easy to implement, as various high-level languages all have arrays
- No extra cost for storing the logical relation between nodes
- Sequential list allows for random access according to the element index, which is simple and convenient

Disadvantages of sequential storage:
- While performing insertion and deletion in sequential lists, on average half of the elements in the list will be moved, thus for sequential lists with relatively big size, the efficiency of these two operations will be low.
- The programmer needs to preallocate enough storage spaces. If the estimate is too high, the later sections of the sequential list will be largely idle. If the estimate is too low, there will be overflow.

Advantages of linked list:
- No need to know the length of the linear list in advance
- Allows for huge variation in the length of the linear list
- Adapts to frequent insertion/deletion of elements
- Able to improve access efficiency by constructing doubly linked lists/circular lists

Both sequential lists and linked lists have pros and cons. In real applications, the choice depends on the requirements and characteristics of the concrete problems. Usually there are the following considerations:

2.5.1 Considerations based on storage

The storage space for sequential lists is allocated statically. Its size must be ascertained before the program executes, that is, there must be an appropriate setting for "MAXSIZE" beforehand. If it is too large there will be wastage, if it is too small there will be overflow. When it is hard to estimate the length or storage size of the linear list, sequential list is not appropriate. For linked lists there is no need to preestimate the storage size.

2.5.2 Considerations based on operations

If the usual operations will be accessing data elements according to indices, then obviously sequential list is better than the linked list. When performing insertion and deletion in linear list, on average half of the elements will be moved; when the amount of data elements is huge and the list is long, this aspect should not be ignored. When inserting and deleting in a linked list, although we still have to find the insertion location, but operations will mostly be comparison operations. In this respect, obviously linked list is better than sequential list.

2.5.3 Considerations based on the environment

Sequential lists are easy to implement, while linked lists are based on pointers; relatively speaking, the first one is easier. Both storage structures have pros and cons, and the choice is mainly determined by the main factors of the concrete problem. Usually, for a "relatively stable" linear list we will choose sequential storage, while linear lists with frequent insertions/deletions, that is, more dynamic ones, will be more suitable for linked storage.

In conclusion, when choosing linear lists, we should comprehensively consider both temporal and spatial factors, and choose the one most suitable to the characteristics of the problem to solve.

2.6 Summary of the chapter

The logical relations between the nodes of a linear list can be connected with "one line" (Fig. 2.52).
The nodes can be either continuously or discretely stored in memory space.
The sequential list occupies continuous memory space.
The logic between the nodes is implicitly contained in the order of the units of storage.
Implementation is done via vectors and operations are simple.
The efficiency depends on what kinds of operations are the most frequent.
The linked list occupies discrete memory space.
The relation between nodes is stored within the pointer field.
Singly linked list, doubly linked list, circularly linked list and so on. There are many varieties.
The implementation is not that straightforward.

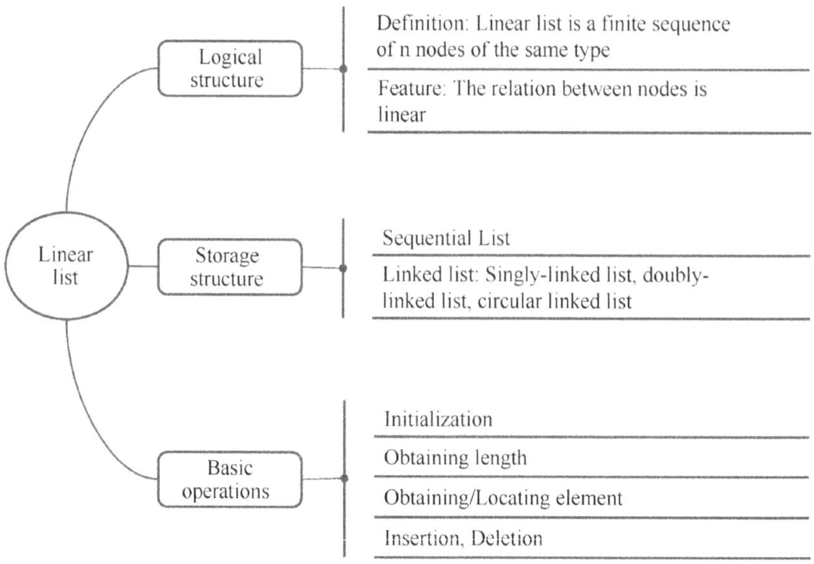

Fig. 2.52: Connections between various concepts of linear list.

Sequential list and linked list have both their advantages and disadvantages. Linked list is convenient for accepting information without predefined length. Sequential list is restricted with a fixed memory space. For frequent lookup via index, sequential list rules. The insertion and deletion on linked list have time complexity $O(1)$, which is amazing.

The choice of storage structure for solving linear problems depends on the functionalities required.

2.7 Exercises

2.7.1 Multiple-choice questions

1. When the data is manifested in the storage devices of the computer, the structure that has adjacent physical addresses, and in which the logical relation between data is expressed via the adjacency of the physical addresses, is called ( ).
   (A) Storage structure
   (B) Logical structure
   (C) Sequential storage structure
   (D) Linked storage structure

2. In a sequential list with n nodes, the operation with time complexity of $O(1)$ is ( ).
   (A) Visit the ith node $(1 \le i \le n)$ and get the immediate predecessor of the ith node $(2 \le i \le n)$
   (B) Insert a new node after the ith node $(1 \le i \le n)$
   (C) Delete the ith node$(1 \le i \le n)$
   (D) Rank the n nodes according to their values

3. To insert a new element and keep the original order of elements to a sequential list with 127 elements, on average how many elements will be moved? ( ).
   (A) 8   (B) 63.5   (C) 63   (D) 7

4. The storage space occupied by linked storage structure ( ).
   (A) Has two parts, one for node value and another for pointer showing the relations between nodes
   (B) Has only one part for node value
   (C) Has only one part for pointer showing the relations between nodes
   (D) Has two parts, one for node value and another for the number of units occupied by the node

5. Linked list is a linear list using which of the following storage structure ( ).
   (A) Sequential   (B) Linked   (C) Star style   (D) Web style

6. If the linear list is stored using linked storage structure, for the addresses of the memory used ( ).
   (A) They must be continuous
   (B) Part of the addresses must be continuous
   (C) They must be noncontinuous
   (D) Either continuous or noncontinuous is okay

7. Under which circumstance is a linear list L suitable to be implemented with linked structure ( ).
   (A) Constant modification on node values in L is needed
   (B) Deletion operations will be constantly applied to L
   (C) L contains a lot of nodes
   (D) The nodes in L have complex structures

8. The storage density of singly linked list ( ).
   (A) is greater than 1
   (B) is equal to 1
   (C) is less than 1
   (D) depends on specific situations

9. Which of the following is the advantage of linear storage structures ( ).
   (A) High storage density
   (B) Easy to perform insertion operations

(C) Easy to perform deletion operations

(D) Can be easily used for the storage and display of various logical structures

10. Which one of the following statements about linear lists is wrong ( )?

   (A) If it employs sequential storage, it must occupy a block of continuous memory units

   (B) If it employs sequential storage, it is easy to perform insertions and deletions

   (C) If it employs linked storage, it does not need to occupy a block of continuous memory units

   (D) If it employs sequential storage, it is easy to perform insertions and deletions

11. If the most common operations on a certain linear list is to save/access an element at any given index, and perform insertion and deletion at the end of the list, then the ( ) storage method will be the most time efficient.

   (A) Sequential list

   (B) Doubly linked list

   (C) Doubly linked circular list with head node

   (D) Singly linked circular list

12. In a certain linear list, the most common operation is to insert an element after the last element and deleting the first element. Then the ( ) storage method is most efficient in time.

   (A) Singly linked list

   (B) Singly linked circular list with only head pointer

   (C) Doubly linked list

   (D) Singly linked circular list with only rear pointer

13. Which of the following is not a characteristic of linked lists ( )?

   (A) No need to move elements with insertion/deletion

   (B) Randomly access any element

   (C) No need to preestimate storage space needed

   (D) Space needed is proportional to the linear length of the list

14. Which of the following is NOT correct ( )?

   (A) For linked storage of linear lists, the time used to look up the ith element is proportional to the value of i

   (B) For linked storage of linear lists, the time used to delete the ith element is not related to the value of this element

   (C) For sequential storage of linear lists, the time used to look up the ith element is proportional to the value of i

   (D) For sequential storage of linear lists, the time used to look up the ith element is not related to the value of i

15. In a singly linked circular list, the condition for p to point to the rear node is ( ).
    (A) P->next=h   (B) p->next=NIL   (C) p->next->next=h   (D) p->data=-1

16. The operation to insert s after the node p in a doubly linked circular list is ( ).
    (A) p->next=s; s->priou=p; p->next->priou=s; s->next=p->next;
    (B) p->next->priou=s; p->next=s; s->priou=p; s->next=p->next;
    (C) s->priou=p; s->next=p->next; p->next=s; p->next->priou=s;
    (D) s->priou=p; s->next=p->next; p->next->priou=s; p->next=s;

17. The correct operation to insert a node pointing to s, after node p, in a singly linked list, is ( ).
    (A) p->next=s;s->next=p->next;
    (B) s->next=p->next;p->next=s;
    (C) p->next=s;p->next=s.next;
    (D) p->next=s->next;p->next=s;

18. For a singly linked list with head node whose head pointer is head, the condition to check this list as an empty list is ( ).
    (A) head==NULL
    (B) head→next==NULL
    (C) head→next==head
    (D) head!=NULL

2.7.2 Algorithm design exercises

1. Suppose in a circular list with length > 1, there is no head node nor head pointer. s is a pointer to a certain node in the list. Try to write an algorithm to delete the predecessor node of s.

2. Suppose it is known that the data element in a singly linked list has three bytes (i.e., alphabet byte, number byte and other byte). Try to write an algorithm to construct three circular lists, so that each circular list only has one type of byte, and use the node space of the original list as the node space of these three lists (the head node can request new space).

3. Suppose there is a linear list $E = \{e_1, e_2, \ldots, e_{n-1}, e_n\}$, try to design an algorithm to reverse the linear list, that is, to reverse the order of the elements, and let it become a reversed linear list $E' = \{e_n, e_{n-1}, \ldots, e_2, e_1\}$. It is required that the reversed linear list occupies the space of the original linear list. Write different processing methods for both sequential list and linked list.

4. It is known that the nodes in a dynamic singly linked list L (with head node) are ordered in the ascending order according to integer values. Try to write an algorithm to insert a node with value x into list L, so that L is still ordered.

5. Suppose there is a doubly linked list, in each node of the list, besides prior, data and next fields, there is a field freq for visit frequency. Before the linked list is used, the value of this field is always initialized to 0. Whenever a LOCATE(L, X) operation is performed on the doubly linked list, the node with value X will have its freq field increased by 1. Also, the nodes in the list should be ordered in the descending order according to the visit frequency, so that the most frequently visited node is always close to the head. Try to write the LOCATE algorithm that satisfies the above requirements.

6. Suppose $A = (a_1, a_2, a_3, \ldots, a_n)$ and $B = (b_1, b_2, \ldots, b_m)$ are two linear lists (suppose all the data elements are integers). If $n = m$ and $a_i = b_i (i = 1, \ldots, n)$, then we say $A = B$. If $a_i = b_i (i = 1, \ldots, j)$ and $a_{j+1} < b_{j+1} (j < n \leq m)$, then we say $A < B$. In other situations, we say $A > B$ (including those where $j < m < b$). Try to write an algorithm to compare A and B, when $A < B$, $A = B$ or $A > B$, output −1, 0 or 1, respectively.

7. Suppose we represent two sets (i.e., all elements are unique) using two linear lists A, B whose element values are sorted in ascending order, now we have to construct a new linear list C, which represents the intersection of sets A and B. The elements in C should also be ordered in ascending order. Try to write algorithms for the above operation in sequential list and singly linked list, respectively.

8. It is known that A, B and C are three linear lists with elements sorted in ascending order. Now we need to perform the following operation on A: delete the elements that appear in both B and C. Try to write algorithms for the above operation in sequential list and singly linked list, respectively.

9. Suppose there are two linear lists A and B with elements sorted in ascending order, and both of which are implemented as singly linked list. Try to write algorithms to merge A and B into one list C sorted in descending order (i.e., non-ascending, allows same values). It is required that the original space used by A and B is used to store C.

10. Suppose it is known that the data element in a singly linked list has data elements of three types of bytes (i.e., alphabet byte, number byte and other byte). Try to write an algorithm to construct three circular lists, so that each circular list only has one type of byte, and use the node space of the original list as the node space of these three lists (the head node can request new space).

11. (Josephus Circle) Given any positive integers n, k, using the following methods we can get a substitution for the arrangement 1, 2,..., n: circularly arrange the numbers 1, 2,..., n, count clockwise starting from 1; when count K is reached, output the number at this position (and delete this number from

the circle), and resume counting from the next number, until all the numbers in the circle have been output. For example, when $n = 10$, $k = 3$, the output substitution should be 3, 6, 9, 2, 7, 1, 8, 5, 10, 4. Try to design an algorithm to output the corresponding substitution based on random input positive integers n, k.

3 Linear list with restricted operations – stack and queue

Main Contents
- The logic structure definition of stack
- The storage structure of stack and the implementation of its operations
- The logic structure definition of queue
- The storage structure of queue and the implementation of its operations

Learning Aims
- Comprehend the features and operation methods of stacks and queues
- Correctly choose them in actual applications

3.1 Stack – a linear list managed in a first-in–last-out manner

The notion of "stack" in data structures comes from the meaning of "stack" in daily lives, which has the characteristic of "first-in–last-out." See Fig. 3.1. For things that can be stacked together, we always put the ones below first, and then the ones above, and the order of retrieval is exactly opposite to the order of storage. We can see the meaning of stack in data structures via the algorithmic implementations of some actual problems.

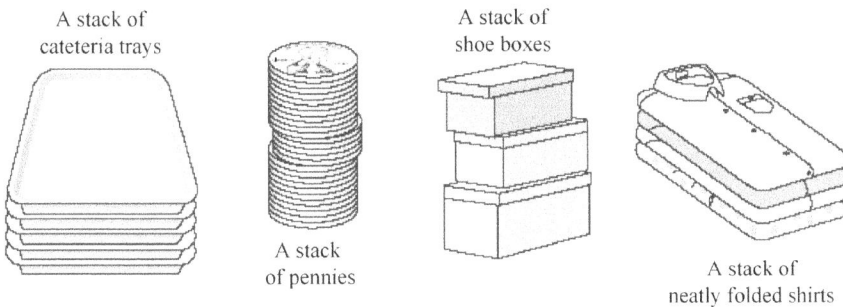

A stack of cateteria trays

A stack of pennies

A stack of shoe boxes

A stack of neatly folded shirts

Fig. 3.1: Stack in daily lives.

3.1.1 Introduction to the operation pattern of stack

3.1.1.1 Introduction to stack 1 – erroneous operation in Word
Word is a commonly used word editing software. If there is some erroneous operation during usage, for example, deleting the wrong content, will you be worried? People

https://doi.org/10.1515/9783110595581-003

familiar with Word will usually say "it doesn't matter," since you can use "undo" tool to restore the content erroneously deleted. The "undo" tool can undo the previous operation. Actually, editing software nowadays all has "undo" functionality. Note that the order of "undo" operations is exactly the opposite of normal operations, as shown in Fig. 3.2. That is to say, the undo operation each time is done to rectify the most recent erroneous operation; this fits our usage habits. Since the computer can undo the previous operation, it must have saved the contents of the operations according to the order of the previous operation, and when undoing, it only needs to cancel the original operations in the reverse order. That is to say, the orders of saving and retrieving information on operations are opposite to each other.

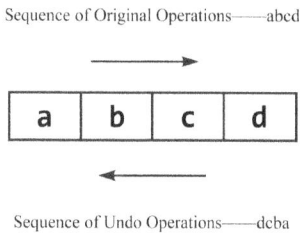

Sequence of Original Operations——abcd

| a | b | c | d |

Sequence of Undo Operations——dcba

Fig. 3.2: The order of "undo" in text editing.

3.1.1.2 Introduction to stack example 2 – bracket matching
Bracket matching is a frequent issue when compiling programs. It is used to detect whether there is some syntactical error. During the syntactic error checking of the compiler, one procedure is checking whether the various brackets are matched.

We can see the general idea from the test case shown in Fig. 3.3. The index in the number is the order of entrance of the brackets.

Index	0	1	2	3	4	5	6	7	8	9
Bracket	{	{	{	}	[	]	}	(	)	}

p q

Fig. 3.3: Test case for bracket matching.

From Fig. 3.3 we can observe that if we scan the cluster of brackets from left to right, then each right bracket will be matched with the most recently encountered unmatched left bracket, for example, "last-in–first-out" (FIFO) or "first-in–last-out." If we record the newest position of the left bracket using p, and point to the most recently entered right bracket with q, compare the contents of p and q. If they match, then we delete this left bracket, and move p one position back, that is to say, we only save the left brackets encountered during the scanning process. The processing flow for the example shown in Fig. 3.3 is shown in Fig. 3.4. We can observe that, in this algorithm for bracket matching, both the insertion and deletion of data occur at the end of the array.

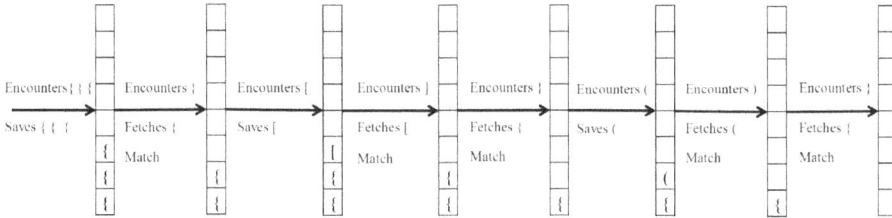

Fig. 3.4: The storage and processing of data in bracket matching algorithms.

3.1.1.3 Introduction to stack example 3 – the recursive invocation of functions

The program for recursively calculating $n!$ is as follows:

```
int fac(int n)
{
    if (n==1) return (1);
    return (n*fac(n-1));
}
```

Using the example of $n = 4$, Fig. 3.5 gives the invocation and returning process of the recursion.

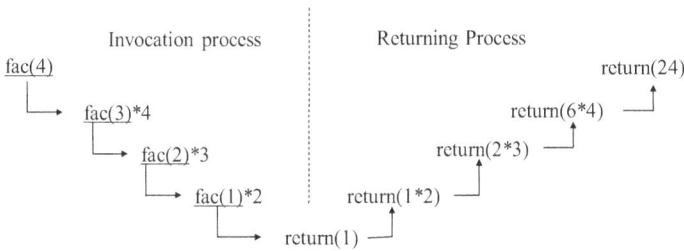

Fig. 3.5: The invocation and returning process of recursively computing $n!$.

Recursive invocation simplifies the problem for the programmers, although there is also risk associated with such layer-by-layer recursive invocation: When the program runs, if the chain of information is damaged, and the function does not know at which layer it currently is, errors will occur in the program.

! **Think and Discuss** How does the embedded invocation mechanism of recursive functions ensure correct return?

Discussion: As we can see from Fig. 3.5, the invocation of a recursive function is a layer-by-layer embedded invocation process. When the function at the next layer runs, the function at the current layer already waits until the function at the next layer returns. The calculations in the function of this layer will only continue after the function at the next layer returns. Therefore, the position for the function to continue its execution, that is, the return address, must be saved.

To ensure the correctness of the value calculation during the returning process, during the execution of fac function and before the execution of the function at the next layer, we must both save the current parameters of the function at the current layer. For example, before executing fac(3), we will need to save parameter 4: before executing fac(2), we will need to save parameter 3 and so on.

Therefore, to ensure the recursive invocation returns correctly, the function invocation mechanism must save the execution environment at the point of invocation, including return address and the parameters of the function, and invoke fac using the parameters of the new layer. When the function invoked finishes, the original environment will be restored. Then the function at this layer will continue its execution until the program ends.

Usually we call the process of saving the information each time "push," and the process of restoring the information "pop."

! **Think and Discuss** What is the order of environment saving and environment restoration during invocation of recursion?

Discussion: Generally speaking, during the preinvocation stage, for each layer of recursion, the local variables, parameter values and return address are all pushed onto the stack. In the returning stage, the local variables, parameter values and return address are ejected, and used to execute the rest of the code in the layer of the caller function. That is to say, it restores the statuses before invocation. Simply speaking, it is a process of layer-by-layer saving and then layer-by-layer restoration, carried out in the order of "first save then restore." This process is similar to the brackets matching in introductory example 3.1. Function invocation is like encountering a left bracket, while function return is like encountering a right bracket.

For modern high-level languages, users do not need to manage the stack during recursion execution. Everything is done by the system.

3.1.1.4 Introduction to stack example 4 – the embedded invocation of functions

In computer programs, one function can call another function inside of its body. The calling mechanism has been widely used since the era of assembly programming: prepare a body of code, the caller can jump to the beginning address of this code according to the predefined steps, and after its execution, return to the succeeding addresses at the moment of jumping.

C programs are executed from the main function. The main function might be called by the operating system. The main function can call other functions, and other functions can call each other. If there is a multilevel embedded invocation of the main function and children functions fa(), fb(), the relations are shown in Fig. 3.6. Combined with introductory example of stack 2, we can see from Fig. 3.6 that the recursive invocation of functions is a special case of embedded invocation of normal multilayer functions. It is just that the function being invoked at each layer is the same one.

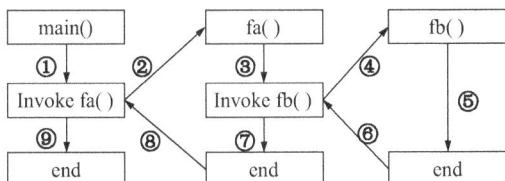

Fig. 3.6: Demonstration of multilevel embedded invocation of functions.

In the same manner as recursive invocation, in order to ensure the correctness of embedded invocation, the environment at the point of invocation (return address, the execution state of the caller function, the parameters of the function being invoked) needs to be saved, and managed according to the principle of "first-in–last-out." The types of data that need to be saved for each environment is the same. An environment information can be viewed as a node. In order to facilitate operations, the insertion and deletion of nodes should be carried out at the same end of the storage space, as shown in Fig. 3.7.

Arguments of fb()
Return the address of fa
Execution status of fa ()
Arguments of fa ()
Return the address of main
Execution status of main ()
Parameters of main()
Address for returning to the operating system
Execution status of operating system

Fig. 3.7: The environment information being saved and the order of saving.

From the previous four introductory examples, we can see that the common feature of these problems is the characteristic of "last-in–first-out" during data processing.

This is a typical type of problems; they are usually summarized to the "stack" type of data structure. The following is the concept of stack.

3.1.2 The logic structure of stack

3.1.2.1 The definition of stack

The illustration of stack is shown in Fig. 3.8.

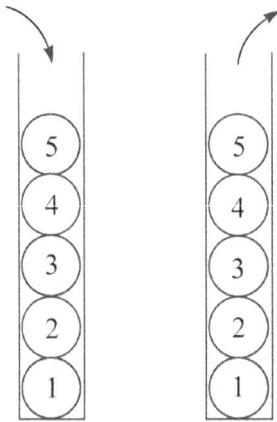

Fig. 3.8: Illustration of stack.

Imagine a bamboo pole that is sealed on one end and open at another. There are some balls with indices. The diameter of the balls is slightly smaller than the diameter of the bamboo pole. Now, when we put the balls with different indices into the bamboo pole, we can discover a rule of thumb: The balls we put in first can only be retrieved later. On the contrary, the balls we put in later can be retrieved first. Putting and retrieving the balls correspond to "insertion" and "deletion" operations. "First-in–last-out" is the characteristic of this type of structure.

When we abstract the balls in the above structure to the nodes in data structures, since the relation between nodes is linear, it is also a linear list. Also, since all the operations happen at one end of the list, "those which came in first can only exit later"; therefore it is a linear list with restricted operations. We call such type of linear list "stack."

> **i** **Definition** Stack is a special type of linear list. All its insertion and deletion operations are restricted to the same end of the list.
>
> The end of the stack which allows for insertion, deletion operations is called top. The other end is called bottom. When there are no elements in the stack, it is called an empty stack.

The insertion operation on stack is normally called "push,", the deletion operation on stack is usually called "pop." See Fig. 3.9.

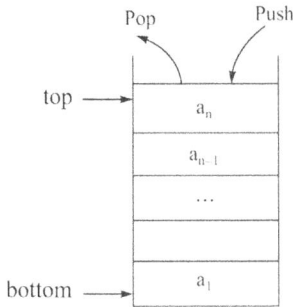

Fig. 3.9: Abstract illustration of stack.

The first element to enter the stack is at the bottom of the stack. The last element to enter the stack is at the top of the stack. The first item to exit the stack is the top element. The last element to exit the stack is the bottom element.

Think and Discuss How many parameters do we need to indicate the state of a stack?
Discussion: To annotate the state of a stack, we must first list all the possible states of the stack. On the premise that the size of the stack is known, there should be three situations: empty, full, neither empty nor full. The parameters we design to indicate the state of the stack should be able to represent all these possible situations of the stack.

According to the definition of stack, the data element that enters the stack each time will be put in front of the top element and thus become the new top element. The data element that exits the stack each time is always the current top element. The various situations and operations on stack are shown in Fig. 3.10, where situation (3) indicates full stack. Therefore, the change of the content of the stack only needs to be indicated by a stack-top pointer.

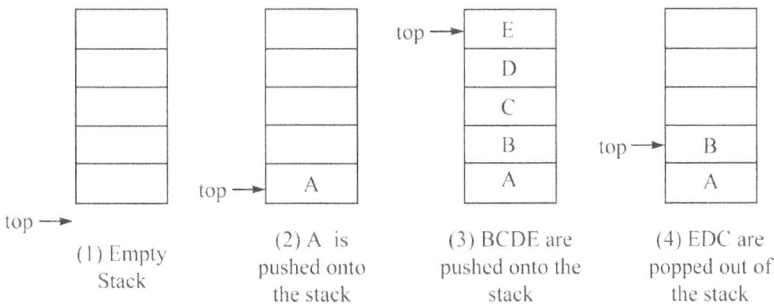

Fig. 3.10: Illustration on stack operations.

3.1.2.2 The differences and connections between stack and linear list

1. Stack is a special case of linear list.
2. The insertion and deletion operations on stack can only be performed at stack top, while the insertion and deletion operations can be performed at arbitrary positions of a linear list.

> **Think and Discuss** Why do we need stack?
>
> **Discussion:** Somebody might think: "can't we just directly use arrays or linked lists to realize the desired functionalities? Why do we introduce such a data structure as stack?
>
> The introduction of stack simplifies program design, designates different layers of concern, narrows down the things to be considered and focuses more on the core problem to be solved. If we use arrays to solve the same problem, since we will need to consider details such as the increment/decrement of the indices of the array, the focus of problem solving will be unclear.
>
> Many high-level languages, such as Java and C#, provide prepackaged stack data structure. We do not need to pay attention to the implementation details of stack, and only need to perform push/pop operations on stacks, which is very convenient.

3.1.2.3 Operations on stack

According to the definition of stack, the basic operations on stack include the following:

(1) Initialization of stack: create an empty stack S.
(2) Deciding emptiness of stack: decide whether the stack is empty.
(3) Get the top element: get the value of the top element of the stack.
(4) Push: insert element e into stack S, making it the new top element of the stack.
(5) Pop: delete the top element of stack S.

3.1.3 The design of the storage structure of stacks

Since stack is a special case of linear list, its storage structure can adapt the storage forms of linear list – sequential structure and linked structure.

3.1.3.1 Sequential stack – use a piece of continuous space to store stack elements

The sequential storage structure of stack needs to be realized with an array and an integer variable. The array is used to store all elements of the stack sequentially; the integer variable is used to store the index of the top element of the stack. We can call this variable top pointer top. The illustration and description of data structure of the stack is shown in Fig. 3.11.

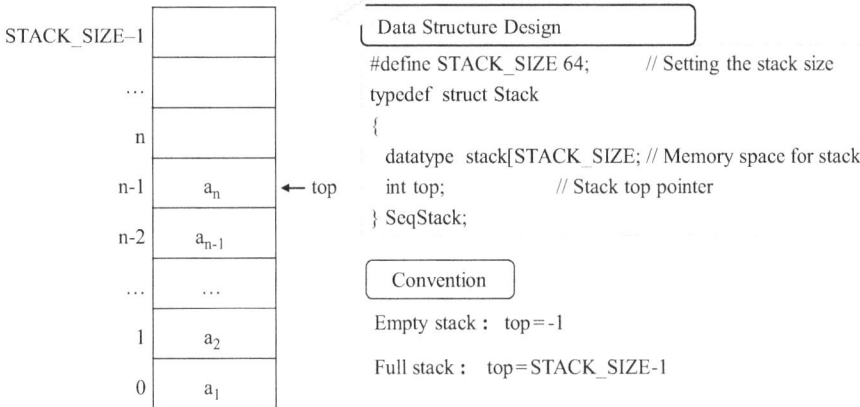

Data Structure Design

```
#define STACK_SIZE 64;        // Setting the stack size
typedef  struct Stack
{
  datatype  stack[STACK_SIZE; // Memory space for stack
  int top;                 // Stack top pointer
} SeqStack;
```

Convention

Empty stack : top=-1

Full stack :   top=STACK_SIZE-1

Fig. 3.11: Description of sequential stack structure.

3.1.3.2 Linked stack – storing stack elements in noncontinuous space

In sequential stack, since the sequential storage structure needs preallocation, and the storage size is usually hard to determine in advance. If the memory allocated is too small, overflow might occur; if the memory allocated is too large, storage space will be wasted. Therefore, in order to overcome the defects of sequential storage, we might use linked storage structure to represent stack. See Fig. 3.12.

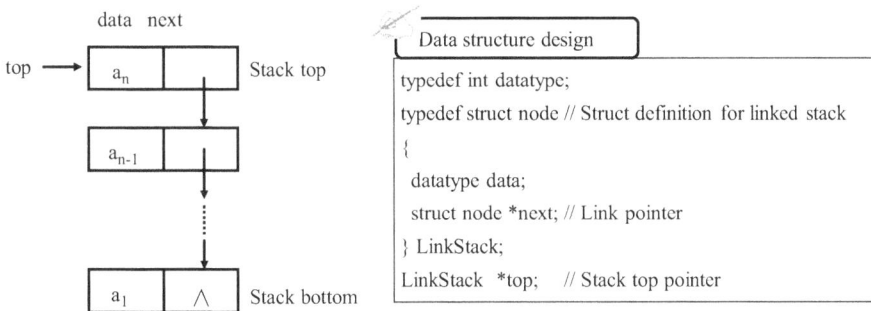

Data structure design

```
typedef int datatype;
typedef struct node // Struct definition for linked stack
{
  datatype data;
  struct node *next; // Link pointer
} LinkStack;
LinkStack  *top;     // Stack top pointer
```

Fig. 3.12: Structure description of linked stack.

A stack using linked storage method is called linked stack or link-style stack. Linked stack is constituted of individual nodes. Each node contains a data field and a pointer field. In the linked stack, the data field of each node is used to store every element in the stack; the pointer field is used to represent relations between elements.

3.1.4 Operations on stack

3.1.4.1 Basic operations on sequential stack
The operations on sequential stack mainly consist of the following. We will detail the implementations of some of those operations.
– Initialization
– Checking the emptiness of the stack
– Push
– Pop
– Retrieving the top element
– Getting the length of the stack

1. Initialization
At the initialization of the stack, we set the top pointer as –1.
(1) Design of test cases and function framework: see Tables 3.1 and 3.2, respectively.

Table 3.1: Test cases for initialization of stack.

Test case	Input	Expected result
Normal case	Address of the sequential stack	Set the top pointer to indicate "stack empty"
Boundary and abnormal cases	None	None

Table 3.2: Function framework for initialization of stack.

Functionality description	Input	Output
Initialization of stack initialize_SqStack	Address of sequential stack SeqStack *	None
Function name	Parameters	Function type

(2) Program implementation

```
/*=====================================================================
Functionality of the function: Set the stack as empty for sequential stack
Function input: Address of the sequential stack
Function output: None
=====================================================================*/
void initialize_SqStack( SeqStack *s )
```

```
{
      s->top = -1;
}
```

2.   Check whether the stack is empty
Check whether the stack is empty, see if there is any element in the stack.
(1) Design of test cases and function framework: see Tables 3.3 and 3.4, respectively.

Table 3.3: Test cases for emptiness check of stack.

Test case	Status	Expected result
Normal case	Nonempty stack	Return nonempty indicator
	Empty stack	Return "stack empty" indicator

Table 3.4: Function framework for emptiness check of stack.

Functionality description	Input	Output
Check emptiness of stack: StackEmpty_SqStack	Address of sequential stack: Seqstack *	Status indicator: int (Empty: 1; Non-empty: 0)
Function name	Parameters	Function type

(2) Program implementation

```
/*=====================================================================
Functionality of the function: Check whether the sequential stack is empty
Function input: Address of the sequential stack
Function output: 1 - Stack is empty; 0 - Stack is non-empty
=====================================================================*/
int StackEmpty_SqStack(SeqStack *s)
{
      return( s->top == -1 );
}
```

3.   Push operation on sequential stack
Push the element with value x into the stack. The illustration of the operation is shown in Fig. 3.13. Before the push, the top pointer top points to the position of the top element a_n. To push the element x, first add 1 to top, in order to point to one position higher than that of a_n, and then push x into this unit.

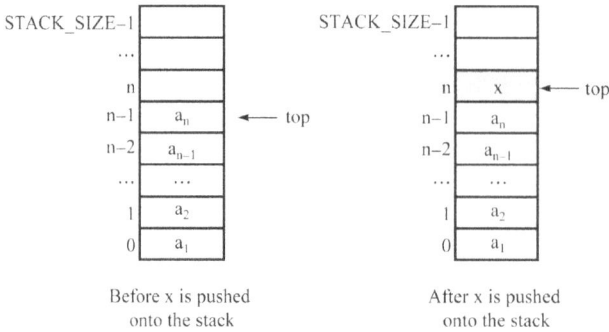

Before x is pushed
onto the stack

After x is pushed
onto the stack

Fig. 3.13: Push operation.

(1) Design of test cases and function outline: see Tables 3.5 and 3.6.

Table 3.5: Test cases for push operation on sequential stack.

Test case	Stack state	Expected result
Normal case	Nonfull	Return indicator of successful push operation
Abnormal case	Full	Return overflow indicator

Table 3.6: Function outline for push operation on sequential stack.

Function description	Input	Output
Push: Push_SqStack	Address of sequential stack: SeqStack * Value of the new element: datatype	Operation status int (Normal: 1; Overflow: 0)
Function name	Parameters	Function type

(2) Pseudocode description of the algorithm, see Table 3.7.

Table 3.7: Pseudocode for push operation on sequential stack.

Top-level pseudocode description	First-level elaboration
Insert new element x at the top of the sequential stack	If stack is full, return FALSE
	Modify top pointer top++
	Put x at the location pointed to by the top pointer
	Return TRUE

(3) Program implementation

```
/*======================================================================
Functionality of the function: Push operation on sequential stack
Function input: Address of the sequential stack, value of the element to be
pushed
Function output: 0 - Overflow, operation failed; 1-Normal operation
====================================================================*/
int Push_SqStack(SeqStack *s, datatype x)
{
     if ( s->top == STACK_SIZE-1)   return FALSE; // Overflow
     else
     {
        s->top++;
        s->stack[s->top]=x;
     }
      return TRUE;
}
```

Think and Discuss Can the following two function structure designs accomplish push on stack?

Structure 1, see Table 3.8.

Table 3.8: Function outline 1 for push operation on sequential stack.

Functionality description	Input	Output	
Push: push	Content of the sequential stack	Operation status	1: Normal
	Value of the new element		0: Overflow
Function name	Parameters	Function type	

```
int push(SeqStack s, datatype x )
```

Structure 2, see Table 3.9.

Table 3.9: Function outline 2 for push operation on sequential stack.

Functionality description	Input	Output	
Push: push	Address of the sequential stack	Normal	Address of the stack
	Value of the new element	Overflow	NULL
Function name	Parameters	Function type	

```
SeqStack *PUSHS( SeqStack *s, datatype e)
```

Verifying Structure 1 in Practice
The source code for verification is as follows:

```c
#include<stdio.h>
#define STACK_SIZE 6
typedef char datatype;
typedef struct Stack
{
    datatype stack[STACK_SIZE];    //Stack space
    int top; //Top pointer
} SeqStack;
void InitStack( SeqStack *s );
int push(SeqStack s, datatype x );

void InitStack( SeqStack *s )     //Initialization
{
   s->top = -1;
}

int push(SeqStack s, datatype x ) //Push
 {
    if ( s.top == STACK_SIZE-1) return FALSE;
    else
    {
       s.top = s.top + 1;
       s.stack[s.top]=x;
    }
    return TRUE;
 }

int main(void)
{
   SeqStack sa;
   int sign;

   InitStack(&sa);
   sign=push(sa,'a');
   sign=push(sa,'b');
   return 0;
}
```

Tracing and Debugging

In Fig. 3.14, before the sa stack in main was initialized, top pointer points to a random value. Note that sa is a struct variable; its address is 0x18ff38.

In Fig. 3.15, after the initialization function InitStack is called, the top pointer is set to −1.

Note: The Chinese characters in Fig. 3.14 and so on are garbled output produced by the system, as the system environment uses GBK character encoding by default.

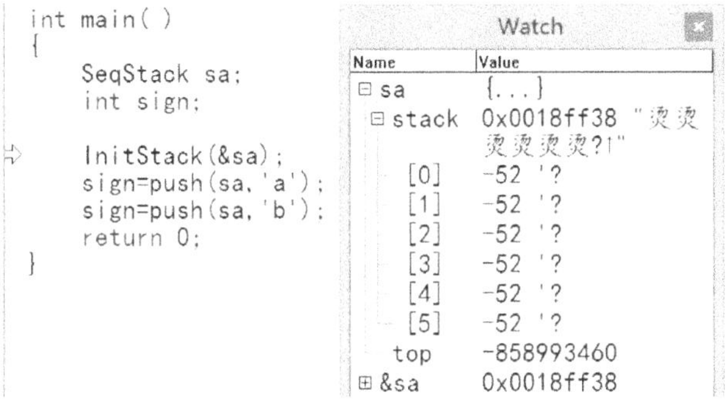

```
int main( )
{
    SeqStack sa;
    int sign;

⇒    InitStack(&sa);
    sign=push(sa, 'a');
    sign=push(sa, 'b');
    return 0;
}
```

Watch	
Name	**Value**
⊟ sa	{...}
⊟ stack	0x0018ff38 "烫烫烫烫烫烫?!"
[0]	−52 '?
[1]	−52 '?
[2]	−52 '?
[3]	−52 '?
[4]	−52 '?
[5]	−52 '?
top	−858993460
⊞ &sa	0x0018ff38

Fig. 3.14: Testing step 1 for structure 1.

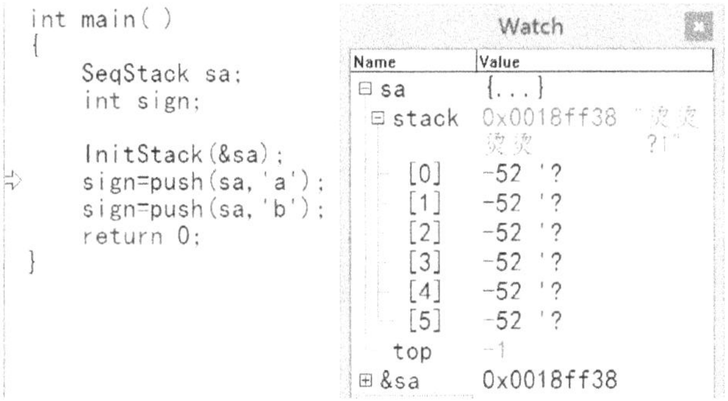

```
int main( )
{
    SeqStack sa;
    int sign;

    InitStack(&sa);
⇒    sign=push(sa, 'a');
    sign=push(sa, 'b');
    return 0;
}
```

Watch	
Name	**Value**
⊟ sa	{...}
⊟ stack	0x0018ff38 "烫烫烫烫?!"
[0]	−52 '?
[1]	−52 '?
[2]	−52 '?
[3]	−52 '?
[4]	−52 '?
[5]	−52 '?
top	−1
⊞ &sa	0x0018ff38

Fig. 3.15: Testing step 2 for structure 1.

In Fig. 3.16, push function is called, and the address of parameter s is 0x18fedc. Note that it is not at the same address as the stack sa in main.

```
void InitStack( SeqStack *s )
    {
        s->top = -1;
    }

int push(SeqStack s, datatype  x )
    {
        if ( s.top == STACK_SIZE-1) return 0;
        else
            {
                s.top = s.top + 1;
                s.stack[s.top]=x;
            }
        return 1;
    }
```

Name	Value
sa	CXX0017: Error:
&sa	CXX0017: Error:
⊟ s	{...}
⊟ stack	0x0018fed8 "烫烫
	烫烫 a"
[0]	-52 '?
[1]	-52 '?
[2]	-52 '?
[3]	-52 '?
[4]	-52 '?
[5]	-52 '?
top	-1
⊞ &s	0x0018fed8

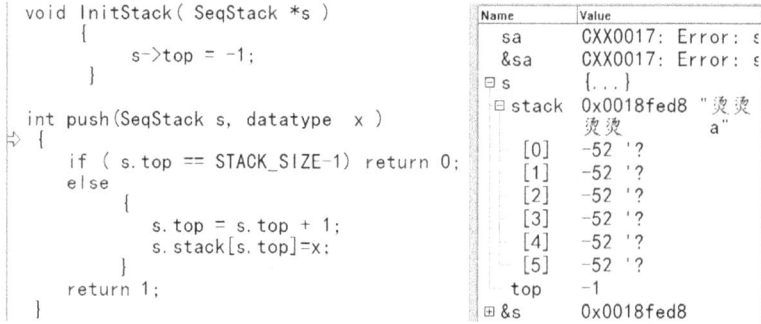

Fig. 3.16: Testing step 3 for structure 1.

In Fig. 3.17, the top pointer is added by 1, the value 'a' of parameter x is pushed into stack[0].

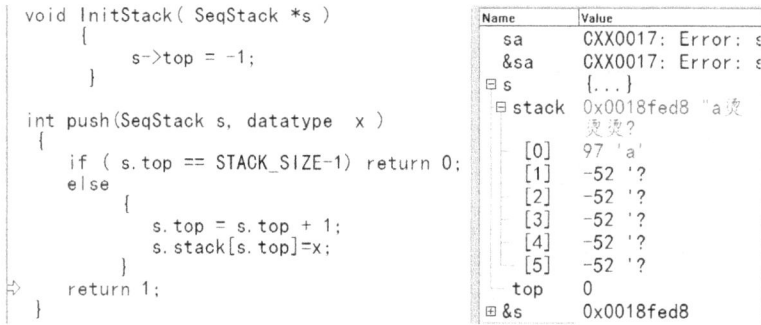

```
void InitStack( SeqStack *s )
    {
        s->top = -1;
    }

int push(SeqStack s, datatype  x )
    {
        if ( s.top == STACK_SIZE-1) return 0;
        else
            {
                s.top = s.top + 1;
                s.stack[s.top]=x;
            }
        return 1;
    }
```

Name	Value
sa	CXX0017: Error:
&sa	CXX0017: Error:
⊟ s	{...}
⊟ stack	0x0018fed8 "a烫
	烫烫?
[0]	97 'a'
[1]	-52 '?
[2]	-52 '?
[3]	-52 '?
[4]	-52 '?
[5]	-52 '?
top	0
⊞ &s	0x0018fed8

Fig. 3.17: Testing step 4 for structure 1.

In Fig. 3.18, returning to main, the value of sign is 1, indicating the push in finished normally. However, the contents in stack sa are not changed at this time.

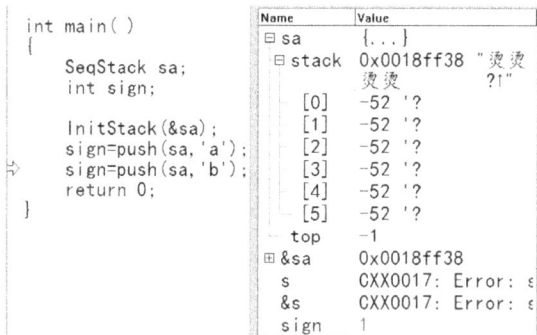

```
int main( )
    {
        SeqStack sa;
        int sign;

        InitStack(&sa);
        sign=push(sa, 'a');
        sign=push(sa, 'b');
        return 0;
    }
```

Name	Value
⊟ sa	{...}
⊟ stack	0x0018ff38 "烫烫
	烫烫 ?↑"
[0]	-52 '?
[1]	-52 '?
[2]	-52 '?
[3]	-52 '?
[4]	-52 '?
[5]	-52 '?
top	-1
⊞ &sa	0x0018ff38
s	CXX0017: Error:
&s	CXX0017: Error:
sign	1

Fig. 3.18: Testing step 5 for structure 1.

In Fig. 3.19, when x parameter is 'b', the top pointer still starts from –1.

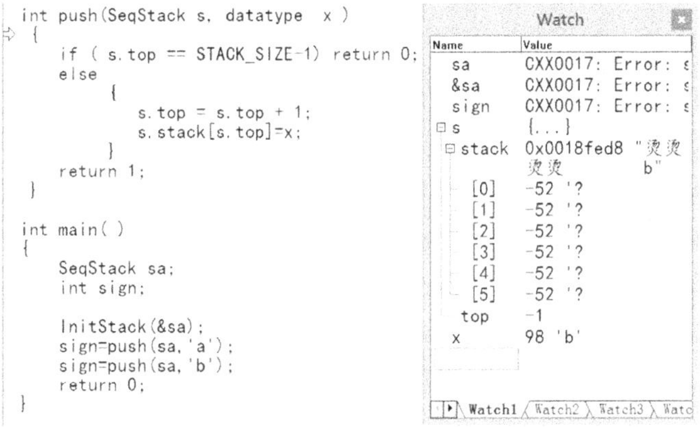

```
  int push(SeqStack s, datatype  x )
  {
      if ( s.top == STACK_SIZE-1) return 0;
      else
          {
              s.top = s.top + 1;
              s.stack[s.top]=x;
          }
      return 1;
  }

  int main( )
  {
      SeqStack sa;
      int sign;

      InitStack(&sa);
      sign=push(sa,'a');
      sign=push(sa,'b');
      return 0;
  }
```

Watch	☒
Name	**Value**
sa	CXX0017: Error: s
&sa	CXX0017: Error: s
sign	CXX0017: Error: s
⊟ s	{...}
⊟ stack	0x0018fed8 "烫 烫
	烫烫 b"
[0]	-52 '?
[1]	-52 '?
[2]	-52 '?
[3]	-52 '?
[4]	-52 '?
[5]	-52 '?
top	-1
x	98 'b'

Watch1 ╱ Watch2 ╲ Watch3 ╲ Watc

Fig. 3.19: Testing step 6 for structure 1.

In Fig. 3.20, x = 'b' is pushed into stack s.

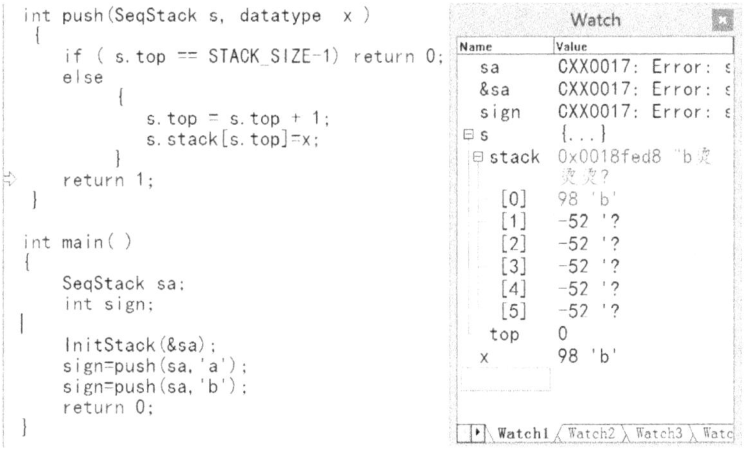

```
  int push(SeqStack s, datatype  x )
  {
      if ( s.top == STACK_SIZE-1) return 0;
      else
          {
              s.top = s.top + 1;
              s.stack[s.top]=x;
          }
      return 1;
  }

  int main( )
  {
      SeqStack sa;
      int sign;

      InitStack(&sa);
      sign=push(sa,'a');
      sign=push(sa,'b');
      return 0;
  }
```

Watch	☒
Name	**Value**
sa	CXX0017: Error: s
&sa	CXX0017: Error: s
sign	CXX0017: Error: s
⊟ s	{...}
⊟ stack	0x0018fed8 "b 烫
	烫 烫?
[0]	98 'b'
[1]	-52 '?
[2]	-52 '?
[3]	-52 '?
[4]	-52 '?
[5]	-52 '?
top	0
x	98 'b'

Watch1 ╱ Watch2 ╲ Watch3 ╲ Watc

Fig. 3.20: Testing step 7 for structure 1.

In Fig. 3.21, the calling of push(sa, 'b') finishes.

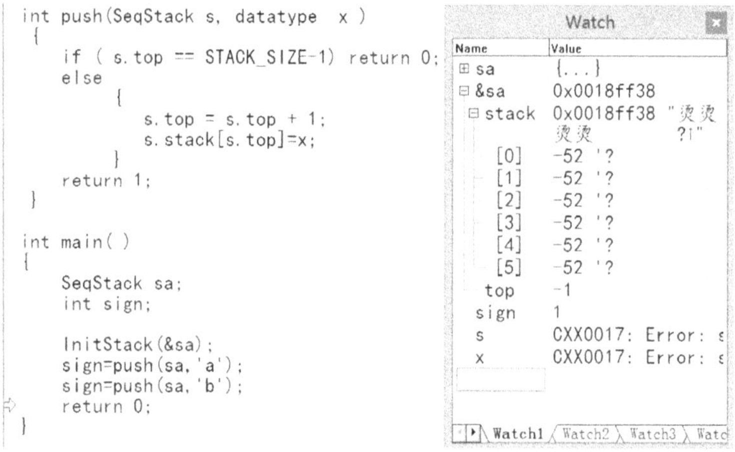

```
int push(SeqStack s, datatype  x )
  {
      if ( s.top == STACK_SIZE-1) return 0;
      else
          {
              s.top = s.top + 1;
              s.stack[s.top]=x;
          }
      return 1;
  }
int main( )
  {
      SeqStack sa;
      int sign;

      InitStack(&sa);
      sign=push(sa, 'a');
      sign=push(sa, 'b');
      return 0;
  }
```

Watch	
Name	Value
⊞ sa	{...}
⊟ &sa	0x0018ff38
⊟ stack	0x0018ff38 "烫烫
	烫烫 ?↑"
[0]	-52 '?
[1]	-52 '?
[2]	-52 '?
[3]	-52 '?
[4]	-52 '?
[5]	-52 '?
top	-1
sign	1
s	CXX0017: Error: s
x	CXX0017: Error: s

Watch1 ⟨ Watch2 ⟩ Watch3 ⟩ Watc

Fig. 3.21: Testing step 8 for structure 1.

Discussion: In the push function, we input a copy of stack sa, s, that is to say, we copied all the information of stack sa into the structure s, and performed push operation on the contents of s, in push function. However, according to the information passing mechanism for functions in C programming language, the caller function will not be able to get the changes on the contents of s via such single-parameter passing mechanism (for the mechanisms of "pass-by-value" and "pass-by-reference," refer to the related contents on the "function" part of C language reference).

Conclusion In designing the structure of a function, we must pay attention to the characteristics of the language used for implementation. In C, there are one-directional and bidirectional restrictions when passing the parameters. We should choose the appropriate information passing mechanism according to the requirements of the functionality of the function. Do not decide on the parameters of the function carelessly.

Verifying Structure 2 in Practice

The source code for structure 2 is as follows:

```
#include<stdio.h>
#define STACK_SIZE 6
typedef char datatype;
typedef struct Stack
{
    datatype stack[STACK_SIZE];  //Stack space
    int top; //Top pointer
} SeqStack;

void InitStack( SeqStack *s );
int push(SeqStack s, datatype x);
```

```
void InitStack( SeqStack *s )  //Initialization
{
    s->top = -1;
}

int push(SeqStack s, datatype x ) //Push
 {
    if ( s.top == STACK_SIZE-1) return FALSE;
    else
    {
        s.top = s.top + 1;
        s.stack[s.top]=x;
    }
    return TRUE;
 }

int main(void)
{
    SeqStack sa;
    int sign;

    InitStack(&sa);
    sign=push(sa,'a');
    sign=push(sa,'b');
    return 0;
}
```

In Fig. 3.22, before the stack sa in main is initialized, top pointer contains some random number. Note sa is a struct variable, with an address 0x18ff38.

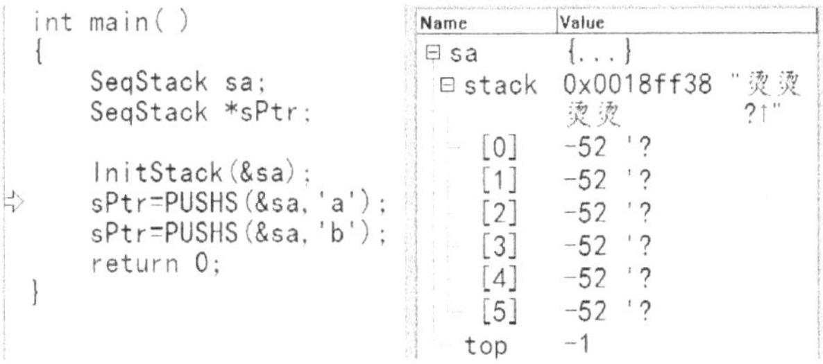

Fig. 3.22: Testing step 1 of structure 2.

In Fig. 3.23, the parameter s in PUSHS function is of pointer type, and it receives the address of stack sa, 0x18ff38, from main.

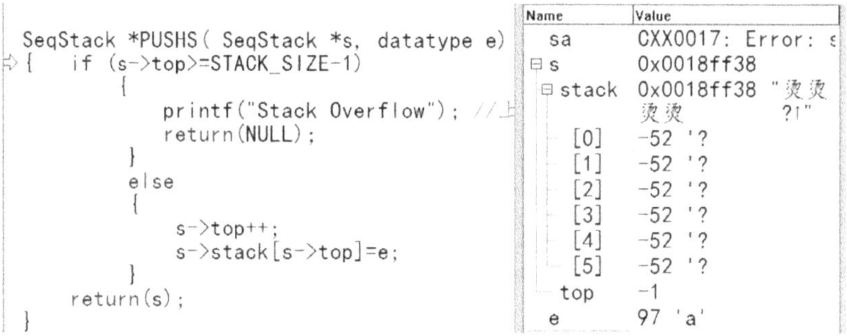

```
SeqStack *PUSHS ( SeqStack *s, datatype e)
{    if (s->top>=STACK_SIZE-1)
     {
          printf("Stack Overflow"); //上
          return(NULL);
     }
     else
     {
          s->top++;
          s->stack[s->top]=e;
     }
     return(s);
}
```

Name	Value
sa	CXX0017: Error: s
⊟ s	0x0018ff38
⊟ stack	0x0018ff38 " 烫烫
	烫烫 ?¦"
[0]	-52 '?
[1]	-52 '?
[2]	-52 '?
[3]	-52 '?
[4]	-52 '?
[5]	-52 '?
top	-1
e	97 'a'

Fig. 3.23: Testing step 2 of structure 2.

In Fig. 3.24, the push operation is finished. Note that the value of pointer s is still 0x18ff38 and has not changed.

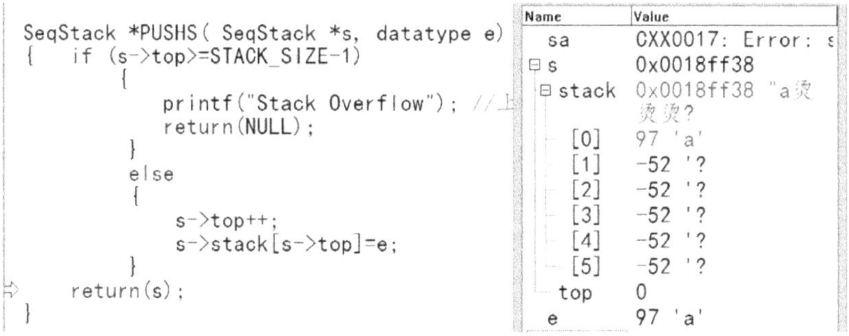

```
SeqStack *PUSHS ( SeqStack *s, datatype e)
{    if (s->top>=STACK_SIZE-1)
     {
          printf("Stack Overflow"); //上
          return(NULL);
     }
     else
     {
          s->top++;
          s->stack[s->top]=e;
     }
     return(s);
}
```

Name	Value
sa	CXX0017: Error: s
⊟ s	0x0018ff38
⊟ stack	0x0018ff38 "a 烫
	烫烫?
[0]	97 'a'
[1]	-52 '?
[2]	-52 '?
[3]	-52 '?
[4]	-52 '?
[5]	-52 '?
top	0
e	97 'a'

Fig. 3.24: Testing step 3 of structure 2.

In Fig. 3.25, the function returns to main. The contents of stack SA has already been modified by function PUSHS, sPtr receives the value returned 0x18ff38.

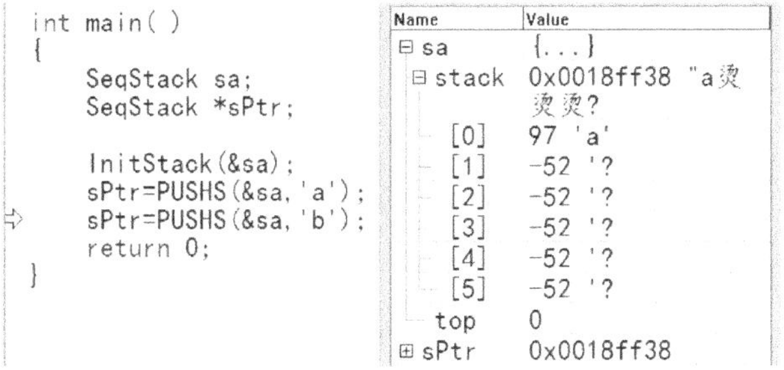

```
int main( )                  Name        Value
{                            ⊟ sa        {...}
    SeqStack sa;             ⊟ stack     0x0018ff38 "a烫
    SeqStack *sPtr;                      烫烫?
                               [0]       97 'a'
    InitStack(&sa);            [1]       -52 '?
    sPtr=PUSHS(&sa,'a');       [2]       -52 '?
⇨   sPtr=PUSHS(&sa,'b');       [3]       -52 '?
    return 0;                  [4]       -52 '?
}                              [5]       -52 '?
                               top       0
                             ⊞ sPtr      0x0018ff38
```

Fig. 3.25: Testing step 4 of structure 2.

In Fig. 3.26, PUSHS(&sa, 'b') finishes execution. The elements 'a' and 'b' are already in stack sa, and the top pointer is 1, which is consistent with what we expected.

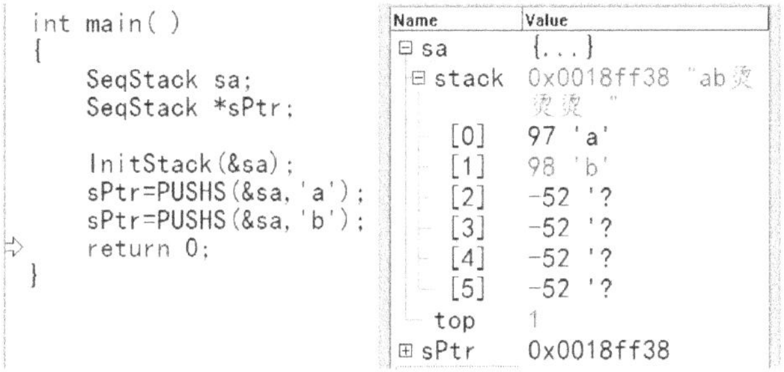

```
int main( )                  Name        Value
{                            ⊟ sa        {...}
    SeqStack sa;             ⊟ stack     0x0018ff38 "ab烫
    SeqStack *sPtr;                      烫烫 "
                               [0]       97 'a'
    InitStack(&sa);            [1]       98 'b'
    sPtr=PUSHS(&sa,'a');       [2]       -52 '?
    sPtr=PUSHS(&sa,'b');       [3]       -52 '?
⇨   return 0;                  [4]       -52 '?
}                              [5]       -52 '?
                               top       1
                             ⊞ sPtr      0x0018ff38
```

Fig. 3.26: Testing step 5 of structure 2.

Discussion: When calling PUSHS function, PUSHS gets the contents of stack sa via s = sa, and thus performs push operation. When the operation is finished, the memory address pointed to by s does not change. Therefore, the caller can get the contents changed in s.
Conclusion We already know that the type of the function is the result type returned to the caller by the function. In this example, we return a special value NULL in the case of abnormality, to mark "overflow" scenario; we use the address of a normal stack structure as the indicator for successful operation. Although this is not erroneous, this is not that straightforward. Also, when the operation is normal, since the memory address pointed to by s did not change anyways, it is unnecessary to return the value of s explicitly. Such a function outline design is neither straightforward nor concise, thus it is not a good design.

4. Pop operation on sequential stack
Pop operation: delete the top data element. For illustration of the operation, see Fig. 3.27.

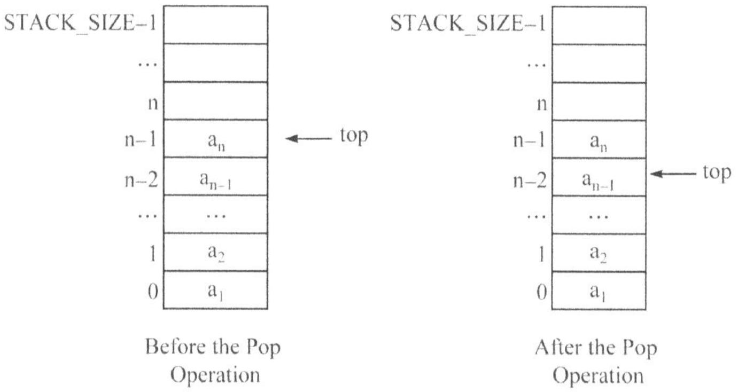

Fig. 3.27: Pop operation.

! **Think and Discuss**

1. Why don't we actually delete the original top element after the pop operation on sequential stack?

Discussion: Because the position of the top element is indicated via the top pointer, instead of via checking the existence of elements in the stack. Therefore, we can also see the convenience of managing the stack using top pointer.

2. When we do not actually delete the original top element, will we impact the next push operation?

Discussion: Push operation is a "write operation," that is, it overwrites the original space. So there is no impact.

(1) Function framework and test cases: see Tables 3.10 and 3.11.

Table 3.10: Test cases for pop operation on sequential stack.

Test case	State	Input	Expected result
Normal case	Stack is non-empty	Top pointer > 0	Return the value of the top element
Boundary case		Top pointer == 0	Return "normal pop operation" indicator
Abnormal case	Stack is empty	Top pointer = −1	Return "abnormal pop operation" indicator

Note: Value of the popped element datatype * is present in both the input and output. It represents the fact that the calling function needs to get the value of the popped element via address passing of the parameter. In the function framework description, this input parameter is specially surrounded with brackets.

Table 3.11: Function framework for pop operation on sequential stack.

Functionality description	Input	Output
Pop: Pop_SqStack	Address of the sequential stack: SeqStack * (Value of the popped element datatype *)	Operation status int (Normal: 1; Underflow: 0) Value of the popped element datatype *
Function name	Parameters	Function type

(2) Pseudocode description of the algorithm: see Table 3.12.

Table 3.12: Pseudocode for pop operation on sequential stack.

Top-level pseudocode description	First-level elaboration
Delete top data element	If stack is empty, return FALSE;
	Record value of the top element x
	Modify top pointer: top–
	Return TRUE

(3) Program implementation

```
/*======================================================================
Functionality of the function: Pop operation on sequential stack
Function input: Address of the sequential stack, (Address of the popped
element)
Function output: 0 - Stack underflow, operation failed; 1 - Normal operation
======================================================================*/
int Pop_SqStack(SeqStack *s, datatype *x)
{
    if ( s->top == -1) return FALSE;
    else
    {
        *x= s-> stack[s-> top];
        s-> top--;
    }
    return TRUE;
}
```

! **Think and Discuss** What is the problem with the design of the below pop function?

```
datatype pop(SeqStack *s)
{
        datatype temp;
        if (StackEmpty(s))
        {
              return(-1);
        }
        else
        {  s->top --;
           return(s->stack[s->top+1]);
        }
}
```

Discussion: Based on the program, we can give the function framework as shown in Table 3.13. We can observe that the type of the stack element being output, datatype, is not necessarily an integer type. No matter whether it is normal or abnormal return, the function can only return one type. Therefore, it is inappropriate to return "−1" in the "underflow" error case.

Table 3.13: Structural design of the pop function.

Functionality description	Input	Output
Pop: pop	Address of the sequential stack: SeqStack *	Normal: Value of the popped element: datatype
		Underflow: -1
Function name	Parameters	Function Type

5. Get the top element
Get the value of the top element without changing the top pointer.

It is similar to the pop function. It is just that we would not modify the top pointer. The description of the implementation can be seen at the section on pop operation and will not be repeated again.

```
/*=================================================================
Functionality of the function: Get top element in sequential stack
Function input: Address of the sequential stack, (address of the element)
Function output: 0 - Stack underflow, operation failed; 1 - Normal operation
=================================================================*/
```

```
int Get_SqStack(SeqStack *s, datatype *x)
  {
      if ( s->top == -1) return FALSE;
      else
      {
          *x= s-> stack[s-> top];
      }
      return TRUE;
}
```

3.1.4.2 Basic operations on linked stack

The problem for sequential stack is that no new element can be pushed once the stack is full. This is because we used fixed-length array to store elements of the stack. One solution is to use linked storage structure, so that the stack can be dynamically expanded.

The linked storage structure for stacks is called linked stack. It is a singly linked list with restricted operations. Its insertion and deletion are restricted to only the head of the list. Since one can only operate at the head of the list, there is no need for linked list to add a head node in the similar fashion as singly linked lists. The stack-top pointer is the head pointer of the linked list, as shown in Fig. 3.28.

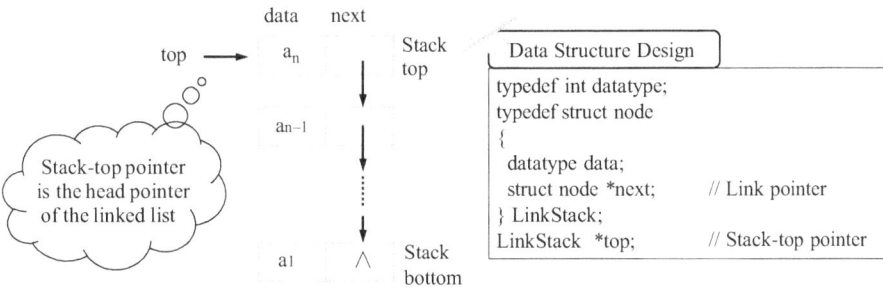

Fig. 3.28: Illustration of linked stack.

We have already learned the algorithm for insertion and deletion operations on a linear linked list, so it is not hard to come up with algorithms for operations such as initialization, push, pop on linked stack.

1. Basic operation on linked stack – push
Insert a new node with value x at the top of the linked stack.
The changes of the linked stack before and after the push are shown in Fig. 3.29.

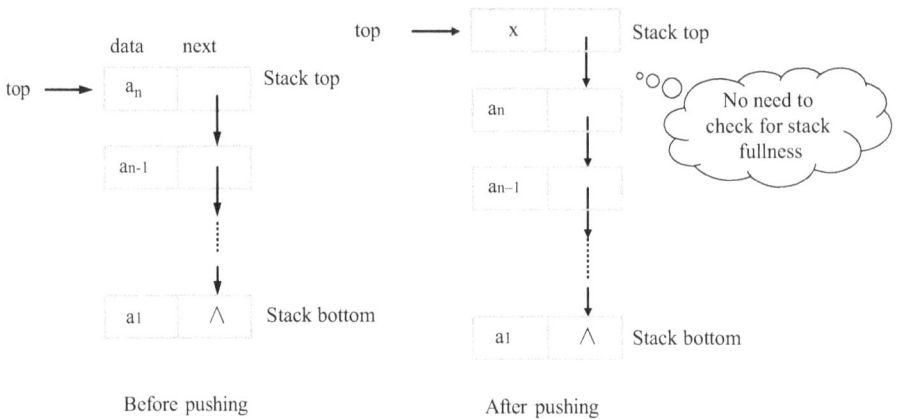

Fig. 3.29: The changes to the linked stack before and after the push.

(1) Design of test cases and function framework: see Tables 3.14 and 3.15.

Table 3.14: Test cases for the push operation on linked stack.

Test case	State	Expected result
Normal case	Linked stack is nonempty	Successful push
Special case	Linked stack is empty	Return top pointer

Table 3.15: Function framework for the push operation on linked stack.

Functionality description	Input	Output
Push PushLStack	(Top pointer LinkStack *) Value of the element pushed datatype	Top pointer LinkStack *
Function name	Parameters	Function type

Think and Discuss Is it necessary to return the struct pointer to the stack?
Discussion: Pass by reference only works on contents based on the same address. If we modified the address inside the function, then this modified address will not be passed back to the caller function. In Fig. 3.29, before push, top points to the address of node a_n, while after push top points to the address of node x. Thus, the address pointed to by top changed, and the new address will not be passed back to the caller via the parameter of the function. Therefore, when designing the function structure, we need to return the top pointer top.

   Note the difference between this situation and the situation where the address pointed to by top does not change, but the content of that address changes.

(2) Pseudocode description of the algorithm: see Table 3.16.

Table 3.16: Pseudocode for basic operation on the stack – push.

Top-level pseudocode	First-level elaboration
Insertion new node with value x at the top position of the linked stack	Apply for allocation of new node p, and give it value x
	Link the p node at the top of the stack
	Modify the top pointer
	Return the top pointer

(3) Program implementation

```
/*============================================================
Functionality of the function: The push operation on linked stack
Function input: (top pointer), element to be pushed.
Function output: Top pointer
============================================================*/
LinkStack * PushLStack(LinkStack *top, datatype x )
{  LinkStack *p;
   p=malloc( sizeof(LinkStack ) );
   p->data=x;
   p->next=top;
   top= p;
   return top;
}
```

Verification Is it necessary to return the struct pointer to stack?
The source code is as follows:

```
#include<stdio.h>
#include<stdlib.h>
typedef int datatype;
typedef struct node // Node
{
   datatype data;
   struct node *next; // Link pointer
} LinkStack;
LinkStack * PushLStack(LinkStack *top, datatype x);
LinkStack * PushLStack(LinkStack *top, datatype x)
```

```
{ LinkStack *p;
  p=(LinkStack *)malloc( sizeof(LinkStack));
  p->data=x;
  p->next=top;
  top= p;
  return top;
}
int main(void)
{
  LinkStack *topPtr; // Stack top pointer
  topPtr=PushLStack(topPtr,'a'); // Push element 'a'
  topPtr=PushLStack(topPtr,'b'); // Push element 'b'
  return 0;
}
```

Note that in Fig. 3.30, we do not initialize the topPtr pointer at its declaration, and thus it has a random value. We can see a warning"Warning C4700: local variable 'topPtr' used without having been initialized."

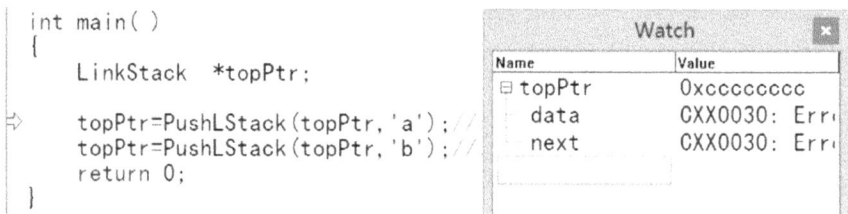

Fig. 3.30: Testing step 1 for push on linked stack.

Figure 3.31: we enter PushLStack function. Note the value of top is 0xcccccccc.

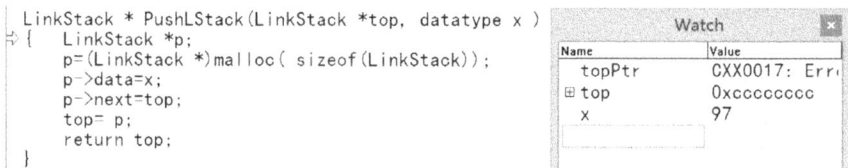

Fig. 3.31: Testing step 2 for push on linked stack.

In Fig. 3.32, we call malloc and created a new node 0x5e1780. The element is given the value 'a' (The ASCII code of 'a' is 97).

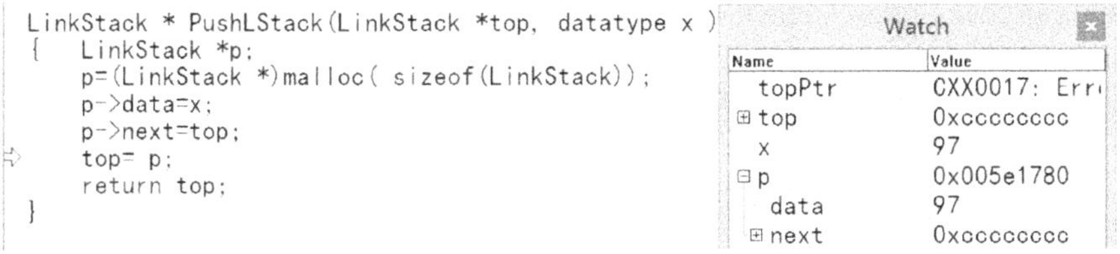

```
LinkStack * PushLStack(LinkStack *top, datatype x )
{   LinkStack *p;
    p=(LinkStack *)malloc( sizeof(LinkStack));
    p->data=x;
    p->next=top;
    top= p;
    return top;
}
```

Watch	
Name	Value
topPtr	CXX0017: Err
⊞ top	0xcccccccc
x	97
⊟ p	0x005e1780
data	97
⊞ next	0xcccccccc

Fig. 3.32: Testing step 3 for push on linked stack.

In Fig. 3.33, top pointers to new node 0x5e1780, and then return to main.

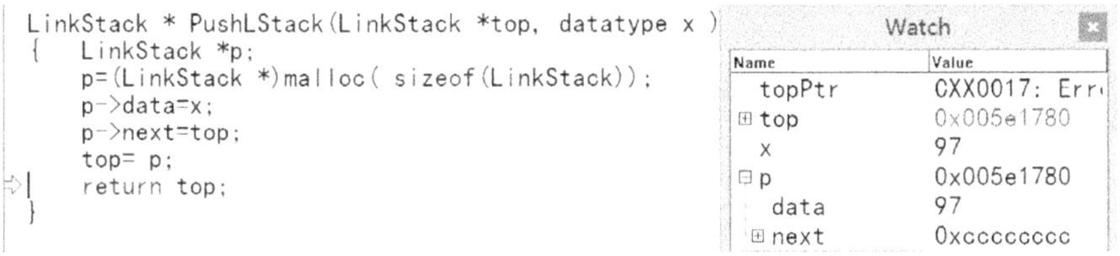

```
LinkStack * PushLStack(LinkStack *top, datatype x )
{   LinkStack *p;
    p=(LinkStack *)malloc( sizeof(LinkStack));
    p->data=x;
    p->next=top;
    top= p;
    return top;
}
```

Watch	
Name	Value
topPtr	CXX0017: Err
⊞ top	0x005e1780
x	97
⊟ p	0x005e1780
data	97
⊞ next	0xcccccccc

Fig. 3.33: Testing step 4 for push on linked stack.

In Fig. 3.34, main gets the returned 0x5e1780 address.

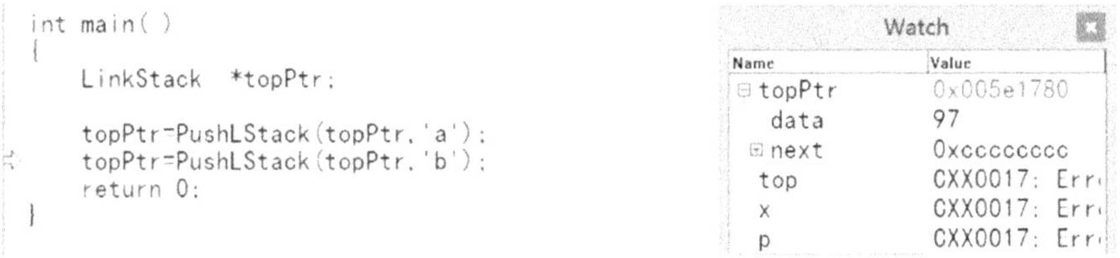

```
int main( )
{
    LinkStack  *topPtr;

    topPtr=PushLStack(topPtr,'a');
    topPtr=PushLStack(topPtr,'b');
    return 0;
}
```

Watch	
Name	Value
⊟ topPtr	0x005e1780
data	97
⊟ next	0xcccccccc
top	CXX0017: Err
x	CXX0017: Err
p	CXX0017: Err

Fig. 3.34: Testing step 5 for push on linked stack.

Figure 3.35 is the situation in the linked stack after element 'b' is pushed.

```
int main( )
{
    LinkStack  *topPtr;

    topPtr=PushLStack(topPtr,'a');
    topPtr=PushLStack(topPtr,'b');
    return 0;
}
```

Name	Value
⊟ topPtr	0x005e1740
data	98
⊟ next	0x005e1780
data	97
⊞ next	0xcccccccc

Fig. 3.35: Testing step 6 for push on linked stack.

Note that the next value at the bottom of the stack is 0xcccccccc (a random value), which does not conform to the restriction about the last node indicator in linked list. We can make improvements before we push the first element 'a' – initialize the top pointer topPtr to NULL at its declaration, then the next value at the bottom of the stack will be 0, as shown in Fig. 3.36.

```
int main( )
{
    LinkStack   *topPtr;

    topPtr=PushLStack(NULL,'a');
    topPtr=PushLStack(topPtr,'b');
    return 0;
}
```

Name	Value
topPtr	0x00551740
data	98
next	0x00551780
data	97
next	0x00000000

Fig. 3.36: Testing step 7 for push on linked stack.

2. Basic operation on linked stack – pop

Delete the node at the stack top position. The state changes of the linked stack before and after the pop are shown in Fig. 3.37.

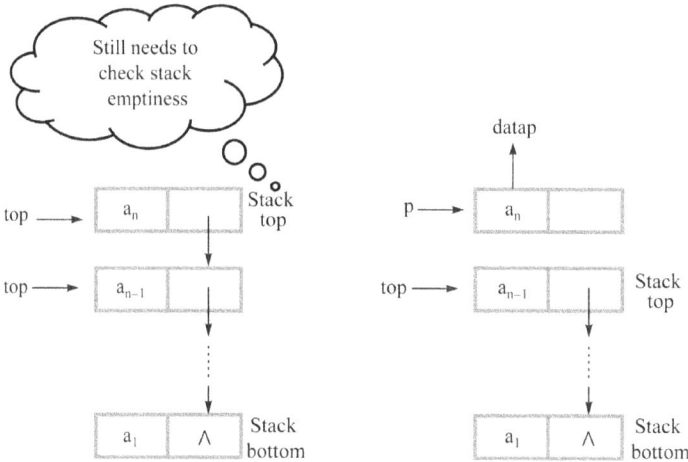

Fig. 3.37: State changes of the linked stack before and after the pop operation.

(1) Design of function structure and test cases: see Tables 3.17 and 3.18.

Table 3.17: Test cases for pop on linked stack.

Test cases	Input/state	Expected results
Normal case	Stack nonempty	Return top pointer, value of the top element
Abnormal case	Stack empty	Return NULL

Table 3.18: The design of function structure of pop operation on linked stack.

Function description	Input	Output
Pop: PopLStack	Stack top pointer: `LinkStack *` (Value of the top element: datatype*)	Stack top pointer: `LinkStack*` Value of the top element: `datatype*`
Function name	Parameters	Function type

(2) Pseudocode description of the algorithm: see Table 3.19.

Table 3.19: Pseudocode design of the pop operation on linked stack.

Top-level pseudocode	First-level elaboration
Delete node at stack top position of linked stack	If stack is nonempty
	Record the address of the stack top node p, value of the element datap
	Modify the stack top pointer top
	Release node p

(3) Program implementation

```
/*===============================================================
Function functionality: pop operation on the top of the linked stack
Function input: Top pointer, (popped element)
Function output: Top pointer
==============================================================*/
LinkStack * PopLStack(LinkStack *top, datatype *datap)
{
  LinkStack *p;
  if ( top != NULL)
  {  *datap=top->data;
     p=top;
     top=top->next;
     free(p);
  }
   return top;
}
```

Think and Discuss Can we deal with the situation where the stack is empty in PopLStack function? **Discussion:** When the stack is empty, NULL will be returned. Therefore, there is no need for special treatment for the empty stack situation.

3.1.5 Comparison of various stack structures

The comparison on time and space complexity between various stack structures is listed in Fig. 3.38.

	Time complexity	Space complexity
Sequential stack	All operations only need constant time	Its length needs to be fixed
Linked stack	The operation is performed on the top of the stack, the efficiency is high	The length of linked stack is extendable, but it adds structural cost
Note	The time complexity of sequential stack and linked stack are about the same	In actual applications, sequential stacks are more widely used.

Fig. 3.38: Comparison of various stack structures.

The shortcoming of sequential stack is that no push operation can be performed after the stack is full. There is no full stack problem on linked stack (when system resources are enough).

3.1.6 Examples of the application of stack

Because of the inherent "first-in–last-out" feature of stack, it has become a very useful tool in program designs. Whenever the solution process for the problem has the "first-in–last-out" characteristic, the algorithm most likely also uses "stack." This section introduces some classical applications of stack.

3.1.6.1 Base conversion

For example, the conversion from base 10 numbers to base R numbers. The conversion between the number N in base 10 and the number d in other bases is a basic problem for the computer to realize computations. There are various solutions. A simple algorithm is based on the below method:

N=(n div d)*d+ n mod d (where div is the division operation and mod is the modulo operation, n is a base-10 number.)

Using the example of converting 1348 in base 10 to base 8, the steps of conversion are shown in Fig. 3.39.

From the conversion steps we can see that the remainder first obtained is the lowest digit of the result; the remainder last obtained is the highest digit of the result, that is, the order of getting the result is the reverse of the order of getting the remainders. It matches the "first-in–last-out" property of stacks. Therefore, we can use stack to implement base conversion.

Stack $(1348)_{10} = (2504)_8$

	n	n div 8	n mod 8
2	1348	168	4	—— Get the lowest digit of base 8
5	168	21	0	—— Get the second digit of base 8
0	21	2	5	—— Get the third digit of base 8
4	2	0	2	—— Get the fourth digit of base 8

Fig. 3.39: Steps of base conversion.

Think and Discuss What is the difference between implementing base conversion between se- ❗
quential stack and sequential list?
Discussion: Some people might say, isn't it also simple to just directly use array to implement
this problem? We can try to use array to rewrite this algorithm, then we will understand the ben-
efits of using stack in this algorithm.

The program to implement base conversion using stack is as follows:

```
// For any non-negative base 10 integer n, print the equivalent base 8 number
/*==============================================================
Functionality of the function: Converting from base 10 to base 8
Function input: Address of the stack structure, number in base 10
Function output: None
==============================================================*/
void conversion(SeqStack *S, int n)
{
    int e;
    while (n)
    {
        Push_SqStack(S,n%8); // "Remainder" is pushed onto the stack
        n = n/8; // The result is non-zero, continue calculation
    }
    while (!StackEmpty_SqStack(S)) // Stack is non-empty, display result
    {
        Pop_SqStack(S,&e);
        printf("%d",e);
    }
}
```

Test program
```
#include <stdio.h>
#define FALSE 0
#define TRUE 1
```

```
#include"stack.h"
int main(void)
{
    SeqStack s;
    initialize_SqStack(&s); // Construct empty stack
    conversion(&s,1348);
    return 0;
}
```

Program result: 2504.

3.1.6.2 Implement recursive functions with stack
We will have an analysis of the execution of recursion. By tracing a concrete recursive program, let us see the role of the system stack and the change of elements in it during a recursive invocation of function. (Note: To view the call stack during debugging, choose View→Debug Windows→Call Stack in the testing environment.)

Functionality of the function: obtain the sum of the expression 1 + 2 + 3 + ... + value

Implementation method of recursion
1. Base case of recursion: iterate=value if value = 1
2. Condition for recursion to continue: iterate=value+iterate(value − 1) if value > 1

```
int iterate(int value);
int sum;
int main(void)
{
    int v;
    v= iterate(4);
    return 0;
}
int iterate(int value)
{
    if(value == 1) return TRUE;
    return sum=value + iterate(value -1);
}
```

The illustration of the execution of iterate is shown in Fig. 3.40.

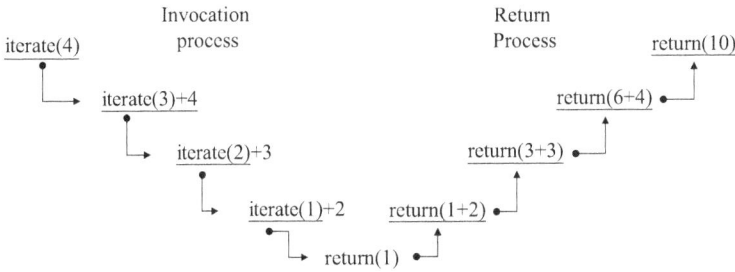

Fig. 3.40: Illustration of the execution of the recursive function.

Before invoking iterate is shown in Fig. 3.41.

```
int iterate(int value);
int sum;
int main()
{
    int v;
    v= iterate(4);
    return 0;
}
```

Name	Value
sum	0
&value	CXX0017: Err
v	-858993460

Fig. 3.41: Before invoking iterate.

The first time invoking iterate(4), value = 4, the address of value is 0x12ff2c, as shown in Fig. 3.42.

```
int iterate(int value)
{
    if(value == 1) return 1;
    return sum=value + iterate(value -1);
}
```

Name	Value
sum	0
&value	0x0012ff2c
	4

Fig. 3.42: Value = 4, the address of value is 0x12ff2c.

Invoke iterate(4–1), value = 3, the address of value is 0x12fed4. Note that now the address with value = 3 and the address with value = 4 are different, as shown in Fig. 3.43.

```
int iterate(int value)
{
    if(value == 1) return 1;
    return sum=value + iterate(value -1);
}
```

Name	Value
sum	0
&value	0x0012fed4
	3

Fig. 3.43: Value = 3, the address of value is 0x12fed4.

Invoke iterate(3–1), value = 2, the address of value is 0x12fe7c, as shown in Fig. 3.44.

```
int iterate(int value)
{
    if(value == 1) return 1;
    return sum=value + iterate(value -1);
}
```

Name	Value
sum	0
&value	0x0012fe7c
	2

Fig. 3.44: Value = 2, the address of value is 0x12fe7c.

Invoke iterate(2–1), value = 1, the address of value is 0x12fe24, as shown in Fig. 3.45.

```
int iterate(int value)
{
    if(value == 1) return 1;
    return sum=value + iterate(value -1);
}
```

Name	Value
sum	0
&value	0x0012fe24
	1

Fig. 3.45: Value = 1, the address of value is 0x12fe24.

value = 1, condition of Call Stack, as shown in Fig. 3.46.

```
iterate(int 1) line 13
iterate(int 2) line 15 + 12 bytes
iterate(int 3) line 15 + 12 bytes
iterate(int 4) line 15 + 12 bytes
main() line 8 + 7 bytes
mainCRTStartup() line 206 + 25 bytes
KERNEL32! 7c81776f()
```

Name	Value
sum	0
&value	0x0012fe24
	1

Fig. 3.46: Value = 1, condition of Call Stack.

Before executing sum = value + iterate(2–1), value = 2, iterate(1) = 1, as shown in Fig. 3.47.

```
int iterate(int value)
{
    if(value == 1) return 1;
    return sum=value + iterate(value -1);
}
```

Name	Value
sum	0
&value	0x0012fe7c
	2

Fig. 3.47: Value = 2, before executing return.

After executing sum = value + iterate(2–1), sum = 3, as shown in Fig. 3.48.

```
int iterate(int value)
{
    if(value == 1) return 1;
    return sum=value + iterate(value -1);
}
```

Name	Value
sum	3
⊟ &value	0x0012fe7c
	2

Fig. 3.48: Value = 2, after executing return, iterate(2) = 3.

After executing sum = value + iterate(2 – 1), before iterate(2) returns, condition of the Call Stack, as shown in Fig. 3.49.

```
⇨ iterate(int 2) line 16
  iterate(int 3) line 15 + 12 bytes
  iterate(int 4) line 15 + 12 bytes
  main() line 8 + 7 bytes
  mainCRTStartup() line 206 + 25 bytes
  KERNEL32! 7c81776f()
```

Name	Value
sum	3
⊟ &value	0x0012fe7c
	2

Fig. 3.49: Value = 2, condition of Call Stack.

Before executing sum = value + iterate(3 – 1), value = 3, iterate(2) = 3, as shown in Fig. 3.50.

```
int iterate(int value)
{
    if(value == 1) return 1;
⇨   return sum=value + iterate(value -1);
}
```

Name	Value
sum	3
⊟ &value	0x0012fed4
	3

Fig. 3.50: Value = 3, before executing return.

After executing sum = value + iterate(3 – 1), sum = 6, as shown in Fig. 3.51.

```
int iterate(int value)
{
    if(value == 1) return 1;
    return sum=value + iterate(value -1);
}
```

Name	Value
sum	6
⊟ &value	0x0012fed4
	3

Fig. 3.51: Value = 3, after executing return, iterate(3) = 6.

After executing sum = value + iterate(3 – 1), before iterate(3) returns, condition of the Call Stack, as shown in Fig. 3.52.

```
⇨ iterate(int 3) line 16
  iterate(int 4) line 15 + 12 bytes
  main() line 8 + 7 bytes
  mainCRTStartup() line 206 + 25 bytes
  KERNEL32! 7c81776f()
```

Name	Value
sum	6
⊟ &value	0x0012fed4
	3

Fig. 3.52: Value = 3, condition of the Call Stack.

Before executing sum = value + iterate(4 − 1), value = 4, iterate(3) = 6, as shown in Fig. 3.53.

```
  int iterate(int value)
  {
      if(value == 1) return 1;
⇨     return sum=value + iterate(value -1);
  }
```

Name	Value
sum	6
⊟ &value	0x0012ff2c
	4

Fig. 3.53: Value = 4, before executing return.

After executing sum = value + iterate(4–1), sum = 10, as shown in Fig. 3.54.

```
  int iterate(int value)
  {
      if(value == 1) return 1;
      return sum=value + iterate(value -1);
⇨ }
```

Name	Value
sum	10
⊟ &value	0x0012ff2c
	4

Fig. 3.54: Value = 4, after executing return, iterate(4) = 10.

After executing sum = value + iterate(3–1), before iterate(4) returns, the condition of the Call Stack, as shown in Fig. 3.55.

```
⇨ iterate(int 4) line 16
  main() line 8 + 7 bytes
  mainCRTStartup() line 206 + 25 bytes
  KERNEL32! 7c81776f()
```

Name	Value
sum	10
⊟ &value	0x0012ff2c
	4

Fig. 3.55: Value = 1, condition of the Call Stack.

The situation of returning to main, as shown in Fig. 3.56.

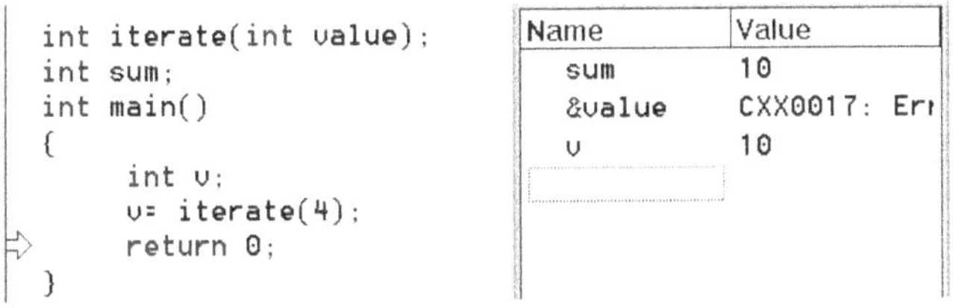

```
int iterate(int value);
int sum;
int main()
{
    int v;
    v= iterate(4);
    return 0;
}
```

Name	Value
sum	10
&value	CXX0017: Err
v	10

Fig. 3.56: The invocation of iterate(4) is finished.

3.1.6.3 Evaluating expressions

When compiling programs, if we want to translate an expression into machine language with correct values, we need to first correctly understand the expressions. Its implementation is a classic example of stack. Interested readers can refer to related materials for in-depth understanding.

Knowledge ABC The representation of arithmetic expressions

Expression: Consists of operands, operators and delimiters.

Operands: can be numbers, constants or variables.

Operators: arithmetic operators (+, −, *, /).

Delimiters: left/right parentheses and termination sign for the expression.

There are three different representational methods for expressions, which are named according to the different positions of the operators: prefix expressions, infix expressions, postfix expressions.

$$\text{Let: Exp} = \underline{S1} \text{ OP } \underline{S2}$$

where Exp means expression, $\underline{S1}$, $\underline{S2}$ are operands, OP is the operator, then

OP $\underline{S1}$ $\underline{S2}$ is prefix representation

$\underline{S1}$ OP $\underline{S2}$ is infix representation

$\underline{S1}$ $\underline{S2}$ OP is postfix representation

For example: Exp = a*b + (c−d/e)*f

Then the three corresponding representations will be respectively:

Prefix expression: +*ab*−c/def

Infix expression: a*b+(c−d/e)*f

Postfix expression: ab*cde/−f*+

The features of various expressions: the relative positions between operands do not change. The relative orders of the operators are different.

The operation rules for prefix expressions are: two continuous operands and the operator immediately before them constitute a minimum expression. The operation rules for postfix expressions are: each operator and the two operands immediately before it constitute a minimum expression.

In computers, using prefix/postfix expressions can simplify the calculation process.

3.1.7 Recursion – a "first-in–last-out" process

The recursion process is a process that sets out first and goes back later. The solution process has a feature of "first-in–last-out." In the computer, it is very convenient to use stack to implement the execution of recursive functions. Since many contents in the ensuing chapters are based on the idea of recursion, in this section, we carry out a comprehensive discussion on recursion.

3.1.7.1 The concept of recursion and its key elements

When you stand between two facing mirrors, what will you see in the mirrors? Yes, the mirrors will show multiple copies of the same image, decreasing in size.

"Mirror within mirror" is a phenomenon in our daily lives. There are similar scenarios in mathematics and programming. Let's first observe two known examples.

Example 1: Factorial

Factorial calculation is a well-known mathematical calculation. We can observe in its definition that one factorial calculation includes an invocation to the factorial calculation itself, just on a decreased scale of $n-1$:

$$n! = \begin{cases} 1 & n = 0 \\ n*(n-1)! & n > 0 \end{cases}$$

Example 2: Definition of linked list nodes

The structure definition of a node of the singly linked list is as follows. Within the struct definition, there is once again a struct reference in the form of `struct node`:

```
typedef struct node
{
  datatype data;
  struct node *next;
} linklist;
```

When there are scenarios in the problem where the computational process directly/indirectly invokes itself, normally such a process is called a recursive process. If the explanation of an object partially contains itself, or it uses itself to define itself, we call this object a recursive object.

Recursive process is a process with back and forth. During the process of the problem becoming smaller and getting farther away, there will be an endpoint, where it cannot become smaller or go farther. From that point, it will go all the way back to the original point.

Term Explanation Recursion

i

In mathematics and computer science, it refers to a method by which the function uses itself in its definition.

The basic idea of recursion is to convert a large-scale problem into small-scale similar subproblems to be solved. In function implementation, since the method to solve the large-scale problem and the method to solve the small-scale problem are usually the same method, the situation where the function calls itself occurs. Also, for the problem-solving function to obtain any result, it must have an obvious termination condition; otherwise, it will carry on the recursion infinitely. Therefore, there must be two elements to recursive processes:
- Boundary condition/base case: a definition of the function that does not use recursion, under the simplest case of the problem.
- Recursion continuation condition: the condition upon which the problem is converted to its base case.

Example 3.1: Obtain the value of the nth item of the Fibonacci sequence
Solution: according to the definition of the Fibonacci sequence, the base cases of recursion are the two special cases where $n = 0$ and $n = 1$. The program implementation is as follows:

```
/*==============================================================================
Functionality of the function: Obtain the value of the nth item of the Fibonacci sequence
Function Output:  The value of the nth item of the Fibonacci sequence
Function input:  Integer n
============================================================================*/
int Fib(n)
{
   int fibn;
   if (n<=1) fibn=n;
   else fibn=Fib(n-1)+Fib(n-2);
   return fibn;
}
```

The mathematical model of recursion is actually mathematical induction method. Induction method applies to one scenario, where one difficult problem can be divided into its subproblems, and those subproblems can be further divided into smaller subproblems to be solved. Those problems are actually the same model, that is, there exists the same logical induction processing item. When the repeated induction reaches the end, the ending processing method must give out the final solution. Otherwise, mathematical induction will become infinite induction, and will never end.

3.1.7.2 Analysis of features of recursion

To use recursive algorithms, we only need to obtain the mathematical expression of recursion to conveniently write out the program. The program is highly readable and easy to comprehend. In the computer, recursion is normally implemented using stack mechanism. Whenever recursion deepens by one level, a stack data area must be assigned in the memory. In this way, when the level of recursion gets relatively deep, a huge amount of memory space will be occupied, and might even result in memory breakdown (stack overflow). Therefore, in occasions that put restrictions on running memory, other nonrecursive methods are needed to replace the recursive algorithm. We normally call it elimination of recursion. Elimination methods are mainly those listed below.

1. Eliminate recursion with stack structure
Use a stack to manually simulate the operational process of system stacks. This method is widely applicable. However, it essentially is still recursive. It is just that it lets tasks originally performed by the computer be performed by men. Therefore, the optimization effect on the algorithm is not significant.

2. Eliminate recursion with iterative method
Iterative algorithm is a basic method which a computer uses to solve problems. It takes advantage of the fact that the computer computes very fast and is suited to repetitive operations. It lets the computer repetitively execute a set of instructions (or certain steps); whenever this set of instructions (or these steps) are executed, a new value is inferred/calculated from the original value of the variable.

Using iterative algorithm to solve problems, the following three aspects of work must be taken care of:
(1) Ascertain the iteration variable. In questions that can be solved with iterative algorithms, there is at least one variable that has its new value directly or indirectly calculated from its old value. This variable is the iteration variable.
(2) Establish iteration equations. The so-called iteration equations refer to the equations (or relations), which can be used to calculate the next value of the variable from its previous value. The construction of iteration equations is the key to solving iterative problems. Normally, it can be done using recurrence relation or reverse recurrence relation.
(3) Control the iteration process. When to end the iteration process? This is a question that must be considered when writing iterative programs. The control of the iterative process can usually be divided into two cases: The first is that the number of iterations needed is a fixed value, which can be calculated. The other is that the number of iterations needed cannot be ascertained. For the former case, we can construct a fixed number of iterations to realize the control on the iterative process. For the latter case, we need to further analyze the condition by which to end the iterative process.

Example 3.2: To calculate the values of the Fibonacci sequence, the implementation with iterative algorithm is as follows:

```
/*==========================================================================
Functionality of the function: Iteratively calculate the Fibonacci sequence
Function output: The value of the nth item of the Fibonacci sequence
Function input: Integer n
==========================================================================*/
long Fib(long n)
{   long F1=0, F2=1, F3;
    if (n<=1) return n;
    for (int i=0;  i<=n;  i++)
    { F3 =F1+ F2;
      F1=F2;
      F2=F3;
    }
    return F3;
}
```

Recursive and iterative methods are both based on one control structure. Iteration uses looping structure; recursion uses branching structure. Iteration and recursion both involve looping. Iteration explicitly uses a looping structure; recursion realizes the looping via repetitive function invocation. Iteration and recursion both involve an ending test. Iteration ends when the looping condition is false; recursion ends when it encounters the base case.

3. Tail recursion elimination method

Tail recursion is a special form of recursion, which only has one statement that invokes recursion. This statement is also at the end of the function, that is, the last action of the function is to call itself. Optimization of tail recursion is usually performed by not adding a new stack frame but instead uses a JUMP/GOTO instruction, and is already implemented in compilers of various programming languages, for example, C programming language. Therefore, programming in this way can lead to considerable performance gain.

Example 3.3: In algorithms using linked lists, find the last node of the linked list and print it.
Nonrecursive implementation
// Print the last node of the linked list

```
void Print ( linklist *f )
{ while ( f ->next != NULL ) f = f->next;
  printf(" f ->data", %c);
}
```

Recursive implementation:

```
// Use recursion to implement the printing of the last node in the linked list
void Print( linklist *f )
{ if ( f ->next == NULL ) printf(" f ->data", %c);
  else Print( f ->next );
}
```

Example 3.4: Use tail recursion to calculate the Fibonacci sequence. The program implementation is as follows:

```
/*=============================================================================
Functionality of the function: Calculate the Fibonacci sequence using tail recursion
Function input: The values of the adjacent two items a and b, the index of the item to
calculate n
Function output: The value of the nth item in the Fibonacci sequence
=============================================================================*/
int fib_rw(int a, int b, int n)
{
   if(n<=1) return b;
   return fib_rw(b, a+b, n-1); // In the last statement of the program, perform pure
invocation of the function itself - tail recursion
}
```

Tail recursion optimization is mainly optimization of stack memory space. This optimization is from $O(n)$ to $O(1)$. In terms of time complexity, the improvement is actually
caused by the reduction of memory allocation work induced by space optimization,
and there would not be qualitative improvements of time complexity.

3.1.7.3 Summary of recursion
Recursion is a nice way to design programs.
   A recursive process must have the following two features:
- Boundary condition/base case: a definition of the function that does not use
  recursion, under the simplest case of the problem.
- Recursion continuation condition: the condition upon which the problem is
  converted to its base case.

When recursive methods can more naturally reflect the problem and make the program easier to understand and test, recursive methods usually replace iterative
methods. A reason to choose recursion for problem solving is that iterative solutions might not look so straightforward.

In cases where program performance is required, recursion should be avoided. Recursion invocation will cost a lot of time, has relatively high space complexity and can easily cause stack overflow.

3.2 Queue – linear list managed in a "FIFO" manner

Queue indicates a sequence that queues up to wait. When the requests for service exceed the maximum service capacity, queue will be needed. The queue in daily lives has the same meaning as the queue in data structures. The illustration of queue is shown in Fig. 3.57.

Fig. 3.57: Illustration of queue.

3.2.1 Introduction to the queue processing model

The queue data structure is normally used for data caching. It can be used to balance two components with different processing speeds so that the quicker component does not need to wait for the slower component. Let's see some practical examples using queue processing model.

3.2.1.1 Introductory example to queue 1 – asynchronous processing of data in computer

3.2.1.1.1 Buffered queues in e-commerce systems

In the order input system of e-commerce websites, the peak order rate can be two to three times of the average order rate. Since order input system must be capable of processing peak load, the processing capability is idle in a lot of time intervals. If we buffer the "send order" task with queue (i.e., store the "send order" instructions in order in a storage area called "buffer zone," but do not process them real time), then the system does not need to have the capability to process peak load. If at peak time interval, we queue up the asynchronous tasks and only execute them later at idle time (asynchronous is a concept relative to synchronous; asynchronous tasks sometimes do not need to be processed and returned immediately), the system will be more efficiently utilized and no longer have a huge contrast between task load at peak time and idle time. See Fig. 3.58.

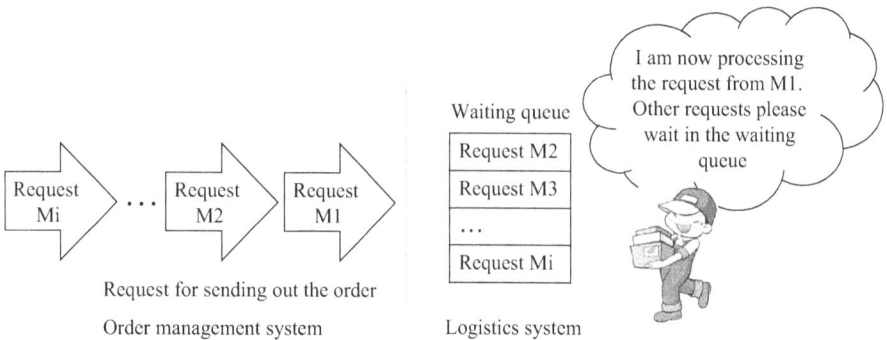

Fig. 3.58: Buffer queue in e-commerce systems.

Here, asynchronous processing can be understood as "accept first, but only process gradually when the system has the resources." The advantage of asynchronous processing is that the work can be done when resources (e.g., CPU time and memory space) are available. In most large-scale systems, many processing tasks can be dealt with asynchronously.

3.2.1.1.2 Mail queues in mail servers
Generally speaking, mail servers will send mails submitted by clients immediately. However, then there is some downtime, for example, connection down or target unreachable, the mail server will put this mail into mail queue, wait for a while and then try sending again.

From the perspective of data structures, queue is a linear list of information. Its visit order is FIFO. That is to say, the first item put into the queue will be the first item to be read out of the queue, the second item put into the queue will be the second item read out of the queue and so on. This is the only save/access operation permitted by queue. Any other random access is not permitted. This data structure ensures that the requests for data resources will be carried out in strict FIFO order. Therefore, it can be used to coordinate events and act as input/output buffering.

3.2.1.2 Introductory example to queue 2 – solution to Pascal's triangle using queue

Pascal's triangle looks as follows:

```
            1
          1   1
        1   2   1
      1   3   3   1
    1   4   6   4   1
```

Pascal's triangle consists of the coefficients of the various items expanded from the nth (n = 1,2,3,...) square of the binary expression ($a + b$). Its feature is that both its left side and right side are always 1. Starting from the second row, each number in the middle will be the sum of the two adjacent numbers in the previous row. The question is to output several rows of Pascal's triangle via programming.

This question is commonly used for practices on program design. There are various solutions. Here we will use the "FIFO" characteristic of the queue to solve this problem.

Algorithm description

As shown in Fig. 3.59, for the convenience of calculation, we insert 0 between each row as the separation indicator. The arrays of coefficients are stored in the array queue[].

queue[]	0	1	1	0	1	2	1	0	1	3	3	1	0	...

Fig. 3.59: The situation where Pascal's triangle is stored in arrays.

In Fig. 3.60, suppose front points to the position of the latter of the two numbers to be used in the summing process (shown by f in the figure), rear points to the position where the sum will be placed (shown by r in the figure).

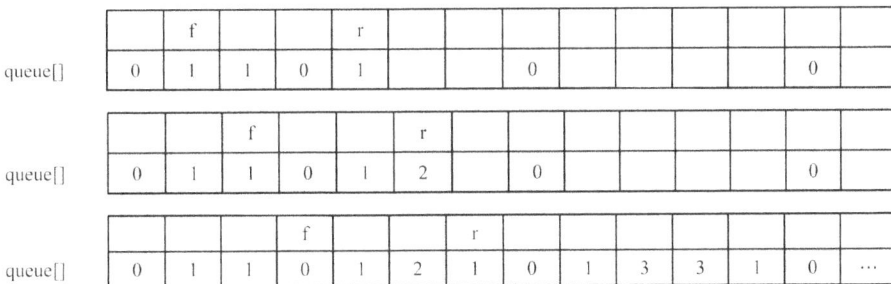

	f			r							
queue[]	0	1	1	0	1			0				0

		f			r						
queue[]	0	1	1	0	1	2		0				0

			f			r					
queue[]	0	1	1	0	1	2	1	0	1	3	3	1	0	...

Fig. 3.60: Calculation rule 1 of the new data item in Pascal's triangle.

Case handling

$$\text{queue[rear]= queue[front-1]+ queue[front]}$$
$$\text{if (queue[front]==0) then queue[++rear]=0}$$

Normally speaking, whenever we calculate a new coefficient, we move the array pointer front by one position; whenever we fill in a new coefficient, we move the rear pointer by one position. This process is the same as the processing of queue, that is, information is processed at the head of the array, then the node is moved out of the queue, and the newly inserted data enters via the end of the queue. The insertion of the separator 0 is a special case. See Fig. 3.61. In this case, front does not move, rear is moved back by one position. As the data filled in increases, the relative distance between front and rear will gradually increase, that is, enqueuing speed is larger than the dequeuing speed.

			f				r						
queue[]	0	1	1	0	1	2	1	0	1	3	3	1	0	...

Fig. 3.61: Calculation rule 2 of the new data item in Pascal's triangle.

Program implementation

```c
#include <stdio.h>
int main(void)
{
    int n=33;
    int queue[49]={0,1,1,0};  // 0 is the row separator
    int front=1,rear=4;
    // front: The position of the current element;
    // rear:  The position of the element about to be inserted into the queue

    for (int i=0; i<n; i++)
    {
        // Insert the sum of the two elements at the end of the queue
        queue[rear]=queue[front-1]+queue[front];
        printf ("%d ", queue[rear]);
        rear++;
        if (queue[front]==0)      //Encountered the separator
        {
            queue[rear]=0;        //Add the separator
            rear++;
```

```
        printf ("\n");          //Output the newline character
    }
    front++;                    //front pointer is moved by one position
  }
  return 0;
}
```

Results

```
                        1 2 1
                        1 3 3 1
                        1 4 6 4 1
                        1 5 10 10 5 1
                        1 6 15 20 15 6 1
                        1 7 21 35 35 21 7 1
```

In this example, front points to the data about to be processed. The result after processing is inserted into the tail of the array pointed to by rear, as the newly inserted data. The whole data processing model is in the form of a queue.

3.2.2 The logical structure of queue

From the two introductory examples of queue, we can summarize the logical structure of queue.

The queue data structure is to list the nodes one by one according to a certain order. Its processing is the same as the processing of the queue in our daily lives. The rules are:

Ordering: All nodes are ordered into one queue. The ones later entered are ordered near the end of the queue.

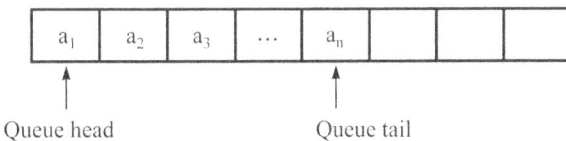

Fig. 3.62: Illustration of queue.

Processing: Process the event at the front of the queue. If there is still element in the queue, continue the processing, until the queue becomes empty or interruption event happens.

Definition of Queue
Queue is a linear list that only allows insertion operation at one end and deletion operation at the other end. In Fig. 3.62, the end where deletion happens is called "queue head," and the end where insertion happens is called "queue tail."

Queue differs from stack in that it is a FIFO linear list. Similar to stack, queue is also an important linear structure. According to the definition of queue, the basic operations on the queue are the following:

1. Empty queue: empty an existing queue.
2. Emptiness check: if the queue is empty, then return 1, otherwise return 0.
3. Dequeue operation: when the queue is not empty, return the value of the head element of the queue and modify the head pointer of the queue.
4. Enqueue operation: insert the node into the queue tail, and modify the tail pointer.
5. Head operation: when the queue is not empty, return the value of the head value, but does not delete the head element.

3.2.3 The sequential storage structure of queue

The implementation of a queue also needs sequential list or linked list as basis. This section discusses the sequential structure of queue.

3.2.3.1 Sequential queue
The sequential storage structure of queue is called sequential queue. Sequential queue is actually sequential list with restricted operations. Same as sequential list, sequential queue also must use one vector space to store the elements in the current queue.

1. Structural design of sequential queue

Question 1: To keep track of the change in state of a queue, how many parameters do we need at least? See Fig. 3.63.

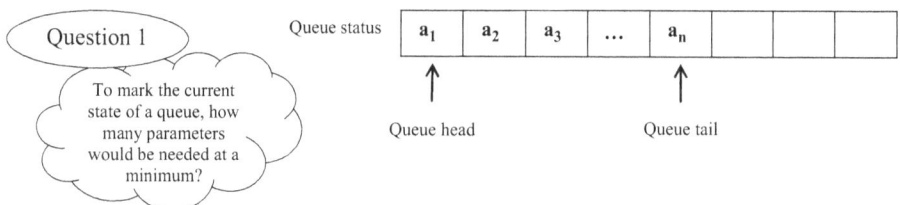

Fig. 3.63: Structural design of queue question 1.

Discussion: As we can see from Fig. 3.63, both the head and tail elements will change. Pop and push operations are relatively independent of each other. Therefore, it is reasonable to set two pointers, head and tail, to keep track of the change of state of the queue.

Question 2: see Fig. 3.64.

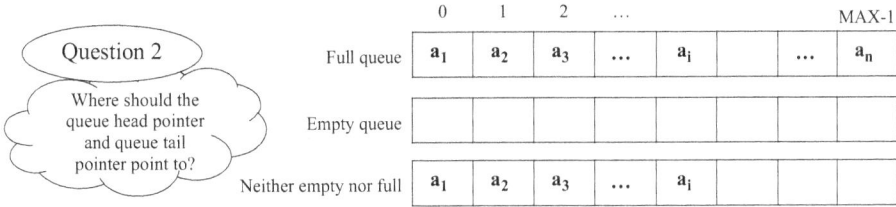

Fig. 3.64: Structural design of queue question 2.

Discussion: If we look at Fig. 3.62, the head pointer points to the first element in the queue a_1, and the tail pointer points to the last element of the queue a_n. This situation should be permissible. But whether such a rule is feasible, the conclusion can only be reached after testing. How to perform the test? We need to consider all possible scenarios of the queue. The head pointer and the tail pointer must both be reasonably and clearly labeled. Only then, we can say that such a rule is feasible. In essence, this is the same kind of idea used when performing tests on programs.

First, look at the situation when the element is popped from the queue in Fig. 3.64. The head pointer is set to front, tail pointer is set to rear. Elements a_1, a_2 are popped one after another. Front moves by one position, respectively. Therefore, we encounter question 3.

Question 3: Do we need to delete an already popped element? See Fig. 3.65.

Discussion: Because the position of the head element is indicated by front, we do not need to actually delete the values of a_1 and a_2. Therefore, we reach our first conclusion.

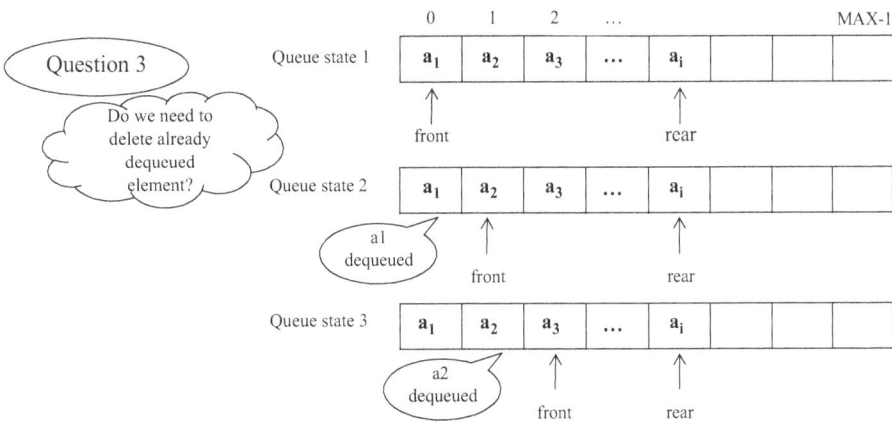

Fig. 3.65: Scenario of element popped from the queue.

Conclusion 1 Already popped elements in sequential queue do not need to be deleted.
In the push scenario shown in Fig. 3.66, rear pointer points to the last position of the sequential list, with element value a_m. At this time, if there is element a_{m+1} being inserted, then we encounter the fourth problem: pseudo-overflow.

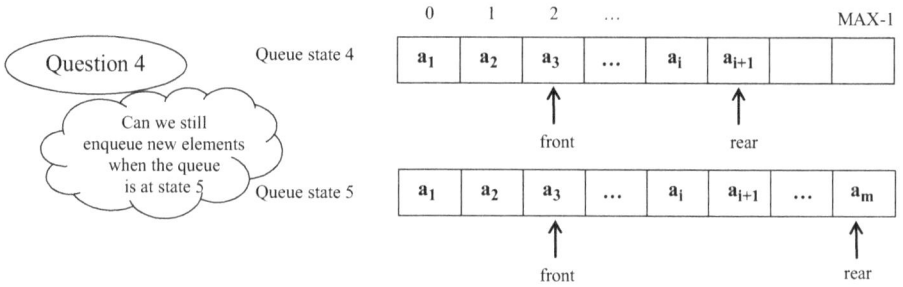

Fig. 3.66: Scenario 1 of element inserted into the list.

Terminology Explanation
Pseudo-overflow indicates the situation where, since we can only insert at one end of the queue and delete at the other end, there will be a situation different to that of stack after continuous pop and push operations: the queue moves constantly toward the tail in of the array; at the front of the queue head, an unusable spare storage area is produced. Eventually, when the rear pointer points to the last position (i.e., rear = MAX−1) and new elements cannot be added, there will however be a storage area in the front of the memory space being wasted. This phenomenon is called "pseudo-overflow."

Question 4: Can we still insert new elements in the case of pseudo-overflow?
Discussion: In the case of pseudo-overflow, if even though the queue is totally empty, we still would not be able to directly insert new elements, then such a queue can only be used once. Therefore, the usage of such a queue is apparently unreasonable. The reasonable design is to let the newly inserted element $a_m + 1$ fit in the idle area. There are two ways to put the element.
(1) Move all the existing elements in the queue toward lower memory addresses. Apparently this method would waste a lot of time.
(2) Regard the storage area of the queue as a ring-shaped area whose head and tail are connected. When we have already used address MAX−1, the next address will be "flipped" to 0, as shown in Fig. 3.67

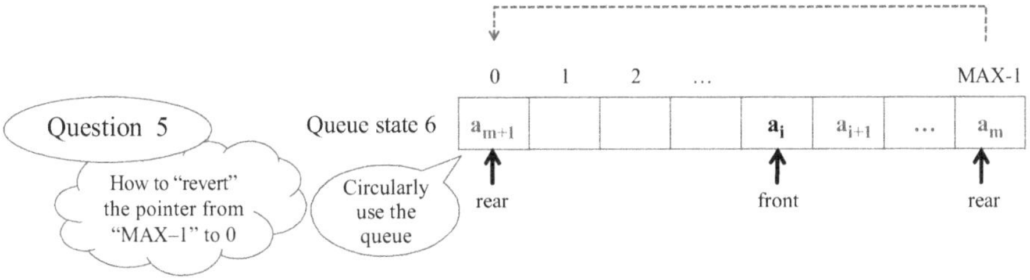

Fig. 3.67: Scenario 2 of element inserted into the list.

We use the second method to solve the reusability problem of queue storage space. Queues that use this skill to store contents structurally are called "circular queues." Apparently, since the space of circular queues can be reused, unless the vector space is truly all occupied by queue elements, there would not be any overflow. Therefore, except for some simple applications, real and practical sequential queues are all circular queues. Hence, we come to the second conclusion.

Conclusion 2 The storage space of a sequential queue should be used circularly.
From the discussion about rear pointer about, we come to the fifth question.
Question 5: how to "flip" the rear pointer?
Discussion: The "flipping" of the rear pointer can be achieved in the following two ways.
  Method 1:
  if (i+1==MAX) i=0; // i represents front or rear
  else i++;

  Method 2: Use modulo operation
  i=(i+1) % MAX

The feature of modulo operation is that whenever we perform the "addition" operation on the array index, we can automatically have the restriction on the length of the array, and we would not need to check every time whether the index is out of bounds. Therefore, we have simplified the calculation. We can arrive at the third conclusion.

Conclusion 3 Rules for calculating the front and rear pointers of a circular queue:
$$rear = (rear + 1) \bmod length\_of\_list$$
front = (front + 1) mod length_of_list
Note: mod – modulo operation. It is represented by % operator in C language.

We have discussed the circular use of the queue when the queue is neither empty nor full. Now we will discuss the special cases of when the queue is full and when the queue is empty.

Suppose the elements in the queue have changed according to the rule of "head-in–tail-out," and here comes a moment, when the situation shown in Fig. 3.68 happens.

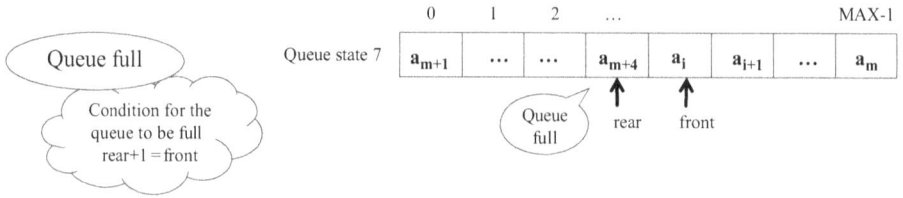

Fig. 3.68: Situation where the queue is full for question 5.

At this time, the queue is at "full" condition. We can define the relation between the current rear and front pointers as the condition of the queue being full.

Condition for the queue being full: rear + 1==front.

Next we discuss the situation when the queue is empty. We start our examination from the condition where the queue still has one element left before it becomes empty, as shown in Fig. 3.69. At this time, head and rear pointers point to the same location. After the last element is popped from the queue, the front pointer will point to one position after rear, that is, at this time the relation between the two pointers is rear + 1 == front. This is the same as the previously discussed condition for the queue being full. Therefore, only from the relation between rear and front, we would not be able to distinguish whether the queue is full or empty.

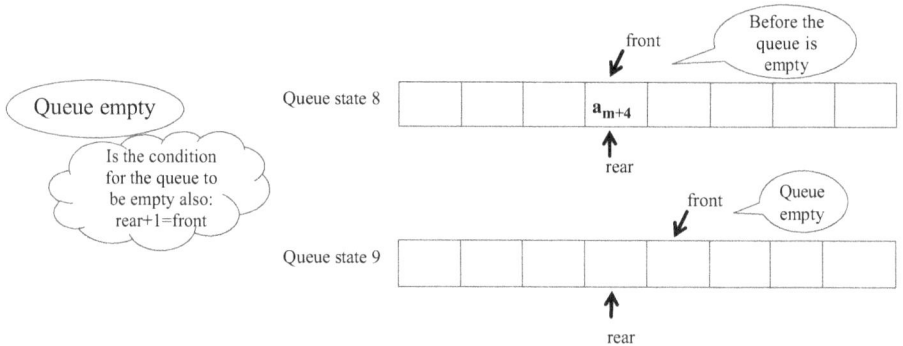

Fig. 3.69: Situation where the queue is empty for question 5.

Thus, we can see that if the head and rear pointers point, respectively, to the first and last elements of the queue, a design plan that only describes the status of the queue with two pointers is infeasible. Therefore, we reach the following question 6:

Question 6: is it okay to use the same condition to check the fullness and emptiness of the queue?

Discussion: We might try to add some additional conditions. For example, use another marker to differentiate between the emptiness and fullness of the queue; use a counter to record the total number of elements in the queue. But such an approach would increase the workload of the program. Therefore, we reach the following question:

Question 7: Can we just use two pointers front and rear to mark the status of the queue?

Discussion: If we only use two pointers as markers, then we must make the conditions for the emptiness and fullness of the queue different, in order to fulfill the above requirement.

Observe Fig. 3.70.

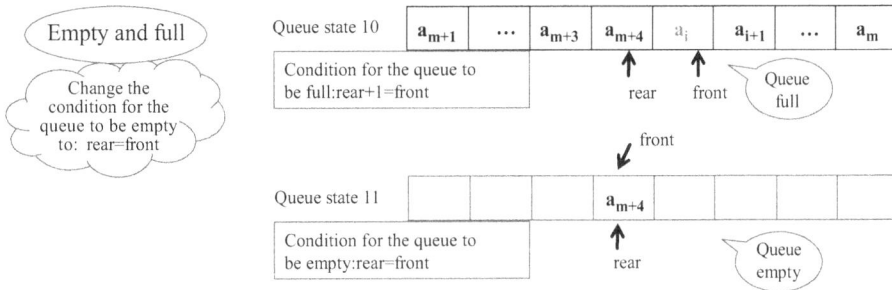

Fig. 3.70: Discussion 1 on the emptiness and fullness of the queue for question 7.

(1) Both the conditions of emptiness and fullness of the queue are rear + 1 == front.
(2) We can try to change the condition for the emptiness of the queue to rear == front.
(3) If the queue is already at "empty" status when rear==front, then the element a_{m+4} which was previously inserted should not be in the queue, that is, a_{m+4} cannot be inserted in the queue. Then, when the queue is full, a_{m+4} also does not exist, as shown in Fig. 3.71.
(4) In order to ensure the condition for queue fullness rear + 1 == front still stands, then we need to move both rear and front; one position to the front, that is, rear points to the tail element, front points to one position prior to the head element. Then, when the queue is full, although the unit pointed to by front is empty, we would not be able to use it. The aim of such a design is to ensure that the conditions for the fullness and emptiness of the queue are different.

Question 8: Let the rear pointer point to the tail element and front pointer point to the position prior to the head element. Then, can we indicate all the change statuses of the queue using only two pointers?

Discussion: We can perform a check. The situation where the queue is full is shown in Fig. 3.71, the situation before the queue is empty is shown in Fig. 3.72. The head element a_{m+3} is popped, the queue becomes empty, and front pointer moves toward the tail by one. At this time, rear = front.

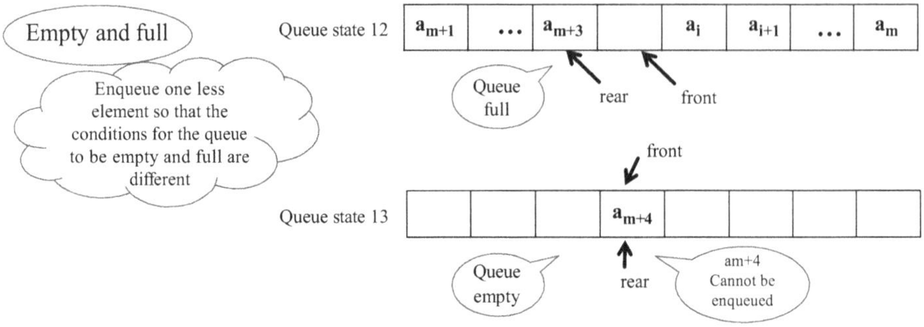

Fig. 3.71: Discussion 2 on the emptiness and fullness of the queue for question 7.

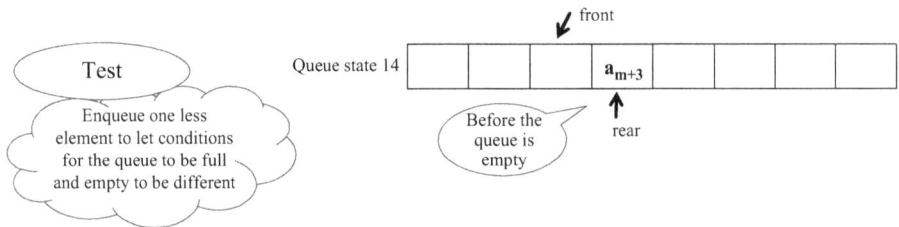

Fig. 3.72: Discussion for the situation where the queue is empty for question 8.

Up to here, we have completely answered the question 2 "What are the appropriate positions for the head/tail pointers to point to?" We can reach the fourth conclusion.

Conclusion 4
(1) The head pointer in the circular queue points to one position prior to the first element in the queue.
(2) The rear pointer points to the position of the last element in the queue.
(3) The queue needs to leave the space for one element empty, in order to ensure that the conditions for the emptiness and fullness of the queue are different.

Think and Discuss The head pointer of a circular queue points to the head element. Is it also okay for the rear pointer to point to the position next to the last element?

Discussion: This situation is similar to the positional design of the head and rear pointers in Conclusion 4; see Fig. 3.73. The conditions for the queue to be full are the same. We can then deduce that the conditions for the queue to be empty are also the same for those two situations. Therefore, this configuration method for the positions of the head and rear pointers is also feasible.

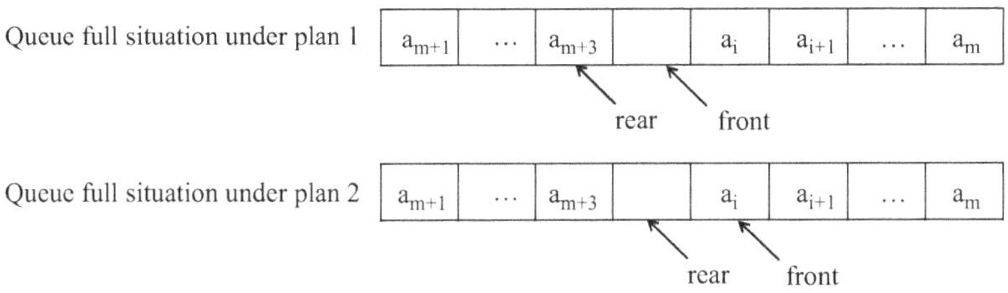

Fig. 3.73: Queue full situation in a circular queue.

2. The structure of circular list and rules of operation
Queue stored with sequential storage structure is called sequential queue. Sequential queue is actually sequential list with limited operations. Similar to sequential list, sequential queue must use one vector space to store the elements of the current queue. The space of the sequential queue is used in a circular fashion. We call such a queue circular queue. The definition of sequential queue and rules of use are shown in Fig. 3.74.

Data structure design

```
#define QUEUE_SIZE 128
typedef struct
{ datatype data[QUEUE_SIZE];
  int front, rear;
} SeqQueue;
```

Whenever there isn't any special declaration in the circular queue, operations all follow these rules

Rules for using circular queue

Initialization of the queue:	front = rear = QUEUE_SIZE-1;
Add 1 to the head pointer:	front = (front+1) %QUEUE_SIZE;
Add one to the tail pointer:	rear = (rear+1) % QUEUE_SIZE;
Condition for the queue to be full:	(rear+1) % QUEUE_SIZE = front;
Condition for the queue to be empty:	front = rear;

Fig. 3.74: The structure and rules of operation of circular queue.

Except for the initial situation, the queue becomes empty/full under the following two situations: if front changes faster than rear, empty queue will be produced; if rear changes faster than front, then full queue is produced.

Example 3.5: The solution using circular queue for Pascal's triangle.
In the introductory example 2 – Pascal's triangle, we did not circularly use the queue in our solution. If the relation between the length of queue[] and the number of iterations is not set properly, then there is a risk for the array queue to have index-out-of-bounds violation. We use tracing to observe such out-of-bounds scenario in the following.

In Fig. 3.75, the front points to the position of the latter number among the two numbers to be calculated (represented in the figure as f) and the rear points to the position where the sum is going to be placed (represented in the figure as r).

								f					r
queue[]	0	1	1	0	1	2	1	0	1	3	3	1	0

Fig. 3.75: Introductory example to queue 2 – queue solution to Pascal's triangle.

Let the length of the queue be 42, then queue is defined as

```
int queue[42]={0,1,1,0};
```

One improvement is to use circular queue to process data. The pushing and popping of elements are processed using the rules of circular queue. The program implementation is as follows:

(1) Let the order of the polynomial be 10, the number of coefficients be n = 63.

```
#include <stdio.h>
#define M 32
int main(void)
{
    int n=63;
    int queue[M]={0,1,1,0};//0 is the row separation indicator
    int front=1,rear=4;
    //front: Position of the current element;
    // rear:  Position of the element to be pushed

    for (int i=0; i<n; i++)
    {
        //Insert the sum of two elements at the tail of the queue
        queue[rear]=queue[(front-1+M)%M]+queue[front];
        printf ("%d ", queue[rear]);
        //rear++;
        rear=(rear+1)% M;
        if (queue[front]==0) //Row separation indicator is encountered
        {
            queue[rear]=0;//Add row separation indicator
            //rear++;
            rear=(rear+1)% M;
```

```
    printf ("\n");//Output new line character
  }
  //front++;//Move the front pointer by one position
  front=(front+1)%M;
}
return 0;
}
```

Result:

1 2 1
1 3 3 1
1 4 6 4 1
1 5 10 10 5 1
1 6 15 20 15 6 1
1 7 21 35 35 21 7 1
1 8 28 56 70 56 28 8 1
1 9 36 84 126 126 84 36 9 1
1 10 45 120 210 252 210 120 45 10 1

(2) Let the length of the circular list be $M = 8$, the coefficients of the polynomial $n = 63$.

The test result of the above program is as follows:

1 2 1
1 3 3 1
1 4 6 4 1
1 5 10 10 5 1
1 6 15 20 15 6 1
1 7 22 42 57 63 64 64 65 72 94 136 193 256 320 384 449 521 615 751 944 1200 1520
1904 2353 2874 3489 4240 5184 6384 7904 9808 12161 15035 18524 22764 27948
3433 2

The result is abnormal starting from row 6. Why? Through tracing, we list part of the results obtained above in the list. See Fig. 3.76. When $i = 27$, the result is erroneous. Therefore, when $i = 26$, we pay attention to the values of front and rear in the queue array.

i	0	1	2	3	4	5	6	7	8	9	10	11	12	13	14	15	16	17	18	19	20	21	22	23	24	25	26	27	28
dequeuing element	1	2	1	1	3	3	1	1	4	6	4	1	1	5	10	10	5	1	1	6	15	20	15	6	1	1	7	22	42

Fig. 3.76: List for testing and analysis on the circular queue solution for Pascal's triangle.

The reason is that when front = rear, the status of the array is "full." If we push an element again, the tail element will overwrite the original head element. One improvement can be to add a check for the fullness of the queue at the first line inside of the for loop. We do not list the detailed program again here.

Conclusion During the use of a circular queue, since the length of the queue is limited, when the speed of pushing is larger than the speed of popping, the new tail element will overwrite the original head element, that is, the queue "overflows."

3.2.4 Basic operations on sequential queue

3.2.4.1 Basic operation on sequential queue – set queue as empty
1. Design of test cases and function framework: see Tables 3.20 and 3.21.

Table 3.20: Basic operation on sequential queue – design of test cases for setting queue as empty.

Test case	Status	Expected result
Normal case	Queue empty or nonempty	The head and rear pointers are set as equal

Table 3.21: Basic operation on sequential queue – design of function framework for setting queue as empty.

Function description	Input	Output
Set queue as empty: initialize_SqQueue	Initial address of the queue: SeqQueue*	None
Function name	Parameters	Function type

2. Pseudocode description of the algorithm
Set head and rear pointers according to the condition of empty queue:

```
front=rear=QUEUE_SIZE - 1
```

3. Program implementation

```
/*================================================================
Functionality of the function: Set the queue as empty in sequential queue
Function input: Initial address of the queue
Function output: None
================================================================*/
```

```
void initialize_SqQueue(SeqQueue *sq)
{
   sq->front = QUEUE_SIZE-1;
   sq->rear = QUEUE_SIZE-1;
}
```

3.2.4.2 Basic operation on sequential queue – check emptiness of queue
1.   Design of test cases and function framework: see Tables 3.22 and 3.23.

Table 3.22: Basic operation on sequential queue – design of test cases for emptiness check of queue.

Test case	Status/input	Expected result
Normal case	Empty queue	Output emptiness indicator
	Nonempty queue	Output nonemptiness indicator

Table 3.23: Basic operation on sequential queue – design of function structure for emptiness check of queue.

Functionality description	Input	Output
Check emptiness of queue: Empty_SqQueue	Starting address of queue: SeqQueue*	Queue status indicator int (Empty: 1; non-empty: 0)
Function name	Parameters	Function type

2.   Pseudocode description of the algorithm
Check whether the queue is empty according to the emptiness condition rear = front: if it is empty, return 1; if it is nonempty, return 0.

3.   Program implementation

```
/*====================================================================
Functionality of the function: Check emptiness of queue on sequential queue
Function input: Starting address of the queue
Function output: 1 - Empty; 0 - Non-empty
=================================================================*/
int Empty_SqQueue(SeqQueue *sq)
{ if ( sq->rear == sq->front ) return TRUE;
```

```
  else return FALSE;
}
```

4. Analysis on the efficiency of the algorithm: time complexity $O(1)$.

3.2.4.3 Basic operation on sequential queue – get the head element
1. Design of test cases and function framework: see Tables 3.24 and 3.25.

Table 3.24: Basic operation on sequential queue – design of test cases for getting the head element of queue.

Test case	Status	Expected result
Normal case	Nonempty queue	Return the position of the head element
Abnormal case	Empty queue	Return emptiness indicator

Table 3.25: Basic operation on sequential queue – design of function structure for getting the head element of queue.

Functionality description	Input	Output
Get head element: get_SqQueue	Starting address of queue: SeqQueue *	Position of head element int (Empty queue: –1; non-empty queue: Position of the head element)
Function name	Parameters	Function type

2. Pseudocode description of the algorithm
If the queue is not empty, return the index of the position of the head element; otherwise, return –1.

3. Program implementation

```
/*=============================================================
Functionality of the function: Get the head element from a sequential queue
Function input: Starting address of the queue
Function output: -1 - Emptiness indicator; other values - position of the head
element
=============================================================*/
int get_SqQueue(SeqQueue *sq )
```

```
{
    if ( ! Empty_SqQueue(sq) )//Queue is not empty
      return (sq->front+1) % QUEUE_SIZE;
    return -1;//Queue is empty
}
```

4. Efficiency of the algorithm: time complexity $O(1)$.

3.2.4.4 Basic operation on sequential queue – insert element
1. Design of test cases and function framework: see Tables 3.26 and 3.27.

Table 3.26: Basic operation on sequential queue – design of test cases for inserting element.

Test case	Status	Expected result
Normal	Nonfull queue	Return successful insertion indicator
Abnormal	Full queue	Return failed insertion indicator

Table 3.27: Basic operation on sequential queue – design of function structure for inserting element.

Functionality description	Input	Output
Insert element Insert_SqQueue	Starting address of queue: SeqQueue * Value of the element to be inserted: datatype	Success indicator of insertion: int (Full: 0 Non-Full: 1)
Function name	Parameters	Function type

2. Pseudocode description of the algorithm
If the queue is full, return FALSE; otherwise, move the tail pointer rear backward by one position, and insert the value of the element at the position pointed to by the rear.

3. Program implementation

```
/*================================================================
Functionality of the function: Insertion of element on sequential queue
Function input: Starting address of the queue, value of the element to be
inserted
Function output: 0 - Full queue, unsuccessful operation;
                 1 - Non-full queue, successful operation
================================================================*/
```

```
int Insert_SqQueue(SeqQueue*sq, datatype x)
{
    if (sq->front == (sq->rear+1)%QUEUE_SIZE )  //Check fullness of queue
      return FALSE;
    else
    {
      sq->rear = (sq->rear+1) % QUEUE_SIZE;
      //Move the rear pointer backwards by one position
      sq->data[sq->rear] = x; //Insert element x
      return TRUE;
    }
}
```

4. Algorithm complexity: time complexity $O(1)$.

3.2.4.5 Basic operation on sequential queue – delete element
1. Design of test cases and function framework: see Tables 3.28 and 3.29.

Table 3.28: Basic operation on sequential queue – design of test cases for deleting element.

Test case	Status	Expected result
Normal case	Queue is nonempty	Return the position of the new head element
Abnormal case	Empty queue	Return the queue emptiness indicator

Table 3.29: Basic operation on sequential queue – design of function structure for deleting element.

Functionality description	Input	Output
Delete element: Delete_SqQueue	Starting address of the queue: SeqQueue *	Head pointer int (Empty queue: −1; nonempty queue: Position of the head element)
Function name	Parameters	Function type

2. Pseudocode description of the algorithm: see Table 3.30.

Table 3.30: Basic operation on sequential queue – pseudocode for deleting element.

Top-level pseudocode	First–level elaboration
Deletion on sequential list	If the queue is nonempty
	Move the head pointer front backward by one position
	Return front;
	Otherwise return emptiness indicator −1

3. Program implementation

Note the difference between deletion and getting the head element

```
/*============================================================
Functionality of the function: Deletion of element on sequential queue
Function input: Starting address of the queue
Function output: -1 - Emptiness indicator; Other values - Position of the head
element
=========================================================*/
int Delete_SqQueue(SeqQueue *sq )
{
    if ( ! Empty_SqQueue(sq) )// Queue is non-empty
    {
     sq->front=(sq->front+1)% QUEUE_SIZE;
     return sq->front;
    }
    return -1;// Queue is empty
}
```

4. Algorithm complexity: time complexity $O(1)$.

3.2.5 Linked storage structure of queue

When we were implementing Pascal's triangle above using circular queue, if there is no check on the queue being full, we will face the problem of array overflow. This makes the size of the computation results relatively limited. Is there any other solution besides circular queue? In the chapter on linear list we have already learned that there is also linked storage besides sequential storage for linear lists. Since a queue is a linear list with special operations, then it should also be able to be stored using linked list. The following is a discussion of queue implemented as linked list – linked queue.

i | **Definition Linked queue**
Queue represented with linked list (the linked storage structure of queue) is singly linked list with the restriction of only allowing deletion at the head of the list and insertion at the end of the list. A linked queue with head node is shown in Fig. 3.77. A linked queue is uniquely determined by one head pointer and one rear pointer.

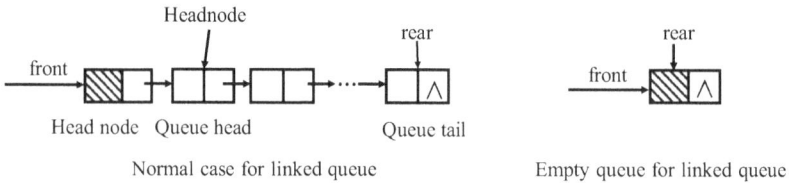

Fig. 3.77: Illustration of linked queue.

Data structure design of linked lists

A linked list consists of a singly linked list shown in Fig. 3.78. The head pointer front points to the head node, and the rear pointer rear points to the tail node. Both the head pointer and the rear pointer are stored in the same struct. The queue pointer l_q points to this structure.

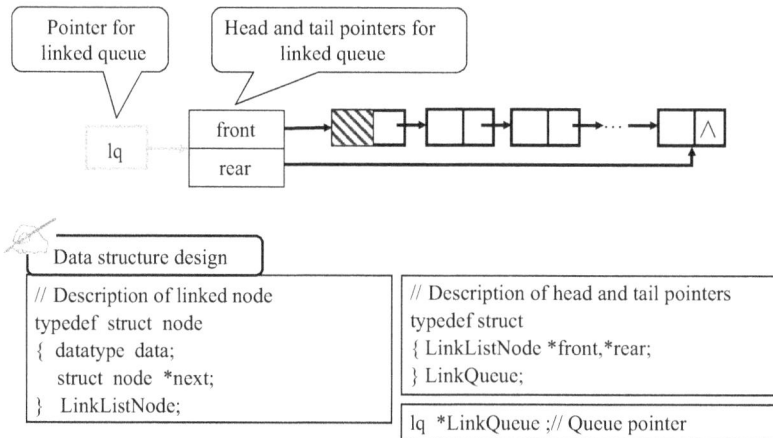

Fig. 3.78: Structure description of linked queue.

Think and Discuss What is the aim of setting up the linked queue pointer, lq?
Discussion: The lq pointer points to the composite structure that contains both the head pointer and the rear pointer. This facilitates the complete passing of queue information.

3.2.6 Basic operations on linked queue

Whenever the solution process of the problem has the characteristic of "FIFO," we can use queue in the solution algorithm. The following are some examples of the application of queue.

3.2.6.1 Basic operations on linked queue – initialize and set the queue as empty

The first time we establish a linked queue with only one head node, the illustration of the operation is shown in Fig. 3.79, and the illustration of the steps is shown in Table 3.31.

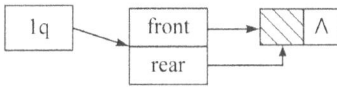

Fig. 3.79: Basic operation of initialization queue linked.

1. Design of the function framework: see Table 3.31.

Table 3.31: Basic operation on linked queue – function framework for initialization.

Functionality description	Input	Output
Initialization: `initialize_LkQueue`	Address of the linked queue: `LinkQueue *`	None
Function name	Parameters	Function type

2. Pseudocode description of the algorithm: see Table 3.32.

Table 3.32: Basic operation on linked queue – pseudocode for initialization.

Top-level pseudocode	First-level elaboration
	Apply for a node
Establishing a linked queue with only one head node for the first time	Set the pointer field of the node to empty
	Both the head pointer and the rear pointer of the queue should point to this node

3. Program implementation

```
/*=======================================================
Functionality of the function: Initialization of linked list
Function input: Starting address of the queue
Function output: None
=======================================================*/
void initialize_LkQueue(LinkQueue *lq)
{  lq->front=(LinkListNode *)malloc(sizeof( LinkListNode));
   lq->front->next=NULL;
   lq->rear=lq->front;
}
```

4. Efficiency of the algorithm: time complexity $O(1)$.

3.2.6.2 Basic operation on linked queue – checking emptiness of queue

1. Design of test cases and function framework: see Tables 3.33 and 3.34.

Table 3.33: Basic operation on linked queue – test cases for checking the emptiness of queue.

Test case	Status	Expected result
Normal case	Empty queue	Return the empty indicator
	Nonempty queue	Return the nonempty indicator

Table 3.34: Basic operation on linked queue – function framework for checking the emptiness of queue.

Functionality description	Input	Output
Check queue emptiness: Empty_LkQueue	Pointer to linked queue: LinkQueue *	Queue status indicator: int (Empty queue: TRUE; Nonempty queue: FALSE)
Function name	Parameters	Function type

2. Pseudocode description of the algorithm: see Table 3.35.

Table 3.35: Basic operation on linked queue – pseudocode for checking the emptiness of queue.

Top-level pseudocode	First-level elaboration
Check emptiness for linked queue	If the head pointer is the same as the rear pointer, return empty indicator TRUE
	Otherwise return nonempty indicator FALSE

3. Program implementation

```
/*===============================================================
Functionality of the function: Check queue emptiness on linked queue
Function input: Starting address of the queue
Function output: 1 - Empty; 0 - Non-empty
===============================================================*/
int Empty_LkQueue( LinkQueue *lq )
{
   if ( lq->front == lq->rear) return TRUE;
   else  return FALSE;
}
```

4. Algorithm efficiency: time complexity $O(1)$.

3.2.6.3 Basic operation on linked queue – retrieve the head node
Head node is shown in Fig. 3.77. Note we are just retrieving the value of the head node instead of dequeuing.
1. Design of test cases and function framework: see Tables 3.36 and 3.37.

Table 3.36: Basic operation on linked queue – test cases for retrieving the head node.

Test case	Status	Expected result
Normal case	Nonempty queue	Return successful operation indicator Return the value of the head node
Abnormal case	Empty queue	Return failed operation indicator

Table 3.37: Basic operation on linked queue – function framework design for retrieving the head node.

Functionality description	Input	Output
Retrieve the head node: Get_LkQueue	Pointer to the linked queue: LinkQueue	Operation successfulness indicator: int Node value: datatype*
	(Value of the node: datatype*)	
Function name	Parameters	Function type

2. Pseudocode description of the algorithm: see Table 3.38.

Table 3.38: Basic operation on linked queue – pseudocode for retrieving the head node.

Top-level pseudocode	First-level elaboration
Retrieve the head node from a linked queue	If the queue is nonempty
	Get the value of the node pointed to by the head pointer;
	Return successful operation indicator TRUE;
	Otherwise return FALSE.

3. Program implementation

```
/*================================================================
Functionality of the function: Retrieve the head node of the linked queue
Function input: Starting address of the queue, (value of the queue node)
Function output: 0 - Empty queue; 1 - non-empty queue
===============================================================*/
int Get_LkQueue(LinkQueue *lq, datatype *x)
{
    if ( Empty_LkQueue(lq)) return FALSE; //Empty queue
    x = lq -> front -> next -> data; //Get the value of the head node
    return TRUE;
}
```

4. Algorithm efficiency: time complexity $O(1)$.

3.2.6.4 Basic operation on linked queue – enqueuing
Illustration of the operation is shown in Fig. 3.80.

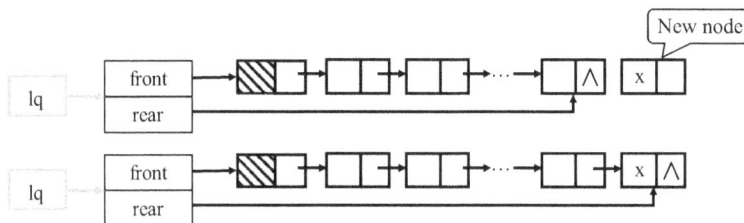

Fig. 3.80: Basic operation on linked queue – enqueuing.

1. Design of test cases and function framework: see Tables 3.39 and 3.40.

Table 3.39: Basic operation on linked queue – test cases for enqueuing.

Test case	Status	Expected result
Normal case	Nonempty queue	Normal enqueue operation
Special case	Empty queue	

Table 3.40: Basic operation on linked queue – design of function framework for enqueuing.

Functionality description	Input	Output
Enqueue: Insert_LkQueue	Pointer to linked queue: `LinkQueue *`	None
	Value of the node to be inserted: `datatype`	
Function name	Parameters	Function type

2. Pseudocode description of the algorithm: see Table 3.41.

Table 3.41: Basic operation on linked queue – pseudocode for enqueuing.

Top-level pseudocode	First-level elaboration
Enqueuing on linked queue	The allocated new node gets linked to the tail of the queue
	Modify the rear pointer of the queue
	Give the new node value x

3. Program implementation

```
/*================================================================
Functionality of the function: Retrieve the head node from linked list
Function input: Starting address of the queue, (Value of the node from the
queue)
Function output: 0 - Empty queue; 1 - Non-empty queue
=============================================================*/
void Insert_LkQueue(LinkQueue *lq, datatype x)
{
   lq->rear->next=(LinkListNode *)malloc(sizeof( LinkListNode ));
   //New node is linked to the tail of the queue
```

```
    lq->rear=lq->rear->next; //Modify the rear pointer of the queue
    lq->rear->data=x; //Gives value to the new node
    lq->rear->next=NULL; //Set the next field of the rear node to NULL
}
```

4. Algorithm complexity: time complexity $O(1)$.

3.2.6.5 Basic operation on linked queue – dequeuing

In Fig. 3.81, s points to the head node of the queue. When the queue has multiple nodes, after s node is deleted, we only need to modify the node pointed to by front -> next, i.e. front -> next = s -> next. When the queue has only one node, we need to deal with rear pointer separately and let it point to the head node, that is, rear = front, to set the queue as empty.

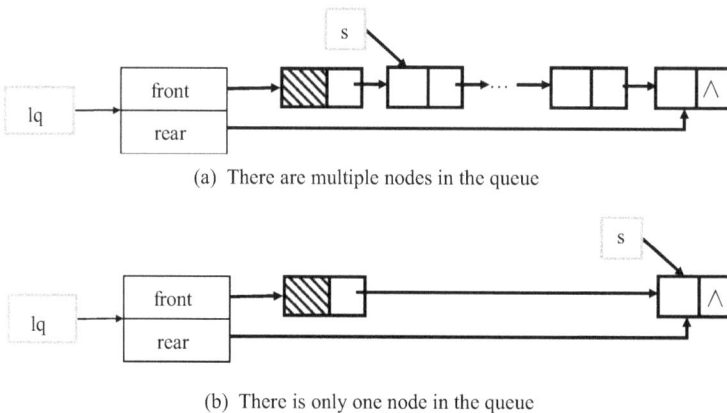

(a) There are multiple nodes in the queue

(b) There is only one node in the queue

Fig. 3.81: Basic operation on linked queue – dequeuing. (a) There are multiple nodes in the queue and (b) there is only one node in the queue.

1. Design of test cases and function framework: see Tables 3.42 and 3.43.

Table 3.42: Basic operation on linked queue – test cases for dequeuing.

Test case	Status	Expected result
Normal case	Nonempty queue with multiple nodes	Dequeue, returns the address of the node retrieved
Special case	Nonempty queue with only one node	Dequeue, set the queue as empty
Abnormal case	Empty queue	Abnormal, return NULL

Table 3.43: Basic operation on linked queue – pseudocode for dequeuing.

Functionality description	Input	Output
Dequeuing	Pointer to the linked queue	Address of the node
Delete_LkQueue	LinkQueue *	LinkList *
Function name	Parameters	Function type

2. Pseudocode description of the algorithm: see Table 3.44.

Table 3.44: Basic operation on linked queue – pseudocode for dequeuing.

Top-level pseudocode	First-level elaboration
Dequeuing on linked queue	If the queue is nonempty, find the head node s
	If the queue has only one node, set the queue as empty
	Dequeue the head node s, modify the pointer field of the head pointer
	Return the address of s
	Return NULL

3. Program implementation

```
/*==================================================
Functionality of the function: Dequeuing on linked queue
Function input: Starting address of the queue
Function output: Address of the head node
==================================================*/
LinkListNode *Delete_LkQueue( LinkQueue *lq )
{
    LinkListNode *s;
    if ( !Empty_LkQueue(lq) )    //Queue is non-empty
    {
        s = lq->front->next;       //s points to the head node
        if (s->next==NULL)         //There's only one node in the queue
            lq->rear =lq->front;   // Set the queue as empty
        else lq->front->next = s->next; // Dequeue the head node
        return(s); //Return the address of the head node being dequeued
    }
    return NULL; //If the queue is empty, return NULL
}
```

4. Algorithm efficiency: time complexity $O(1)$.

! **Think and Discuss** In the dequeue function, is it okay to not free the node being dequeued?
Discussion: When we create a linked queue, all the nodes are dynamically allocated via the malloc function. When we perform the dequeue operation on linked queue, we are actually performing deletion on a node. If the node deleted will no longer be used, then we need to free
the node immediately via free function; otherwise, we might cause memory leak. If the node
being dequeued still has some other uses in the main caller function, then we cannot free it in
the dequeue function. Whether to free the node being dequeued or not, should depend on the
overall system functionality. The basic principle is that, once a dynamically allocated node is
no longer used, it must be freed. If memory leak is caused, then it will be very hard to debug.
   Memory leak can cause serious consequences. The reader can refer to related materials for
further reading.

3.2.6.6 Destroying the linked queue

Considering that after a certain point in time the program might never use this
queue again, we need to perform the destruction of the queue in order to prevent
memory leak.

```
/*===========================================================
Functionality of the function: Destruction of the linked queue
Function input: Starting address of the queue
Function output: None
=========================================================*/
void Destory_LkQueue(LinkQueue *lq)
{
   LinkListNode *s;
   while ( ! Empty_LkQueue(lq) )
   {
      s = Delete_LkQueue(lq);
      free(s);
   }
   free(lq->front);
   lq->front = NULL;
   lq->rear = NULL;
}
```

We can put all the functions mentioned previously about operations on linked
queue into the file LinkQueue.h, then we can directly include this header file in the
subsequent programs using linked queues.

Example 3.6: Linked queue solution to Pascal's Triangle
Previously, when we are using circular queue to construct Pascal's triangle, since there is a restriction on the queue being full, we faced the problem of array overflow. The size of the pro-
cessable result will be limited. In the following we do it again using linked queue.

The program is as follows:

```c
#include <stdio.h>
#include <stdlib.h>
#include "LinkQueue.h"
#define N 42

int main(void)
{
    LinkQueue node;
    LinkQueue *lqPtr=&node;
    LinkList *sPtr;
    datatype value;

    Initial(lqPtr);   //Initialization
    //0,1,1,0 Enqueue
    EnQueue(lqPtr, 0);
    EnQueue(lqPtr, 1);
    EnQueue(lqPtr, 1);
    EnQueue(lqPtr, 0);

    for (int i=0 ; i<N; i++)
    {
        //Dequeue the head element
        sPtr = DeQueue(lqPtr);
        if (sPtr!=NULL)
        {
            //Sum the two elements at the head of the queue
            // to get the new coefficient
            value=sPtr->data+lqPtr->front->next->data;
            if (sPtr->data!= 0) printf("%d ",sPtr->data);
                EnQueue (lqPtr, value); //Enqueue the new coefficient
        }
        //The head element is the separator
        if( lqPtr->front->next->data==0 )
        {
            EnQueue (lqPtr, 0); //Enqueue the separator
```

```
        printf("\n");
    }
}
return 0;
}
```

Result when $N = 42$:

```
1 1
1 2 1
1 3 3 1
1 4 6 4 1
1 5 10 10 5 1
1 6 15 20 15 6 1
1 7 21 35 35 21 7 1
```

Result when $N = 188$:

```
1 1
1 2 1
1 3 3 1
1 4 6 4 1
1 5 10 10 5 1
1 6 15 20 15 6 1
1 7 21 35 35 21 7 1
1 8 28 56 70 56 28 8 1
1 9 36 84 126 126 84 36 9 1
1 10 45 120 210 252 210 120 45 10 1
1 11 55 165 330 462 462 330 165 55 11 1
1 12 66 220 495 792 924 792 495 220 66 12 1
1 13 78 286 715 1287 1716 1716 1287 715 286 78 13 1
1 14 91 364 1001 2002 3003 3432 3003 2002 1001 364 91 14 1
1 15 105 455 1365 3003 5005 6435 6435 5005 3003 1365 455 105 15 1
1 16 120 560 1820 4368 8008 11440 12870 11440 8008 4368 1820 560 120 16 1
1 17 136 680 2380 6188 12376 19448 24310 24310 19448 12376 6188 2380 680 136 17 1
```

3.2.7 Comparison of different queue structures

The features of sequential queue and linked queue are given in Table 3.45. For the comparison between circular queue and linked queue, we can consider two aspects.

Table 3.45: Features of sequential queue and linked queue.

	Storage space	Operation efficiency	Characteristic
Circular queue	Statically allocated memory space	$O(1)$	Has the danger of overflow
Linked queue	Dynamically allocated memory space, which is expandable	$O(1)$	No fear of the queue being overfull

In terms of time efficiency, the basic operations on both types are basically all constant time, that is, $O(1)$, although circular queue applies for memory space first and never releases it during its life span, while linked list will incur some time cost each time it applies for and releases a node. If the pushing and popping operations are frequent, there will be slight performance differences.

In terms of space efficiency, circular queue must have a fixed length, and thus might have the problem of limited space utilization rate, while there is no such problem for linked queue. Although it requires a pointer field, which produces extra space cost, this cost is generally acceptable. Therefore, linked queue is more flexible. In general, if the maximum length of the queue can be ascertained, circular queue is recommended. If the length cannot be preestimated, then linked queue is recommended.

3.2.8 Examples of the application of queue

3.2.8.1 Application of queue 1 – radix sort

Radix sort is an ordering method realized by the methods of "distribute" and "collect." Radix sort is also called "bucket method"; it is achieved via distributing the elements to be sorted into certain "buckets" using partial information from the keywords. The following is a concrete example. In Fig. 3.82, there are 12 two-digit numbers that are to be sorted in ascending order.

0	1	2	3	4	5	6	7	8	9	10	11
78	09	63	30	74	89	94	25	05	69	18	83

Fig. 3.82: Initial state for radix sort.

Sorting step 1: first, according to the value of the last digit, distribute the numbers into buckets with indices 0–9 (which should correspond to the value of the last digit), as shown in Fig. 3.83.

0	1	2	3	4	5	6	7	8	9
30			63	74	25			78	09
			83	94	05			18	89
									69

Fig. 3.83: The result of the first "distribution" in radix sort.

Sorting step 2: after the distribution is over, re-collect the numbers in all buckets in ascending order (in a top-down order within each bucket), and we get a still unordered number sequence, as shown in Fig. 3.84.

0	1	2	3	4	5	6	7	8	9	10	11
30	63	83	74	94	25	05	78	18	09	89	69

Fig. 3.84: The result of the first "collection" in radix sort.

Sorting step 3: perform a distribution again according to the value of the tens digit. The result of the distribution is shown in Fig. 3.85.

0	1	2	3	4	5	6	7	8	9
05	18	25	30			63	74	83	94
09						69	78	89	

Fig. 3.85: The result of the second "distribution" of radix sort.

Sorting step 4: after the distribution is over, re-collect the numbers in all buckets, and we arrive at the number sequence shown in Fig. 3.86.

0	1	2	3	4	5	6	7	8	9	10	11
05	09	18	25	30	63	69	74	78	83	89	94

Fig. 3.86: The result of the second "collection" of radix sort.

Through our observation, we can see that the originally unordered number sequence is now already ordered. If the number sequence to be sorted has numbers with more than three digits, then we repeat the above steps until we are finished with the highest digit.

Algorithm Design Using the example of the above-mentioned sorting of two-digit decimal numbers.

We can represent these buckets with arrays. Design ten arrays with numberings 0–9. The arrays 0–9 correspond, respectively, to the value 0–9 of a certain digit of the two-digit number. The illustration of the related data structure is shown in Fig. 3.87.

1. Scan each two-digit number sequentially. If the last digit is k, then we insert it into array with numbering k.
2. Retrieve the second-digit numbers sequentially from the arrays 0–9.
3. Repeat steps 1 and 2 on the tens digit.

When we retrieve the numbers for the second time, the sorting is over.

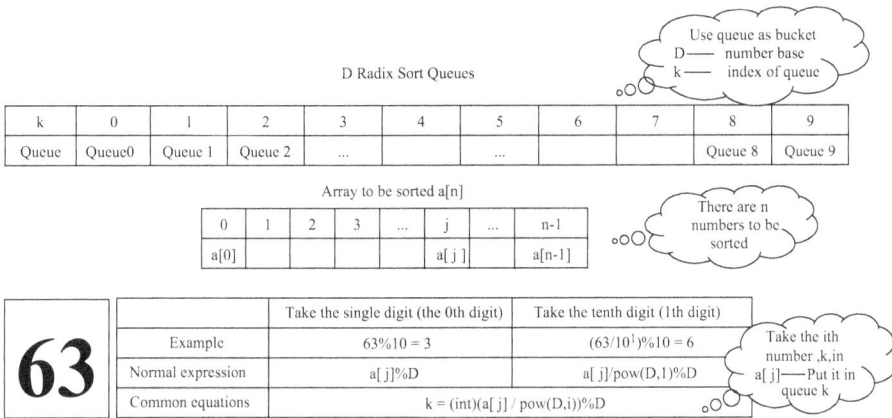

Fig. 3.87 content:

Use queue as bucket
D —— number base
k —— index of queue

D Radix Sort Queues

k	0	1	2	3	4	5	6	7	8	9
Queue	Queue0	Queue 1	Queue 2	...		...			Queue 8	Queue 9

Array to be sorted a[n]

0	1	2	3	...	j	...	n-1
a[0]					a[j]		a[n-1]

There are n numbers to be sorted

	Take the single digit (the 0th digit)	Take the tenth digit (1th digit)
Example	$63\%10 = 3$	$(63/10^1)\%10 = 6$
Normal expression	$a[j]\%D$	$a[j]/pow(D,1)\%D$
Common equations	$k = (int)(a[j] / pow(D,i))\%D$	

63

Take the ith number ,k,in
a[j]—Put it in queue k

Fig. 3.87: Illustration of the data structure for radix sort.

The program implementation is as follows:

```
/*================================================================
Functionality of the function: Radix sort
Function input: Array to be sorted, number of numbers to be sorted n, the
highest digit m among the numbers to be sorted
Function output: (array to be sorted)
================================================================*/
void RadixSort(int a[], int n, int m)
{
  int i, j, k, t;
  SeqQueue tub[D]; // Define D radix queues
//Initialize D queues
  for(i = 0; i < D; i++)
  {
    initialize_SqQueue(&tub[i]);
  }
  //Perform m times distribution and collection
```

```
  for(i = 0; i < m; i++)
  {
    for(j = 0; j < n; j++) //Process n numbers
    {
      k =(int)(a[j]/pow(D,i))% D; //Get the ith number in a[j]
      Insert_SqQueue(&tub[k], a[j]); //Put a[j] into the kth array
    }
    t=0;
//Collect the number from D queues into array a
    for(j = 0; j < D; j++)
    {
      while( ! Empty_SqQueue(&tub[j]))
      {
        k=Delete_SqQueue(&tub[j]);
        a[t]=tub[j].data[k];
        t++;
      }
    }
  }
}
```

Program test:

```
#include <stdio.h>
#include <stdlib.h>
#include <math.h>
#define FALSE 0
#define TRUE 1
#define D 10 //Number of buckets
#define N 9 //Number of numbers to be sorted
#include "SeqQueue.h" //Definition of the queue to be used
int main(void)
{
  int test[N]={710, 342, 45, 686, 6, 429, 134, 68, 246};
  int i, m = 3;
  RadixSort(test, N, m);
  for(i = 0; i < N; i++)
  printf("%d ", test[i]);
  return 0;
}
```

Result: 6 45 68 134 246 342 429 686 710

3.2.8.2 Application of queue 2 – card game

There is a set of cards on the desk, numbered 1–n from top to bottom. The way to distribute the cards is to retrieve two cards from above each time, distribute the first card retrieved to the customer and put the second card retrieved to the bottom of the set of cards. Input n, output the numbering of the card distributed to the customer each time and the last two cards left.

Sample input: 7

Sample output: 1 3 5 7 4 2 6

If we use circular queue, the implementation is as follows:

```c
#include <stdio.h>
#define MAXN 50
int queue[MAXN];
int main(void)
{
    int n, front, rear;
    char ch;
    printf("Please enter y for the first-time entry\n");
    ch=getchar();

    while (ch=='y')
    {
        printf("Please input the total number of cards\n");
        scanf("%d",&n);
        while(n<2||n>=50)
        //n needs to be bigger than 1 and smaller than 50
        {
            printf("The total number of cards should be between 2 and 50 \n");
            scanf("%d",&n);
        }
        for (int i=0; i<n; ++i) //Initialize array
        {
            queue[i]=i+1;
        }
        front=0;
        rear=n;
        while (front!=rear)
        {
            printf("%d ",queue[front]);
            //Output the numbering of the card distributed
            //to the customer each time
```

```
        //When the front pointer has not exceeded the length of the list,
        // move it backwards by one
        front==n-1 ? front%=n-1 : ++front;
        if (rear==n) rear=0; //Otherwise, it should point to queue[0]
        queue[rear]=queue[front];
        //Put the card retrieved later to the bottom of the whole set of cards
        rear==n-1 ? rear%=n-1 : ++rear;
        //Move the front pointer backwards by one position,
        // then the content it points to will be the numbering of the card
        retrieved first.
            front==n-1 ? front%=n-1 : ++front;
        }
        fflush(stdin); //Flush the screen
        printf("\n If you want to continue the test, please input y\n");
        ch=getchar();
    }
    return FALSE;
}
```

Method 2: Use linked queue.

```
#include <stdio.h>
#include <stdlib.h>
#include"LinkQueue.h"

int main(void)
{
    char ch;
    int n;
    datatype *x=(datatype *)malloc(sizeof( datatype));
    //x is the pointer to the head element
    LinkQueue * lq= (LinkQueue *)malloc(sizeof( LinkQueue));//lq is the queue
    Initial(lq);

    printf("To continue, please enter y\n");
    ch=getchar();

    while (ch=='y')
    {
        printf("Please input the total number of cards\n");
        scanf("%d",&n);
        while(n<2||n>=50) //n needs to be bigger than 1 and smaller than 50
```

```
    {
        printf("The total number of cards should be between 2 and 50 \n");
        scanf("%d",&n);
    }
    for (int i=0; i<n; ++i) //Initialize the queue
    {
        EnQueue(lq,i+1);
    }
    while ( Front(lq,x))
    {
        //Output the numbering of the card
        // to be distributed to the customer each time
        printf("%d ",*x);
        DeQueue(lq);      //Retrieve the head node
        if (!Empty(lq)) //Check if the queue is empty
        {
            Front(lq,x);
            //Put the card retrieved later to the bottom of the whole set of cards
            EnQueue(lq,*x);
            DeQueue(lq);
        }
    }
    fflush(stdin); //Flush the screen
    printf("\n If you want to continue the test, please input y\n");
    ch=getchar();
    }
    return 0;
}
```

3.3 Chapter summary

The connections between the main contents of this chapter are shown in Figs. 3.88 and 3.89.

Comparison of the implementation methods of sequential stack and linked stack

From the comparison of the time complexities of push and pop, we can see that the array implementation still has a considerable advantage in terms of perfor-mance. This is because a stack implemented as array does not need to move a large quantity of elements when adding and deleting elements. It only needs to perform copying when expanding the array capacity.

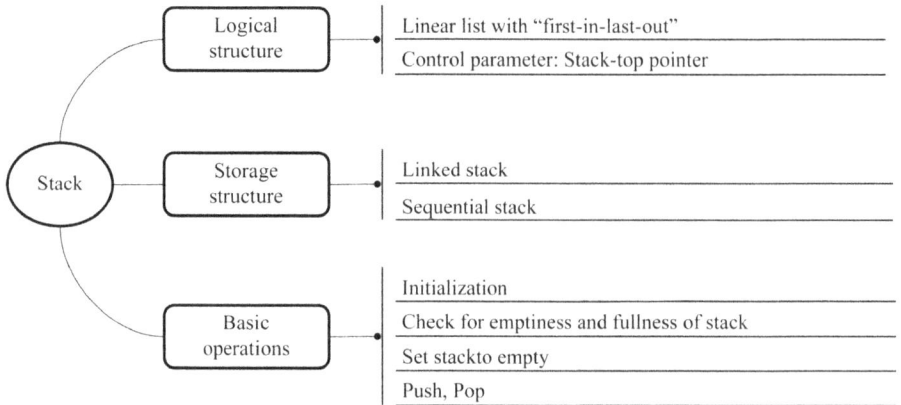

Fig. 3.88: The connections between concepts on stack.

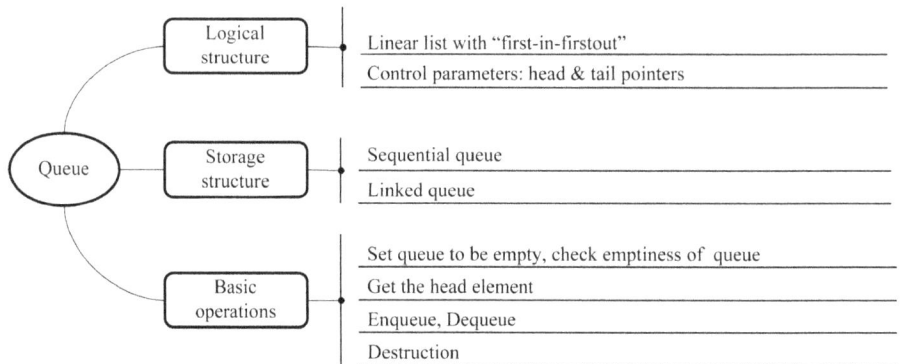

Fig. 3.89: The connections between concepts on queue.

On the contrary, a stack implemented as linked list will need to package the data into a node when pushing, and will need to retrieve the data from the node when popping. At the time it also needs to maintain top pointer and front pointer.

Comparison of linked queue and circular queue:

1. In terms of time: circular queue needs to be preallocated memory space, which will not be released during its lifetime. The allocation and destruction of nodes each time incur some time cost. If the enqueue and dequeue operations are frequent, the performance of linked queue will be slightly worse.

2. In terms of space: circular queue must have a fixed length. Therefore, there might be underutilization of queue space. There is no such problem for linked queue, which is more flexible.

Principle for choosing between circular queue and linked queue:
(1) Whenever you can know the maximum length of the queue, prefer circular queue.
(2) If you cannot preestimate the length of the queue, prefer linked queue.

A linear list has two ends, and there is no restriction on the positions where a node can be inserted or deleted.

If operations are only specifically allowed on one end, it becomes a stack.

The enqueue and dequeue operations of a queue happen, respectively, at two ends of a linear list.

If you store the nodes sequentially; for a stack it's a sequential stack; for a queue it is a circular queue.

If you store the nodes discretely, linked by pointer fields, then the structure is said to be "linked."

You can understand what do "linked stack" and "linked queue" mean just by looking at their names.

If you familiarize yourself with the operations of a linear list, then stack and queue will not be difficult.

Recursive invocations use exactly stack.

Whenever data enters in one end and exits another, we can directly apply queue to the problem.

Pay attention to the special cases of the emptiness and fullness of storage space.

3.4 Exercises

3.4.1 Multiple choice questions

1. Suppose abcdef are pushed into the stack successively in order. If we also allow pop operation in between push operations, then which of the following sequence is impossible to obtain ( ).
   (A) fedcba   (B) bcafed   (C) dcefba   (D) cabdef

2. If we already know the order of push operations for a stack is 1, 2, 3,..., n, and the order of pop operations is $p_1, p_2, p_3, \ldots, p_N$, if p_N is n, then p_i is ( ).
   (A) i (B) $n-i$ (C) $n-i+1$ (D) Cannot be determined

3. To design an algorithm to check whether left and right brackets are matched, it is best to use ( ).
   (A) Sequential linear list   (B) Queue   (C) Linked linear list   (D) Stack

4.   A linked queue needs to ( ) during deletion operation.
     (A) Only modify the head pointer
     (B) Only modify the rear pointer
     (C) Modify both head and read pointers
     (D) Potentially modify both the head and the rear pointer

5.   One needs to use ( ) data structure to deal with the parameter passing and return address during recursion/invocation of function.
     (A) Queue   (B) Multidimensional array   (C) Stack   (D) Linear list

6.   Suppose we store elements of a circular queue using array $A[m]$, with head and rear pointers being front and rear, then the number of current elements in the queue is ( )
     (A) $(rear-front+m)\%m$
     (B) $rear-front+1$
     (C) $(front-rear+m)\%m$
     (D) $(rear-front)\%m$

7.   If we use an array with length 6 to implement circular queue, and currently the values of rear and front are, respectively, 0 and 3, then after we delete one element and then add two elements in the queue, what will the values of rear and front be? ( )
     (A) 1 and 5   (B) 2 and 4   (C) 4 and 2   (D) 5 and 1

8.   For a circular queue with a maximum capacity of n, the rear pointer is rear and the head pointer is front, then the condition for the queue to be empty is: ( ).
     (A) $(rear+1)$ MOD $n=front$
     (B) $rear = front$
     (C) $rear+1=front$
     (D) $(rear-1)$ MOD $n = front$

9.   The commonality between stack and queue is ( ).
     (A) Both are FIFO
     (B) Both are first-in–last-out
     (C) Only allow element insertion and deletion at ends
     (D) No commonality

10. Suppose the initial status of stack S and queue Q are empty, elements e_1, e_2, e_3, e_4, e_5 and e_6 are allowed to pass through the stack S, respectively; an element enters the queue Q immediately after popping from the stack. If we want the order of retrieval from the queue of the six elements to be e_2, e_4, e_3, e_6, e_5, e_1, then the capacity of the stack S should at least be: ( ).
     (A) 6   (B) 4   (C) 3   (D) 2

3.4.2 Practical questions

1. Suppose there are four trains numbered 1, 2, 3, 4 which enter a station with stack structure in order. Write all possible orders of exit for these four trains. Suppose the capacity of the stack is 2.
2. The railroad often designs the station to be stack-like when managing train rides, as shown in Fig. 3.90. The questions are:
    (1) If there are six trains numbered 1, 2, 3, 4, 5, 6 which enter the station in order, then how many possible orders of exiting the station exist?
    (2) If the six trains that enter the station are as described above, then can we obtain the exiting orders: 435612, 325641, 154623 and 135426? If we can't, describe why not. If we can, illustrate how (i.e., write out the order of "push" and "pop").

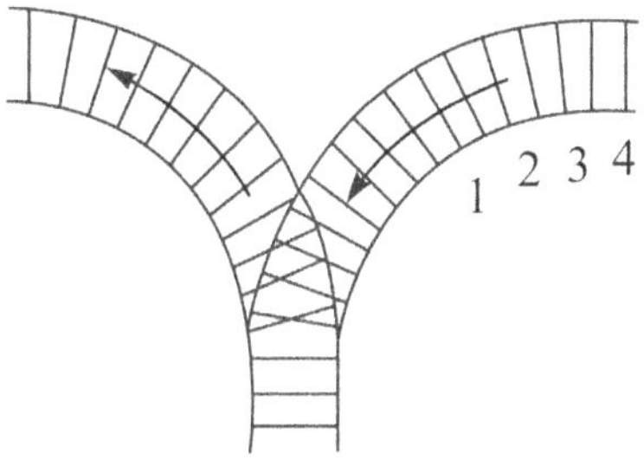

Fig. 3.90: Stack-like train station.

3.4.3 Algorithm design

1. Suppose n chars are stored in a singly linked list. Try to write an algorithm to judge whether there is a symmetry in the chars, for example, xyzzyx and xyzyx are symmetrical. You should use the least time possible to finish the checking. (Hint: Enter half of the chars into the stack first.)
2. Store two stacks with numberings 0 and 1 in an array space $V[m]$. The two bottoms of two stacks are, respectively, at two ends of the array. When the top pointer of stack 0 top[0] is −1, this stack is empty. When the top pointer of stack 1 top[1] is m, this stack is empty. Both stacks grow from both ends toward the center. When we insert a new element into the stack 0, top[0] should be incremented by one to obtain the location of the new stack top; when we insert a new element into stack 1, top[1] should be decremented by one to obtain the location of the new stack top. When top[0] + 1 == top[1] or top[0] == top[1] − 1, the spaces in two stacks are full, and we cannot add any new element to either of the stacks. Try to define the type definition of such a double stack structure and implement the algorithms for emptiness check, fullness check, insertion and deletion.

3. Suppose we store the elements of a circular queue with the array sequ[m], we set variables rear and quelen to indicate the location of the rear element in the circular queue and the number of elements contained within, respectively. Try to give the condition for checking the fullness of this circular queue and write out the corresponding algorithms for push and pop operations. (In the pop operation you need to return the head element.)

4. Suppose we represent a queue using a circular linked list with a head node, and we only set one pointer to point to the tail element node. (Attention: we did not set any head pointer.) Try to write the corresponding initialization, push and pop algorithms.

5. Suppose we represent a double-ended queue with linked list, which allows insertion at both ends of the list, but only allows deletion at one end of the list. Try to write the algorithms for enqueue and dequeue operations on the queue based on this structure and give the conditions for the queue to be empty and full.

6. Implement the insertion and deletion functionalities of a queue using two stacks.

7. Implement the functionalities of a stack using two queues.

4 Sequential list with special contents – multidimensional arrays and strings

Main Contents
- Use two-dimensional arrays to represent matrices and calculations
- The storage method with compression for special matrices
- The definition and storage methods of strings
- Pattern matching

Learning Aims
- Comprehend the storage structure of multidimensional arrays, familiarize yourselves with the storage method with compression for special matrices and sparse matrices
- Understand the features of operations on string. Understand string-matching algorithms

Array in the context of computer science refers to a collection of data of the same type. They fit well with the way data is organized naturally in actual applications and have various usages. The concept of multidimensional arrays is very useful especially in scientific computing and computer graphics. String is an important data structure based on arrays. Database is also an amplification and extension of the concept of array. The contiguous storage of array in computer memory reflects the low-level mechanism of data organization in memory.

The data structures discussed in the previous chapters such as sequential list, stack and array are all linear structures, the data elements in which can be regarded as nondivisible atoms. The arrays to be discussed in this chapter can be viewed as an extension of linear list, that is, the elements in the list are themselves a type of data structure.

4.1 Multidimensional arrays

Array is one of our most familiar organizational forms of data. Since all the elements in an array have a unified type, and the subscript of an element in an array normally has a fixed lower and upper bound, the operations on array are normally simpler than those on other more complex structures. Almost all high-level programming languages offer array. The sequential storage distribution of various data structures also makes use of one-dimensional arrays to describe their storage structures. Multidimensional array is an extension of one-dimensional array.

This section will discuss the logical structure and storage method of arrays from the perspective of data structure.

https://doi.org/10.1515/9783110595581-004

4.1.1 The concept of arrays

In program design, for the convenience of processing, we organize several variables with the same type in an orderly way. This collection of data elements of the same type listed in order is called array.

From the perspective of data structure, array is a finite sequence constituted of n ($n \geq 0$) data elements of the same data type. Array can be viewed as a type of special linear list; it is an extension of linear list.

> **i** **Definition of Array**
> Array is a collection constituted of data elements with the same type. Each data element is called an array element (simplified as element).

One-dimensional array is a linear list with fixed length. Two-dimensional array is also a linear list with fixed length, with each element being a one-dimensional array.

An n-dimensional array is a linear list, whose each element is an $n - 1$ – dimensional array.

For example, a two-dimensional array of size $m \times n$ $A[m, n]$ can be viewed as m rows of one-dimensional arrays, or n columns of one-dimensional arrays, as shown in Fig. 4.1.

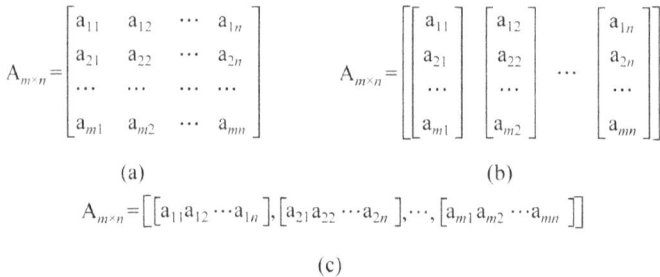

$$A_{m \times n} = \begin{bmatrix} a_{11} & a_{12} & \cdots & a_{1n} \\ a_{21} & a_{22} & \cdots & a_{2n} \\ \cdots & \cdots & \cdots & \cdots \\ a_{m1} & a_{m2} & \cdots & a_{mn} \end{bmatrix}$$

(a)

$$A_{m \times n} = \begin{bmatrix} \begin{bmatrix} a_{11} \\ a_{21} \\ \cdots \\ a_{m1} \end{bmatrix} & \begin{bmatrix} a_{12} \\ a_{22} \\ \cdots \\ a_{m2} \end{bmatrix} & \cdots & \begin{bmatrix} a_{1n} \\ a_{2n} \\ \cdots \\ a_{mn} \end{bmatrix} \end{bmatrix}$$

(b)

$$A_{m \times n} = \begin{bmatrix} [a_{11} a_{12} \cdots a_{1n}], [a_{21} a_{22} \cdots a_{2n}], \cdots, [a_{m1} a_{m2} \cdots a_{mn}] \end{bmatrix}$$

(c)

Fig. 4.1: The relation between arrays and linear lists.

A can be viewed as a linear list in the form of row-vectors

$$A_{m \times n} = [[a_{11} a_{12} \ldots a_{1n}], [a_{21} a_{22} \ldots a_{2n}], \ldots, [a_{m1} a_{m2} \ldots a_{mn}]]$$

or a linear list in the form of column-vectors

$$A_{m \times n} = [[a_{11} a_{21} \ldots a_{m1}], [a_{12} a_{22} \ldots a_{m2}], \ldots, [a_{1n} a_{2n} \ldots a_{mn}]]$$

The appearance of the computer was initially aimed at solving problems of mathematical computations. Therefore, many concepts come from mathematics, for example, function and vector. One might say that one-dimensional arrays correspond to "vector" and that two-dimensional arrays correspond to "matrix."

4.1.2 The storage structure of arrays

With such an organization form of data as array, we can refer to a series of variables with the same name, differentiating them only with the subscript (index).

The array elements in normal programming languages are stored in contiguous memory. They are just adjacent to each other. Note that while arrays can be multidimensional, memory addresses are always one-dimensional.

Think and Discuss The storage structure of the computer is one-dimensional, yet arrays can usually be multidimensional. How to store them?

Discussion: According to the data storage principle of "able to be stored and able to be retrieved," we need to find the correspondence relation between the array subscript and storage address. Since the memory structure of computer is one-dimensional and linear, therefore, when storing multidimensional arrays, we need to solve the problem of mapping a multidimensional relation to a one-dimensional relation, that is, order the elements of the array according to some sequence, and then store this linear sequence in the storage container.

To list the array elements into a linear sequence, then we will have a problem of the specification of the order. Because multidimensional arrays are defined by the arrays one dimension lower. Thinking in this way, using such a relation of induction, we can order the data elements in a multidimensional array into a linear sequence. The storage of one-dimensional array in memory is very simple; we only need to store the elements in contiguous memory units. How do we represent two-dimensional arrays with sequential structure? There are two possible ways, as shown in Fig. 4.2.

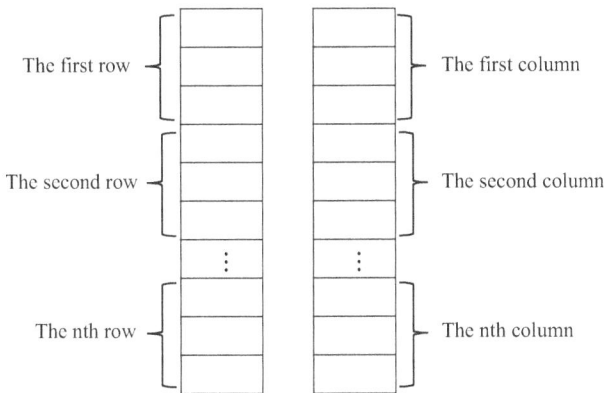

Fig. 4.2: The two storage structures of two-dimensional arrays.

In languages such as C++ and Pascal, arrays are all stored in a row-based manner; in languages such as Fortran, arrays are stored in a column-based manner.

The above rules can be extended to the situation with multidimensional arrays: a row-based order can be defined as first storing the rightmost subscript, from right to left, and storing the leftmost subscript in the end. The row-based order is the opposite: store first the leftmost subscript, from left to right, and store the rightmost subscript the latest.

The features of the array structure are as follows:

1. Extensibility of element: the element itself can have some structure, and it is not just restricted to one singular data element.
2. Homogeneity of elements: elements have the same data type.
3. Fixedness of relation: the number of data elements is fixed. Once an array structure is defined, there would not be any increase or decrease in the number of elements. The subscript relation of data elements is restricted by upper and lower bounds, and the subscripts are ordered.

The two basic operations on arrays:

1. Given a set of subscripts, save the corresponding data elements.
2. Given a set of subscripts, modify the value of a certain data item in the corresponding data element.

The features of arrays determine that it is most suited to sequential storage structure. We will discuss the location of elements of two-dimensional arrays in the memory, that is, the mapping between the subscripts of arrays and the memory addresses.

Suppose that each data element of a two-dimensional array occupies L elements. m, n are the number of rows and columns of the array. $\text{Loc}(a_{11})$ refers to the memory location of the element a_{11}. The storage is row-based –the principle is to store the ith row before storing the $i+1$th row in succession. The illustration can be seen is Fig. 4.3.

According to Fig. 4.4, we can obtain the formula for calculating the memory address of data elements stored in a row-based manner:

$$\text{Loc}(a_{ij}) = \text{Loc}(a_{11}) + ((i-1)*n + (j-1))*L$$

The address of a certain element is the sum of the base address (the starting address of the array), the units occupied by all rows before it and the units occupied by all elements before it in the same row.

In the same manner, we can obtain the formula for calculating data elements stored in a column-based manner as

$$\text{Loc}(a_{ij}) = \text{Loc}(a_{11}) + ((j-1)*m + (i-1))*L$$

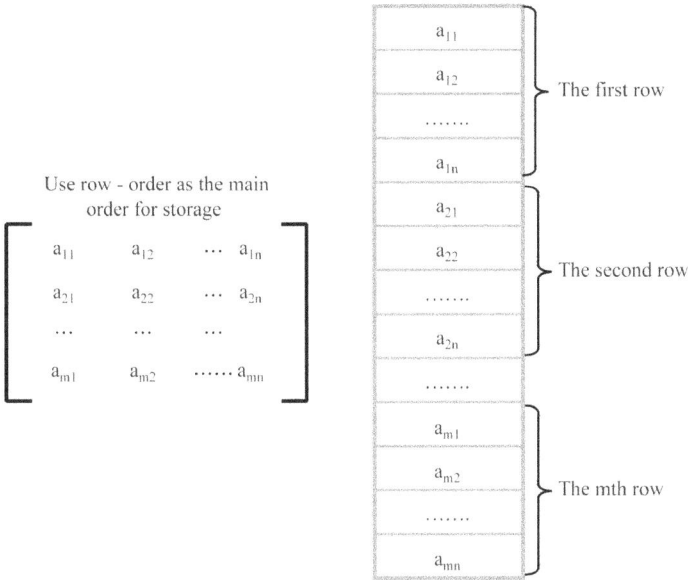

Use row - order as the main order for storage

$$\begin{bmatrix} a_{11} & a_{12} & \cdots & a_{1n} \\ a_{21} & a_{22} & \cdots & a_{2n} \\ \cdots & \cdots & \cdots & \\ a_{m1} & a_{m2} & \cdots\cdots & a_{mn} \end{bmatrix}$$

Fig. 4.3: Illustration of row-based storage of two-dimensional arrays.

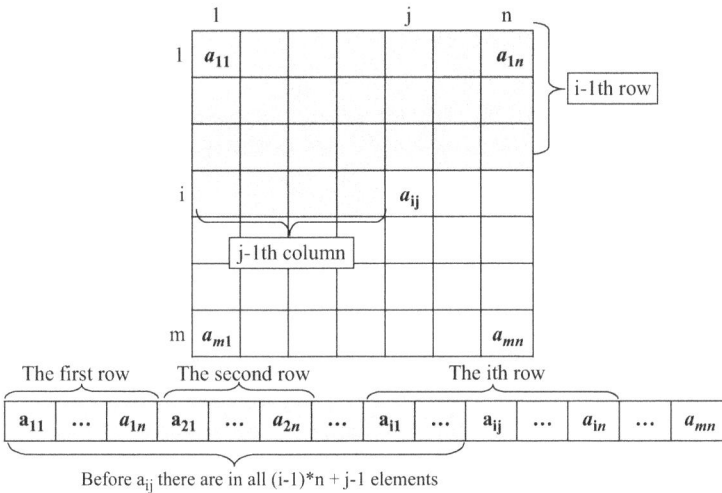

Before a_{ij} there are in all $(i-1)*n + j-1$ elements

Fig. 4.4: Memory address calculation of data elements stored in a row-based manner.

For the arrays stored in the previous two methods, we can express the memory address of the array element as a linear function of its subscript, as long as we know the base address of the array, number of dimensions and the lower and upper bounds of each dimension, as well as the number of memory units occupied by each array element. An array stored sequentially is a random access structure.

> **Term Explanation**
> For the sequential storage of arrays, the storage location of array element is the linear function of its subscript. Since it takes the same amount of time to calculate the storage location of each element, it takes the same amount of time to save/retrieve any element in the array as well. We call storage structures with such a feature as random access storage structure.

Normally during program designs, it is more common to use one-dimensional and two-dimensional arrays, and it is relatively rare to use multidimensional arrays that exceed two dimensions. The storage methods for high-dimensional arrays can be obtained by extending the case for two-dimensional arrays.

Example 4.1: Calculate the address of an array element.
Suppose the base address of the array $a[1 \dots 60, 1 \dots 70]$ is 2048, each element occupies two storage units. If it is stored in a column-based manner, calculate the storage address of element $a[32,58]$.

Note: $a[1 \dots 60, 1 \dots 70]$ is a notation for representing arrays. The range of subscripts for rows is from 1 to 60, and the range of subscripts for columns is 1 to 70.
Solution: The number of rows in the array: $m = 60 - 1 + 1 = 60$; number of columns is $n = 70 - 1 + 1 = 70$; the subscript for row is $i = 32$; the subscript for column is $j = 58$; the length of element is $L = 2$.

Using the formula for obtaining the address of array elements with column-based storage
$$\text{Loc}(a_{ij}) = \text{Loc}(a_{11}) + [(j - 1) * m + (i - 1)] * L$$

We obtain: $\text{LOC}(a32,58) = 2048 + [(58 - 1) * 60 + (32 - 1)] * 2 = 8950$.

> **Think and Discuss** If the array is $a[0 \dots 59, 0 \dots 69]$, will the result still be 8950?
> **Discussion:** Since i and j both start from 0, the formula for memory address is $\text{Loc}(a_{ij}) = \text{Loc}(a_{00}) + [j * m + i] * L$ (see Fig. 4.5).
>
> $$\text{LOC}(a32,58) = 2048 + [58 * 60 + 32] * 2 = 9072$$

4.2 The compressional storage of matrices

The matrix is a mathematical model frequently used in the design of programs that involve numerical calculations. It consists of values of m rows and n columns. In programs written in high-level programming languages, it is common to use two-dimensional arrays to represent matrices. This makes it possible to find the corresponding storage location for each element of the matrix.

For symmetrical matrices, there is no need to store each element using n^2 storage units. If we use row-based storage method, then the mapping of the storage is in shown as Fig. 4.6(a) (the ^ sign in the figure indicates that the element is omitted). To store all the elements in the matrix, it is only necessary to store the elements in the triangle. There are then $(n(n + 1)/2)$ elements in total.

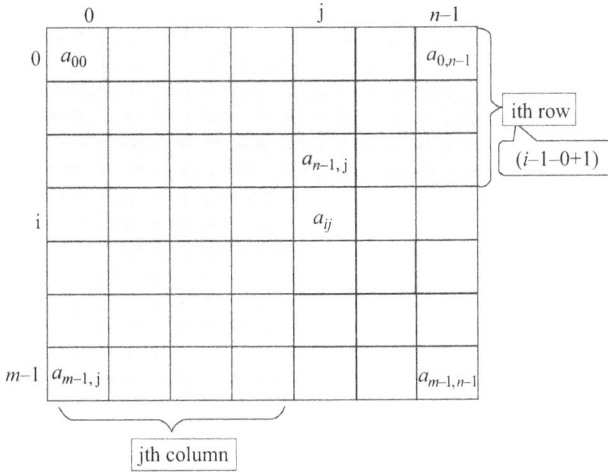

Fig. 4.5: Obtaining the address when the subscript starts from 0.

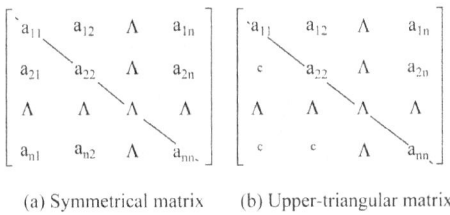

(a) Symmetrical matrix (b) Upper-triangular matrix

Fig. 4.6: Examples of special matrices: (a) symmetrical matrix and (b) upper triangular matrix.

In calculations involving numerical analysis, the high-ranked matrices with the following features are usually used: there are a lot of same or zero-valued elements, for example, the triangle matrix in Fig. 4.6(b), the values in the lower triangle part are all the same (the "c" in the figure represents the same value). In this scenario, if we store the whole matrix with a two-dimensional array, the efficiency would not be high. Suppose that we store the same data only once, that is, compress the data, this will not only save storage space, but also save data transmission time. When the matrix is very large (i.e., high-ranked matrices), we can obtain very high efficiencies.

We call matrices with certain regularity in the distribution of nonzero or zero elements "special matrices." This section discusses the compressional storage of several special matrices and sparse matrices.

i **Knowledge ABC** Data compression

Data compression refers to a technical method that, with the premise of not losing information, decreases the amount of data in order to decrease storage space, and increase the efficiency of transmission, storage and processing. Data compression reorganizes the data according to certain algorithms, in order to reduce the redundancy of data and storage space needed. From the perspective of information, compression is to get rid of the redundancy in information, that is, get rid of ascertained or deducible information, and conserve the uncertain information.

Data compression is composed of lossy compression and lossless compression. If the data compressed can be restored to the complete original data, such a compression method is called lossless data compression. If we allow data loss to a certain degree in order to achieve a higher compression rate, such a method is called lossy data compression.

! **Think and Discuss** What could be the potential issues when storing matrices with compression? What are the possible methods to use?

Discussion: First we should be clear that there are two problems to be solved by compression: first is what type of data to store and how to store them, and second is being able to recover the stored data to its original form.

Analysis and solution for the first problem:

(1) The same data needs only to be stored once; (2) zero element should not occupy storage space.

We can put the data to be stored into a one-dimensional array.

Analysis and solution for the second problem:

This is to solve the "being able to be stored, also being able to be retrieved" problem of data. We only need to find the mapping relation between the same element in the one-dimensional array and in the matrix, in order to recover the original matrix form. After the restoration, the "empty" positions in the matrix will by default be recognized as zero elements mentioned in the first problem.

According to the analysis and discussion of the problems, we can arrive at the following implementation method of the compressional storage of matrices:

(1) Ascertain the number of dimensions of the vector used to store the compressed data.
(2) Ascertain the relation between the subscripts in the two-dimensional array i, j and the subscript of the vector k.

4.2.1 The compressional storage of symmetric matrix

i **Definition of Symmetric Matrix**

In an n-ranked square matrix A, if the elements satisfy the below property, then we call A a symmetric matrix:

$$a_{ij} = a_{ji} \ (0 \leq i, j \leq n - 1)$$

The elements in a symmetric matrix are symmetric with regard to the main diagonal line. Therefore, as long as we can store the elements in the upper triangle or the lower triangle, and let each two symmetric elements share one storage space, we can save half of the storage space. Without loss of generality, we can use "column-based order" to store the elements below the main diagonal (including elements on the main diagonal), as shown in Fig. 4.7. We use one-dimensional array sa[M] as the storage structure of the n-ranked symmetric matrix A. If we want to find sa[k] = a_{ij}, then we need to find the correspondence between i, j and k.

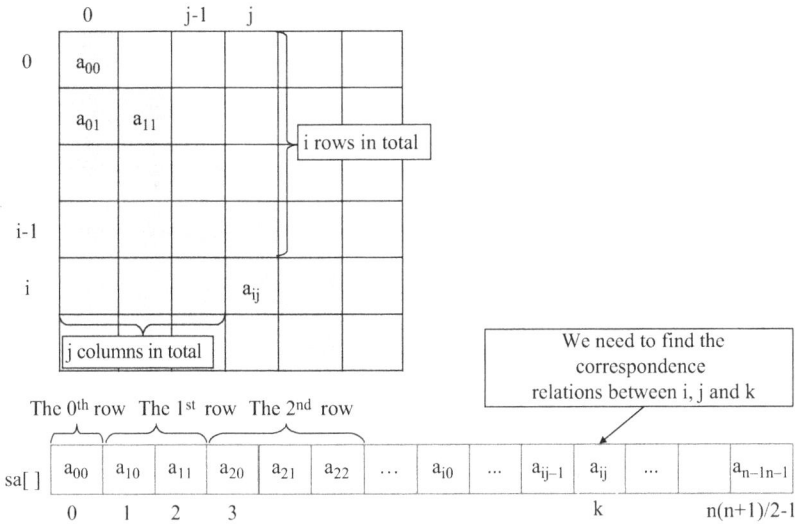

Fig. 4.7: Analysis and illustration of storage of symmetric matrix.

Total number of elements to be stored M: $M = n(1 + n)/2$.

From Fig. 4.8 we can see that k is equal to the number of elements before a_{ij} (note the value of k starts from 0). Therefore, the relation when we store the lower triangle:

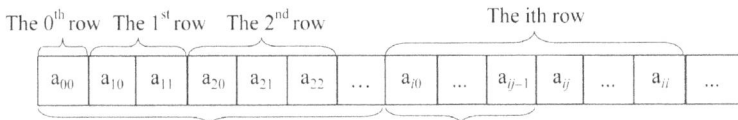

Fig. 4.8: The mapping relation in the storage of symmetric matrix.

$$k = 1 + 2 + 3 + \cdots + i + j = i(1+i)/2 + j \, (i \geq j)$$

In the same way, we can infer the relation when we store the upper triangle:

$$k = j * (j+1)/2 + i(i \le j)$$

4.2.2 The compressional storage of triangular matrix

i

Definition of Triangular Matrix
For a n-ranked square matrix A, if the elements in its lower triangle, except for those on the main diagonal, are all a constant c, that is, $a_{ij} = c$, $0 \le j < i < n$, then we call this matrix *upper triangular matrix*.
  Triangular matrix is classified into upper triangular matrix and lower triangular matrix, as shown in Fig. 4.9.

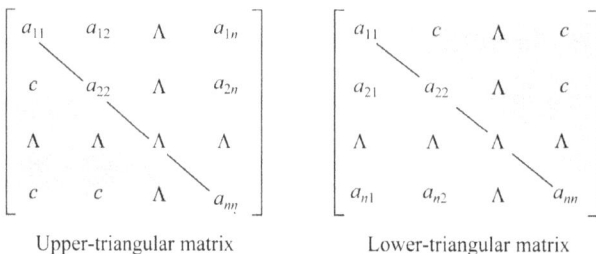

Upper-triangular matrix   Lower-triangular matrix

Fig. 4.9: Triangular matrices.

The Compressional Storage Method of Triangular Matrix
Besides storing the elements in the main diagonal as well as the elements in the upper (lower) triangle, we should also add a space to store the constant c.
  The repetitious element c in the triangular matrix needs only to occupy one storage unit. There are $n(n + 1)/2$ remaining elements. Therefore, triangular matrix can be compressed to be stored in a vector with length $n(n + 1)/2 + 1$, where c is stored at the last position of the vector. The relation between the subscripts of a lower triangular matrix and the subscripts of the vector is shown in Fig. 4.10. The reader can infer the compressional relation of an upper triangular matrix by itself.

		Value of k	Relation of i, j
a[i, j] =	sa[k]	$i(i+1)/2 + j$	When a_{ij} is in the lower triangular area, $i >= j$
	c	$n(n+1)/2$	When a_{ij} is in the upper triangular area, $i < j$

Fig. 4.10: The compressional relation for triangular matrix.

4.2.3 The compressional storage of diagonal matrix

Definition of Diagonal Matrix
A square matrix whose all nonzero elements are concentrated in a band-sized area centered around the main diagonal is called diagonal matrix; it is also called *band-sized matrix*. Figure 4.11 shows a three-diagonal matrix.

In a diagonal matrix, except for the elements on the main diagonal and on the several lines directly above/below the main diagonal, all the elements are 0. For this type of matrix, we can also store it into a one-dimensional matrix with compressional storage, using row-based storage.

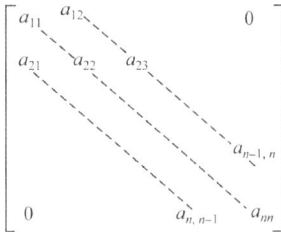

Fig. 4.11: Three-diagonal matrix.

Compression Method 1 for 3-Diagonal Matrix
Suppose we have an n-ranked three-diagonal matrix $A[n][n]$. We store the elements on the three diagonal lines row-by-row into the array $B[M]$, to let $B[k] = A[i][j]$. Give the correspondence relation between i, j and k.

In Fig. 4.12, except for the first and nth row, where both have two elements, each row has exactly three nonzero elements. Therefore, the number of elements to be stored is $M = 3n - 2$.

00	01	02	03	04
10	11	12	13	14
20	21	22	23	24
30	31	32	33	34
40	41	42	43	44

Fig. 4.12: Relation of subscripts in diagonal matrix.

From the correspondence relation in Fig. 4.13, we can get the descriptive formula of the relation:

Element	a_{00}	a_{01}	a_{10}	a_{11}	a_{12}	...	a_{ij}	...	$a_{n-1\,n-2}$	$a_{n-1\,n-1}$
k	0	1	2	3	4				$3n-4$	$3n-3$

i	0	0	1	1	1	2	2	2	3	3	3	...	$n-1$	$n-1$
j	0	1	0	1	2	1	2	3	2	3	4		$n-2$	$n-1$
k	0	1	2	3	4	5	6	7	8	9	10		$3n-4$	$3n-3$

Fig. 4.13: Table of values for the subscripts of the matrix i, j and the subscript of the vector k.

$$K = a_i + b_j + c \ (a, b, c \text{ are all integers})$$

Substitute the actual values of i, j, k back into the formula; we can obtain the values of a, b, c.

Solution: $a = 2$; $b = 1$; $c = 0$.

Therefore: $k = 2i + j$ $(0 \leq I < n; 0 \leq j < n)$

From Fig. 4.13 we can get the regularity of change for k, as shown in Fig. 4.14. According to these values, we can obtain the relation between i, j and k:

$$i = (k + 1)/3 \quad 0 \leq k < 3n - 2 \quad \text{(note how this is integer division)}$$
$$j = (k + 1)/3 + (k + 1)\%3 - 1 \quad \text{or} \quad j = k - 2i = k - [(k + 1)/3] * 2$$

(Note this division is integer division, which would not help obtain a result in fractional form.)

i	0	0	1	1	1	2	2	2	3	3	3	...	$n-1$	$n-1$
j	0	1	0	1	2	1	2	3	2	3	4		$n-2$	$n-1$
k	0	1	2	3	4	5	6	7	8	9	10		$3n-4$	$3n-3$
$(k+1)/3$	0	0	1	1	1	2	2	2	3	3	3			
$(k+1)\%3$	1	2	0	1	2	0	1	2	0	1	2			

Fig. 4.14: The relation between i, j and k in the compression of three-diagonal matrix.

Compression Method 2 for Triangular Matrix

Only store the elements within the band. We can use equi-bandwidth storage method, adding several random elements at the top left corner and bottom right corner, storing the elements within the band in the square array, as shown in Fig. 4.15.

4.2.4 Compressional storage of sparse matrix

4.2.4.1 Definition of sparse matrix

Suppose that there are s nonzero elements in the matrix $A_{m \times n}$, if s is far smaller than the total number of elements in the matrix (i.e., $s = m \times n$), then we call A a *sparse matrix*.

1	3	0	0	0
2	4	6	0	0
0	5	7	9	0
0	0	8	6	4
0	0	0	7	5

x	1	3
2	4	6
5	7	9
8	6	4
7	5	x

Fig. 4.15: Equi-bandwidth storage of diagonal matrix.

Let $e = s/(m * n)$, then we call the e *the sparse factor of the matrix*. Normally we consider a matrix to be sparse when $e \leq 0.05$.

In science and engineering, when solving linear models, large-scale sparse matrices are usual. An example is solving differential equations with value method. Another example is the scanning of handwritten signature: This is a black-white picture, as shown in Fig. 4.16; therefore if we store it directly as a bitmap, then white pixels will far exceed black pixels. Therefore we can also consider it a sparse matrix.

Fig. 4.16: Scanned signature.

When using the computer to store and operate on sparse matrix, since the matrix is too big, it is hard for standard algorithms to be applied. We can save a lot of memory cost via compression, and thus we will also need to modify the algorithms correspondingly in order to operate on the compressed matrix.

Knowledge ABC Sparse matrix and its applications

Sparse matrix refers to a matrix whose nonzero elements constitute a very small percentage of all the elements (e.g., smaller than 5%). Some matrices have nonzero elements constituting a relatively large percentage of all elements (e.g., nearly 50%), but their distribution is quite regular. If we take advantage of this feature, we can avoid storing zero elements, or avoid operations on these zero elements. Therefore, such matrices can still be called *sparse matrices*. Figure 4.17 is a common sparse matrix. We use shades to represent the distribution of the nonzero elements in some common sparse matrices [5].

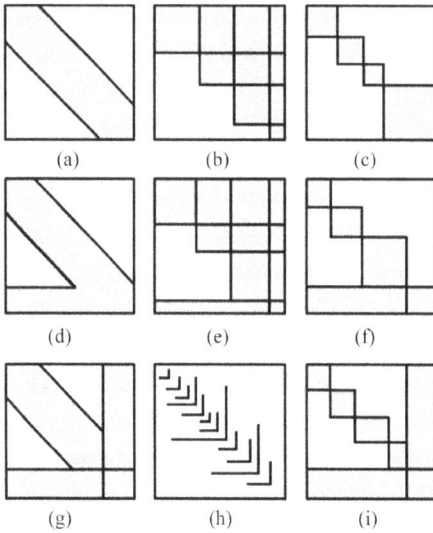

Fig. 4.17: Common sparse matrices.

The modern sparse matrix technology was developed mainly after the 1960s. In research in fields such as structural analysis, network theory, electricity system, chemical engineering, cartography and managerial science, there are all sparse matrices with thousands and even hundreds of thousands of ranks.

The famous PageRank algorithm is a method to indicate the level or importance of web pages; it is the standard used by Google to evaluate the quality of a website. PageRank algorithm first needs to store the webpages and the connections between webpages into the computer. The storage can be realized by matrix (related contents can be seen in Volume 2 of this book.). Since there are massive amounts of webpages on the Internet, then the number of elements in such a matrix will be the square of the number of webpages. Suppose that there are 1 billion webpages, then this matrix will have 10^{18} elements. PageRank algorithm involves multiplication of matrices. To multiply such a huge matrix, the amount of calculation will be huge. The creators of PageRank, Larry Page and Sergey Brin largely reduced the amount of calculation using techniques related to sparse matrix calculation.

Example 4.2: Sparse matrix in actual problems.
Let us look at the problem of communication between the central telecommunication station to each of its subsidiaries [5] Suppose that there are five subsidiaries, numbered 1, 2, 3, 4, 5, while the central station is numbered 6. We represent them using six points ①, ②,..., ⑥ on the plane; see Fig. 4.18.

If there is a communication relation between station i and station j, then we connect points i and j. This corresponds to the entries A_{ij} and A_{ji} being nonzero in the matrix. If there is a communication relation inside of station i, then it corresponds to the entry A_{ii} being nonzero. The matrix deduced from this problem is a diagonal matrix with two sides filled, as shown in Fig. 4.19. This is a sparse matrix.

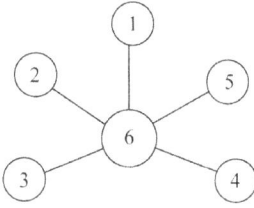

Fig. 4.18: The communication relations between the central station and its subsidiaries.

$$\begin{bmatrix} A_{11} & & & & & A_{16} \\ & A_{22} & & & & A_{26} \\ & & A_{33} & & & A_{36} \\ & & & A_{44} & & A_{46} \\ & & & & A_{55} & A_{56} \\ A_{61} & A_{62} & A_{63} & A_{64} & A_{65} & A_{66} \end{bmatrix}$$

Fig. 4.19: Diagonal matrix with two sides filled.

4.2.4.2 The compressional storage of sparse matrix

There is not one best way to store sparse matrix. Under different specific circumstances, the best way is related to the structure and usage of the matrix to be stored. A good evaluation standard is to make the elements in the matrix easy to look up and occupy little space. The storage is basically in compressed form, excluding large amounts of zero elements in the matrix from calculation, in order to reduce the processing time of the machine, and increase the ability of the machine to process problems regarding high-ranked matrices.

For the various special matrices mentioned previously, their nonzero elements are all regularly distributed; therefore, we can always find a way to store them with compression into a vector, and we can normally find the correspondence relation between the elements in the matrix and this vector. Through this relation, we can still achieve random access on elements of the matrix. In the following, we discuss the storage methods for sparse matrices whose nonzero elements are not regularly distributed.

Think and Discuss How to perform the compressional storage of sparse matrix?

Discussion: When storing sparse matrix, in order to save storage units, we will naturally think of compressional storage methods. Since the number of nonzero elements is relatively small compared with the size of the matrix, we can store just the nonzero elements. Considering the fact that nonzero elements are normally nonregularly distributed, we must also record the row and column (i, j) that element was originally in when storing it. That is to say, a triple (i, j, a_{ij}) can uniquely determine an nonzero element of matrix A. Therefore, sparse matrix can be uniquely determined by the triples representing nonzero elements and the total number of rows and columns of the matrix.

From the discussions above, we can ascertain that the principle for the compressional storage of sparse matrix is to store all the nonzero elements.

After we have ascertained the content to be stored, we can choose either sequential structure or linked structure for the method of storage.

The common forms of compressional storage of sparse matrix are (1) triple list and (2) linked list.

4.2.4.2.1 Triple list

If we order the triples that represent the nonzero elements in a sparse matrix in a row-based order, then we can obtain a linear list with all the nodes being triples. This sequential storage structure is called *triple list*.

Apparently, to uniquely determine a sparse matrix, we must also store the number of rows and columns of this matrix. They, together with the nonzero elements themselves, constitute the triple list.

Example 4.3: Store sparse matrix using triple list.
Solution: Suppose the sparse matrix is M [2, 5], as shown in Fig. 4.20.

In order to facilitate management, we can store information about the number of rows, columns and nonzero elements specifically in the 0th row of the triple list, as shown in Fig. 4.21.

$$M = \begin{bmatrix} 0 & 12 & 9 & 0 & 0 & 0 & 0 \\ 0 & 0 & 0 & 0 & 0 & 0 & 0 \\ -3 & 0 & 0 & 0 & 0 & 14 & 0 \\ 0 & 0 & 24 & 0 & 0 & 0 & 0 \\ 0 & 18 & 0 & 0 & 0 & 0 & 0 \\ 15 & 0 & 0 & -7 & 0 & 0 & 0 \end{bmatrix}$$

Fig. 4.20: Sparse matrix M.

According to Fig. 4.21, we can easily give the type description of the data structure of triple list, as shown in Fig. 4.22.

4.2.4.2.2 The linked list storage method of sparse matrix

For a sparse matrix stored as a triple list, if the positions of nonzero elements change frequently during calculations, the array elements will move frequently. Under such circumstances, a static storage structure such as triple list is not very appropriate. To solve this problem, we can adopt the storage structure of linked list. There can be various forms of linked storage based on different linking methods.

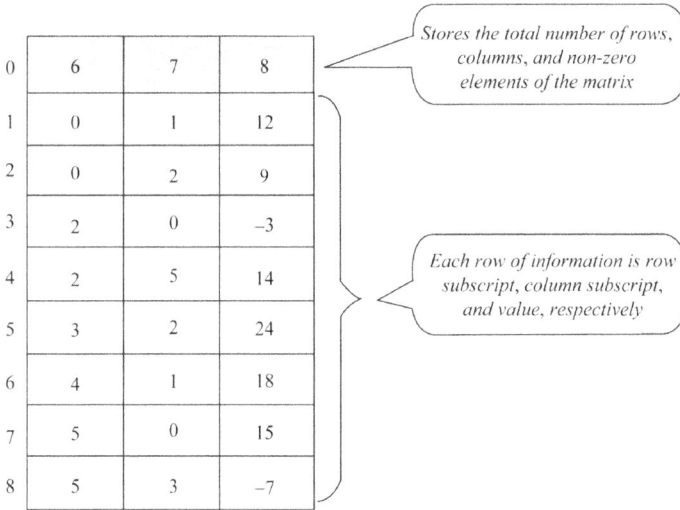

Fig. 4.21: Illustration of triple list storage structure.

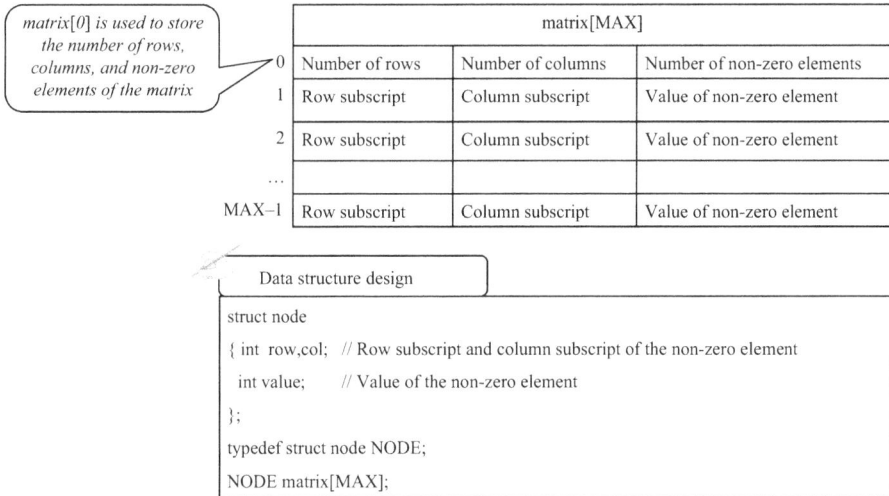

Fig. 4.22: The type description for the data structure of triple list.

1. Singly linked list with a vector of row pointers

The structural design and type description is shown in Fig. 4.23. Each nonzero element can be represented with a node. The nonzero elements of each row of the matrix can be stored in a singly linked list. When the matrix has ROW rows, then there will be ROW-linked lists. The member col of the node struct node records

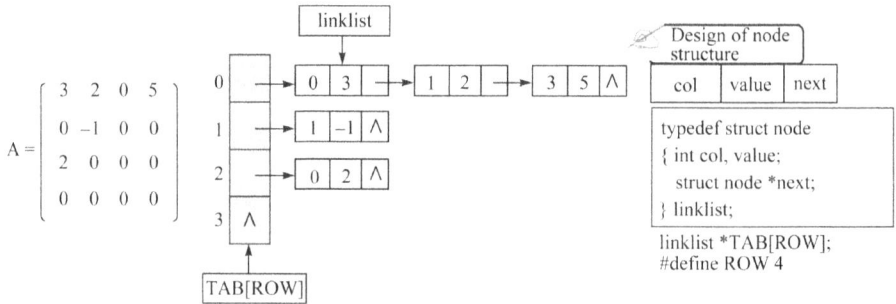

Fig. 4.23: Representation with singly linked list for sparse matrix.

the information about the column that the element is in, value records the value of the element. The information about the head addresses of all the linked lists is collected in the array TAB[ROW], which facilitates unified management.

2. Cross-shaped linked list

An example of representation with cross-shaped linked list can be seen in Fig. 4.24. It represents each nonzero element with a node. In each node, besides the triple representing the row, column and value, there are two additional fields: row pointer field right, used to point to the next nonzero element in this row; column pointer field down, used to point to the next nonzero element in this column. The structural design of the node can be seen in Fig. 4.25. The nonzero element nodes in the same row of the sparse matrix are linked via the row pointer field into a circular linked list with head node. The nonzero element nodes in the same column are linked via the column pointer field into a circular linked list with head node.

4.3 String

The early computers were mostly used for scientific and engineering calculations when invented. They processed numerical data, that is, they performed the jobs of calculators. It is just that they were more powerful and faster than normal calculators. Later, with the strengthening of the functionalities of the computers, people managed to let the computers perform jobs such as alphabet editing, machine translation and document query. All these jobs need to process sequences of text; the information to be processed is string. A string is any finite sequence of letters composed of the letters from the alphabet. This type of information is classified as nonnumerical data in data structure.

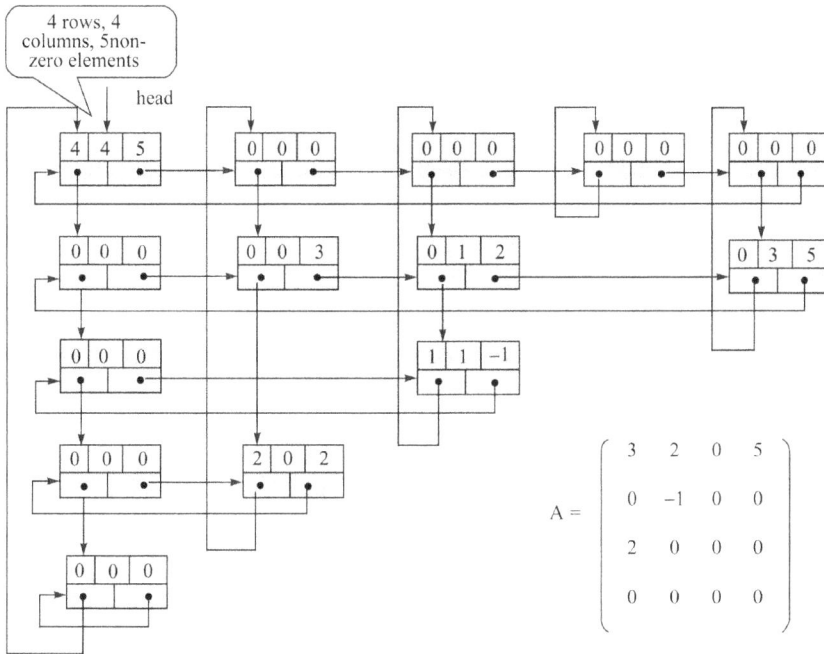

Fig. 4.24: Illustration of the structure of cross-shaped linked list.

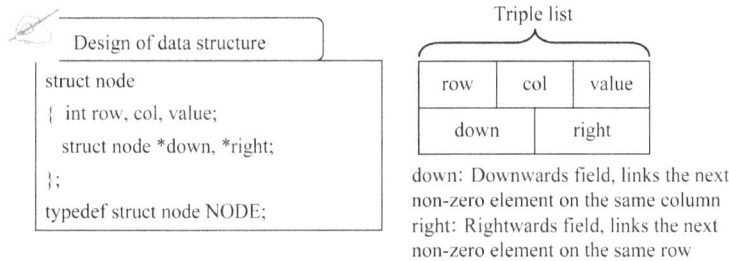

Fig. 4.25: Structure of the node in a cross-shaped linked list.

The application of string is nowadays very widespread. Many high-level languages, including C, provide string processing functionalities.

From the perspective of data structure, string is a linear list with special content. The specialness lies in the fact that the data objects are restricted to the alphabet, that is, the elements of the linear list are letters. The basic operations on linear list mostly have "single element" as object to be operated on, while the basic operations on strings usually have "the whole string" as the object to be operated on. The basic operations on strings differ significantly from those on linear lists. Thus we discuss it separately.

4.3.1 The definition of string

String is a special kind of linear list. It is a finite sequence constituted of n ($n \geq 0$) letters, noted as:

$$s = \text{``}a_1, a_2, a_3, \ldots, a_n\text{''}$$

where s is the name of the string, a_1, a_2, a_3,..., a_n is the value of the string, a_i is a letter within the string, n is the length of the string.

For example, S = "This is a string"

Note: The sequence of letters included within the quotation marks constitutes the value of the string. The quotation marks themselves are not a component of the string.

The above is string defined from the perspective of data structure. From the perspective of programming language, we can have this definition: string is a complex data structure constituted of zero or multiple letters listed in order.

The various scenarios and examples of string can be seen in Fig. 4.26.

Examples of string	Length of string n	Note
"This is a string"	16	Space is also a character
"string"	6	
" "	1	String of spaces: String constituted only of one or multiple spaces
""	0	Empty string: String with length 0 is called empty string. It doesn't include any characters.
"你好"	4	The characters included in the string can be letters, numbers or other characters. This depends on the character set allowed by the specific computer/programming language.

Fig. 4.26: Examples of string.

Note that the strings with values of spaces are not the same as empty strings. String of spaces has contents and nonzero length, and it can contain more than one spaces. The string with one single character is not the same as one single character itself. In C language, strings have a termination indicator.

There are some other concepts to be explained. For example, for the sentences below:

Even friendship may come to an end.

Even when you believe in someone, lies may exist.

The "end," "lie" here can actually be considered as the substrings of strings of words "friend," "believe." Some concepts of string are as follows.

4.3.1.1 Substring
The subsequence constituted of any continuous characters in the string is called the *substring of this string.*

For example, c = "DATA STRUCTURE", f = "DATA," f is a substring of c.

4.3.1.2 The position of the substring

The location of substring t in the main string s refers to the position of the first letter of the first substring, which is the same as t in the main string.

Example: s = "ababccabcac", t = "abc". The location of substring t in the main string s is 2 (the index starts from 0).

4.3.1.3 Equivalence of string

The two strings are equal, if and only if the two strings have the same length, and the characters at each corresponding position are the same.

Since many high-level languages provide functionalities to operate on strings, we do not describe operations on strings here in details. However, due to the importance and widespread use of string-matching (string-searching) algorithms, we specifically introduce them here.

4.3.2 The storage structure of string

Since string is a special type of linear list, with each of its nodes constituting of one character, it can also be stored in sequential storage or linked storage.

4.3.2.1 The sequential storage of string

The most common way to store string is sequential storage, that is, storing the characters in the string in order in continuous memory space. This is called *sequential string*.

Think and Discuss Is there any difference in the design of storage structure between sequential list and sequential string?
Discussion: We can first review the storage structure of sequential list:

```
typedef struct
{
  ElemType   data[LIST_SIZE];
  int last;
} SequenList;
```

The setup of the backup space in the sequential list is to allow for some space for extension when new elements are inserted. Since there is backup space, the actual length of the string is a parameter that must be already known when storing the string. We can design the following storage plan.

1. Use one pointer to indicate the position of the last character.
2. Use a counter to record the number of string elements directly.
3. Add an end indicator at the end of the string: store at the end of the string a special character that will not appear within the string, in order to indicate the end of the string. C language uses this method to deal with strings with fixed lengths. It uses "\0" to indicate the end of a string. By searching for the end indicator, we can get the length of the string indirectly.

Storage plan 1 of sequential string: use a pointer to indicate the last character, as shown in Fig. 4.27.

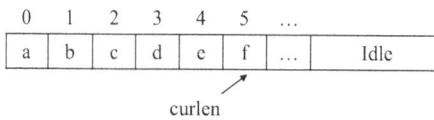

Fig. 4.27: Storage plan 1 of sequential string.

Description of structure:

```
typedef struct
{
  char data[MAXSIZE];
  int   curlen;          // Record the subscript of the last character
} SeqString;
```

Storage plan 2 of sequential string: directly record the length of the string, as shown in Fig. 4.28.

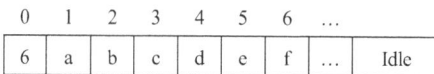

Fig. 4.28: Storage plan 2 for sequential string.

Structure description: char s[MAXSIZE+1];

Note: We use s[0] to store the actual length of the string, the value of the string is stored in s[1]~s[MAXSIZE]. The index of the character corresponds with the storage location. We save the length of the string and the value of the string in the same array, so that the management and calculation will be more convenient.

Storage plan 3 of sequential string: store a special character at the end of the string as the end indicator for the string. In C language the "\0" will be automatically added as the end indicator of the string. It is convenient to directly utilize this functionality, as shown in Fig. 4.29.

0	1	2	3	4	5	6	
a	b	c	d	e	f	\0	Idle

Fig. 4.29: Storage plan 3 for sequential string.

Structure description: char s[MAXSIZE+1];
   Note: MAXSIZE is the length of the string, while "\0" occupies another position.

4.3.2.2 The block link storage structure of string

In sequential string, we need to define the maximum length of the string in advance. This will restrict some of the operations on the string, for example, the concatenation, insertion and replacement. In addition, the insertion and deletion operations on sequential string are inconvenient, since they need to move a large amount of characters. According to the characteristic of the linked storage of linear list, we can store the value of the string using singly linked list. The linked storage structure of string is called *linked string*. The difference between linked string and singly-linked list is only that the data field of each node is a character. Figure 4.30 shows the linked list and its data structure design when the data field of each node has a size of 1.

Linked string with node size of 1

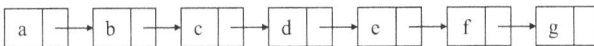

Data structure design
```
typedef struct linknode
{ char data;
  struct linknode *next;
} linkstring;
```

Fig. 4.30: Block link storage structure with single character per node.

! **Think and Discuss** What are the advantages of disadvantages of the linked string structure? **Discussion:** Each linked node will only store one character. Operations such as insertion, deletion and length calculation will be very convenient, but the storage efficiency will be low.

One way for improvement can be to store multiple characters in one single linked node. This can improve the storage efficiency. This is effective when processing big strings with uncertain lengths. This is a compromise between sequential string and linked string, called *block link structure*. The illustration is in Fig. 4.31.

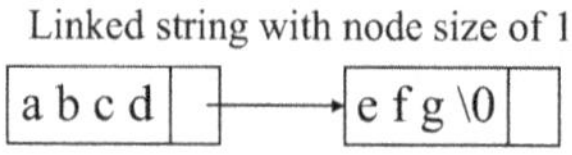

Linked string with node size of 1

```
| a b c d | •|——————→| e f g \0 | |
```

Data structure design

```
typedef struct linknode
{ char data[4];
    struct linknode *next;
} linkstring;
```

Fig. 4.31: Block link storage structure with multiple characters per node.

In actual applications, we can set the size of the node according to the need of the problem. For example, in editors, the whole editing area can be viewed as a string, while each row is a substring, which constitutes a node. That is to say, the string on the same row uses a fixed length structure (80 characters), while rows are connected with pointers.

Since the length of the string is not necessarily an exact multiple of the size of the node, the last node of the linked list will not necessarily be totally occupied by the contents of the string. We can just use "\0" as a filler in this case.

Example 4.4: On a linked string with a node size of 4 "abcdefg," we want to insert "xyz" after the *n*th character. For example, *n* = 3, which corresponds to the character c in the linked string. Design the plan for insertion.
Solution: There are usually two types of insertion plans, "seamless insertion" and "insertion with seam," as shown in Fig. 4.32.

In situation (a), we inserted string xyz "seamlessly" into the required position *n* = 3, that is, in the linked list after insertion, except for the last node, data in other nodes will all have four characters. We will want to consider adapting to all kinds of insertion locations without loss of generality, which will make the calculation quite inconvenient.

In situation (b), we can use a special symbol (□ in the figure), for example space, to fill in nodes not fully utilized. In this scenario the processing will be relatively simple.

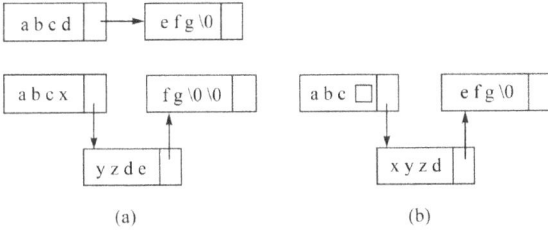

Fig. 4.32: Insertion on linked string.

4.3.2.3 The indexed storage method of string

We use the name of the string variable as the keyword to organize this index list. In the list, the name of the string and the values of the string correspond one by one. There are multiple ways for indexed storage.

1. String index list with length information

$$\text{Let: } S1 = \text{"please"}, S2 = \text{"seek"}$$

The illustration of the storage can be seen in Fig. 4.33. We record the beginning address and length of each string and put them in the index – an array structure, to facilitate management.

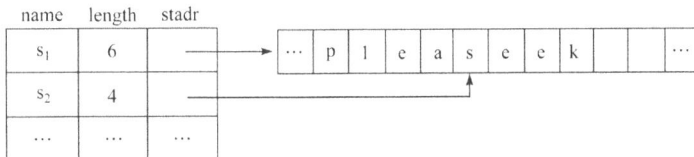

Fig. 4.33: String index list with length information.

Structure description:

```
typedef struct
{
    char name[maxsize];// Name of the string
    int length; // Length of the string
    char * stadr; // Beginning address of the string
} lnode;
```

2. String index list with head and rear pointers

Let S1 ="abcdefg", S2 ="bcd"

We set two pointers for one string, one points to the beginning of the string, the other points to the end. The illustration of the storage is shown in Fig. 4.34.

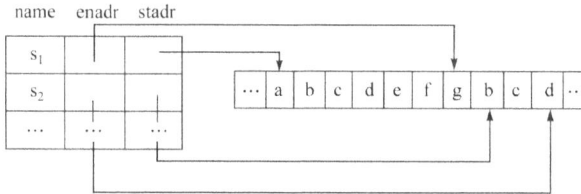

Fig. 4.34: String index list with head and rear pointers.

Structure description:

```
typedef struct
{
  char name[maxsize]; // Name of the string
  char *stadr;        // Address of the beginning of the string
  char *enadr;        // Address of the end of the string
} enode;
```

3. String index list with label variable

Let S1="abcdefg", S2="bcd"

The illustration of the storage can be seen in Fig. 4.35. We set a label variable tag to indicate whether we stored the address of the string or the content of the string. Such a design can facilitate the operations on relatively short strings.

```
typedef struct
{
  char name[maxsize];
  int  tag;                // Feature variable
  union
  {
    char *stadr;           // Label variable is 0, we store the beginning address
    of the string
    char value[4];         // Label variable is 1, we store the value of the string
  } uval;
} tagnode;
```

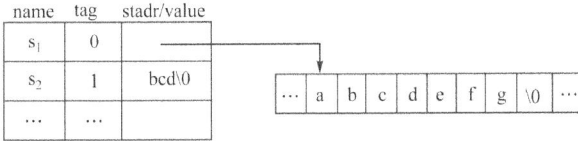

Fig. 4.35: String index list with label variable.

4. Linked string index list

Let S1="GOOD", S2="DAY"

The illustration of the storage can be seen in Fig. 4.36.

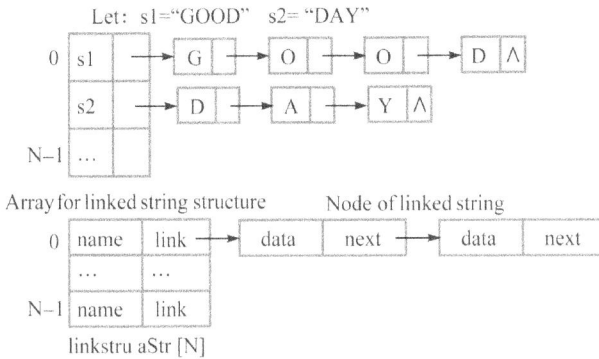

Fig. 4.36: Linked string index list.

```
//Definition of the node
typedef struct linknode
{
  char data;
  struct linknode *next;
} linkstring;
//Definition of the array
typedef struct
{
  char name[maxsize]; //Name of the string
  linkstring *link;
} linkstru;
linkstru aStr [N];
```

4.3.3 Search on strings – pattern matching

A common operation when we browse the web is to search for information we are interested in. For this purpose we use search engines. If we enter the keyword "data structure string," the webpage will list the information containing the keyword; see Fig. 4.37 [1]. Here, the website performed a search and matching on the string. Pattern matching algorithm is key to a search engine, it directly impacts the real-time performance of the system.

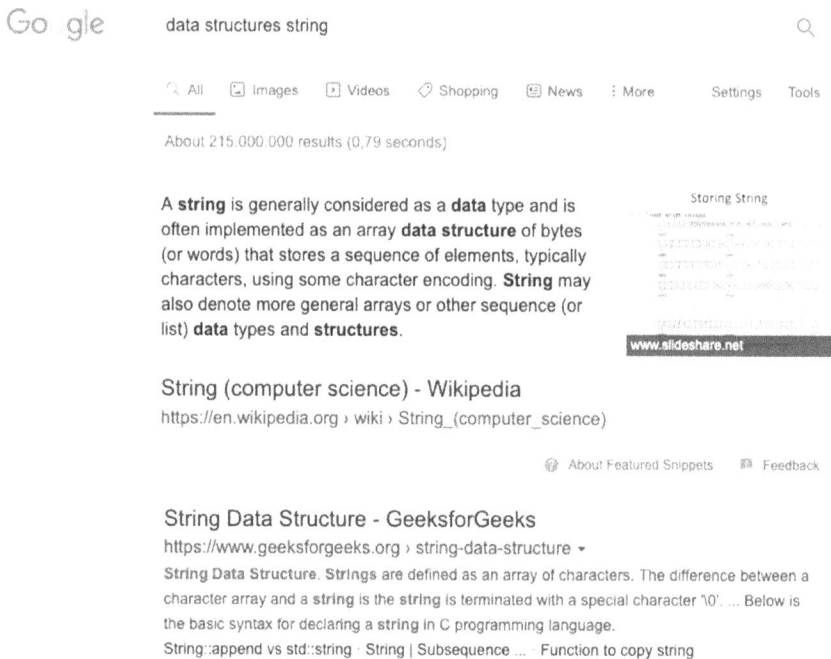

Go gle   data structures string

🔍 All   🖼 Images   ▶ Videos   ♡ Shopping   📰 News   ⋮ More   Settings   Tools

About 215.000.000 results (0,79 seconds)

A **string** is generally considered as a **data** type and is often implemented as an array **data structure** of bytes (or words) that stores a sequence of elements, typically characters, using some character encoding. **String** may also denote more general arrays or other sequence (or list) **data** types and **structures**.

Storing String

www.slideshare.net

String (computer science) - Wikipedia
https://en.wikipedia.org › wiki › String_(computer_science)

❔ About Featured Snippets   📷 Feedback

String Data Structure - GeeksforGeeks
https://www.geeksforgeeks.org › string-data-structure ▾
String Data Structure. Strings are defined as an array of characters. The difference between a character array and a **string** is the **string** is terminated with a special character '\0'. ... Below is the basic syntax for declaring a string in C programming language.
String::append vs std::string · String | Subsequence ... · Function to copy string

Fig. 4.37: Search results from the search engine.

ℹ

Term Explanation Pattern matching
The locating operation of the substring (pattern string) in the main string (target string) is also called *string matching*.

Suppose that there are two strings S and T. The locating of substring is to find out a substring in main string S that is identical to substring T.

Normally, we call the main string S "target string," and the substring T "pattern string." We call the locating process of substring T in target string S the "pattern matching" of string.

There are two results of pattern matching: matching success or matching failure. If we find a substring with pattern T within the main string S, then we return the starting position of substring T in S. When there are multiple substrings with pattern T in S, we usually only find out the beginning position of the first substring.

Knowledge ABC Matching algorithms

The application of matching algorithms is very broad. Examples include searching for virus strings in a file, searching for indicators of an attack in web data packs, searching for keyword or data in a database, searching for the position of a certain word in a word processing program, matching DNA in computational biology and so on. Such searching operations usually involve a huge amount of data, and require a high level of performance.

In many applications, the matching of string constitutes a large portion of operations (as high as 60%–70%). Therefore, the speed of string matching algorithm largely impacts the performance of the whole system.

There has been more than 30 years of research on string matching algorithms. Famous algorithms include BF algorithm, KMP algorithm, BM algorithm, BMH algorithm, RK algorithm and SUNDAY algorithm. Computer scientists have recently come up with a lot of excellent algorithms, such as Aho-Corasick algorithm, Wu-Manber algorithm. AC algorithm is an extension of KMP algorithm in multimodal matching. Wu-Manber is based on the ideas in BM algorithm.

Although string matching is a very classic problem, it faces huge challenges nowadays on its performance. Classic algorithms are not able to satisfy the requirements anymore. Improving string matching algorithms and increasing speed of query is an important field of research in algorithms.

The matching of string is a relatively complex operation on strings. There are various solutions with different efficiencies. Here we only introduce the BF pattern matching algorithm and an improved algorithm based on BF algorithm – KMP pattern matching algorithm.

4.3.3.1 BF algorithm

We first discuss the most simple string matching algorithm, brute force algorithm, which can be abbreviated as BF algorithm. It has relatively low efficiency.

1. The analysis of ideas behind BF algorithm

We match the first character of the target string S with the first character of the pattern string T. If they are equal, then we continue to compare the second character of S and the second character of T. If they are not equal, then we compare the second character of S and the first character of T and so on, until we get the final result.

The following is an actual example of the matching process of BF algorithm, as shown in Fig. 4.38.

Let S = "ababcabcacbab", T = "abcac"

The description of general steps of comparison is below.

Substring T	a	b	c	a	c								
	0	1	2	3	4	5	6	7	8	9	10	11	12
Main String S	a	b	a	b	c	a	b	c	a	c	b	a	b
step1	a	b	c										
step2		a											
step3			a	b	c	a	c						
step4				a									
step5					a								
step6						a	b	c	a	c			

Fig. 4.38: The matching process on strings of BF algorithm.

We start from the beginning of both S and T, and compare the characters at each corresponding position in order. If they are not equal, then we record the subscript of the nonequal characters, and start the comparison again. If they are all equal, then the match is found, and the algorithm stops. If even after we have scanned the whole string S, we still cannot find a scenario of full match, then there is not any match.

Step 1: Compare the characters at each corresponding position of S and T. At the subscript "2," the character "c" in T is not equal to the character "a" in S. The character "c" is noted in gray. After we record the ending positions of S and T (see Fig. 4.39), we enter the next step (Step 2).

Step 2: Move T by one position, compare S and T from the beginning. The processing is the same as in Step 1.

		step1	step2	step3	step4	step5	step6
Starting position	Main string subscript i	0	1	2	3	4	5
	Sub-string subscript j	0	0	0	0	0	0
End position	i	2	1	6	3	4	9
	j	2	0	4	0	0	4

Fig. 4.39: Record of the ending positions during the process of BF matching.

From Fig. 4.40 we can trace the change of the subscript i of the main string.

For each new comparison, the substring starts from 0. Sometimes we need to backtrace for the relation between the position of the main string to start comparison again and the position it ended at the last time. That is to say, we need to move backward from the position it ended at the last time, that is, "backtrace" to a previous position. For example, the ending position of Step 1 is 2, the beginning position of Step 2 is 1; the ending position of Step 3 is 6, the beginning position of Step 4 is 3. Of course there are also moments without backtracking, for example, the ending

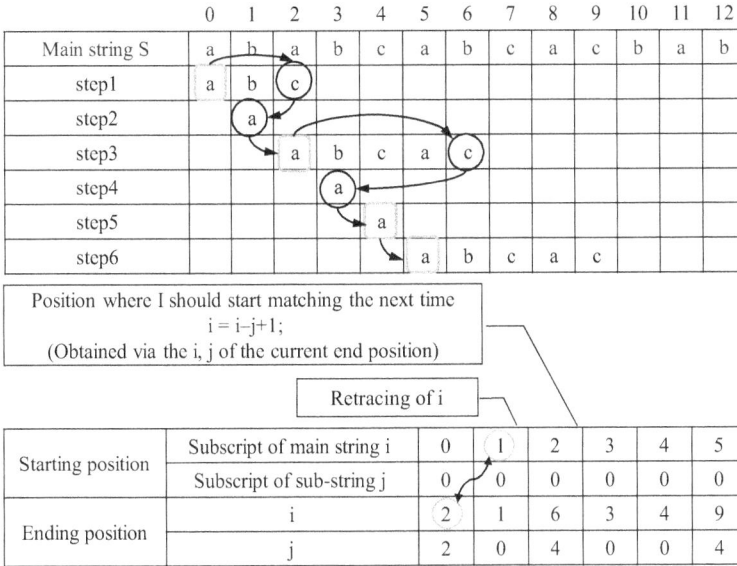

	0	1	2	3	4	5	6	7	8	9	10	11	12
Main string S	a	b	a	b	c	a	b	c	a	c	b	a	b
step1	a	b	c										
step2		a											
step3			a	b	c	a	c						
step4				a									
step5					a								
step6						a	b	c	a	c			

Position where I should start matching the next time
$i = i-j+1$;
(Obtained via the i, j of the current end position)

Retracing of i

Starting position	Subscript of main string i	0	1	2	3	4	5
	Subscript of sub-string j	0	0	0	0	0	0
Ending position	i	2	1	6	3	4	9
	j	2	0	4	0	0	4

Fig. 4.40: The position analysis of the matching process of BF.

position of Step 2 is 1, the beginning position of Step 3 is 2; the ending position of Step 4 is 3, the beginning position of Step 5 is 4. According to the current ending values of *i* and *j*, we can deduce that the position formula for *i* in the new round of matching is $i = i - j + 1$.

2. The design framework of the function is listed in Table. 4.1.

Table 4.1: The design framework of the function for BF algorithm 1.

Functionality description	Input		Output
index BF pattern matching	Contents of main string S	Int	No match: −1
	Contents of substring T		Match: The position of the substring in the main string
Function name	Parameters		Function type

3. The pseudocode description of the algorithm can be seen in Table. 4.2.

Table 4.2: Pseudocode for BF algorithm 1.

First-level elaboration	Second-level elaboration
Initialization	Set the subscript of main string S $i = 0$; the subscript of substring T $j = 0$
Compare the first character of the main string S and the pattern T	When i, j are smaller than the lengths of S, T respectively
First-level elaboration	Second-level elaboration
If they are the same, then continue to compare subsequent characters	If: Si matches Tj, then i++, j++;
Otherwise, starting from the next character of the main string S, compare the characters of pattern T again	Otherwise: Set i, j as the positions where the next matching should start Main string: $i = i-j+1$; substring: $j = 0$
Until the whole string T is scanned	If T string is totally scanned, then we return "match"
Return the result	Otherwise, return "No match"

4. Description of data structure

```
#define MaxSize 100
typedef struct
{ char ch[ MaxSize ];
  int len;
} SqString;
```

5. Program implementation

```
/*=========================================================================
Functionality of the function: BF Algorithm - Calculate whether the pattern T
is matched in the target string S
Function input: Target string S, Pattern string T
Function output: Successful match: Return the position of first occurrence of
pattern string T in S. Unsuccessful: Return -1


=========================================================================*/
```

```
int index( SqString s, SqString t )
{    int i=0, j=0, k;
     while ( i < s.len && j < t.len ) // i, j within normal range?
     {
        if ( s.ch[i] == t.ch [j] ) //If the characters are equal, continue
        {
            i++; j++;
            //Main string and substring match the next character respectively
        }
        else    //Reset the pointers for main string and substring
        {
            i=i-j+1; //Start the matching on main string from the next position
            j=0;        //Start the matching on substring from its beginning
        }
     }
     if ( j >= t.len) k=i - t.len;
     //Return the subscript of the first character matched
     else     k = -1; //Pattern matching is not successful
     return k;
}
```

6. Analysis of algorithm efficiency
Set N is the length of string S, M is the length of string T.

(1) Best-case scenario
Let us analyze through an actual example.

Example 4.5: Analyze the number of executions of BF algorithm when given the strings S and T. The strings S and T are respectively:

S ="abcdgggkh"   (N=9)
T ="gggk"   (M=4)

Discussion on the general case for best-case scenario: see Fig. 4.41, each unsuccessful matching occurs immediately when the first character of pattern T and the corresponding character in string S.

Suppose that the matching is successful from the ith position of S, then the total number of character comparisons in the previous $i - 1$ matchings is $i - 1$. When the matching succeeds at the ith attempt, the total number of comparisons of characters is M. Therefore, the total number of comparisons is $i - 1 + M$. Since when the

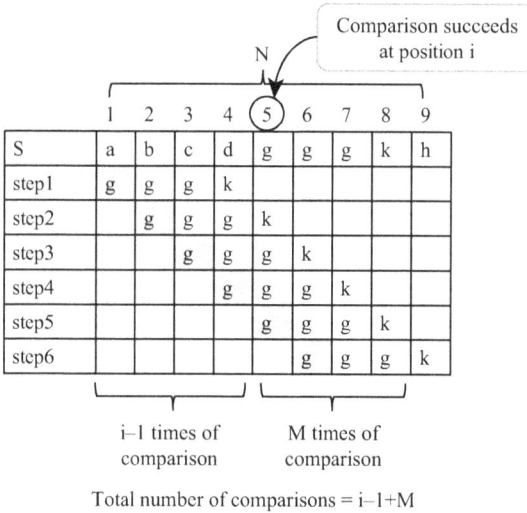

Fig. 4.41: Analysis of matching under the best case.

matching succeeds, the beginning position of S can only be between 1 and
N − M + 1, if for all these N − M + 1 beginning positions, the probabilities of a successful match are all equally P_i, then under the best-case scenario, the average
number of comparisons C_{min} is

$$C_{min} = \sum_{i=1}^{n-m+1} P_i \times (i-1+m) = \frac{1}{n-m+1} \sum_{i=1}^{n-m+1} (i-1+m) = \frac{n+m}{2}$$

Therefore, the average time complexity of the algorithm under the best-case scenario is O(N + M). (Note: Here the uppercase and lower-case n and m have the same
meaning.)

(2)   Worst-case scenario

Example 4.6: Analyze the number of executions of BF algorithm when given the strings S and T.
The strings S and T are, respectively:

S = "gggggggk" (N=9)
T = "gggk"   (M=4)

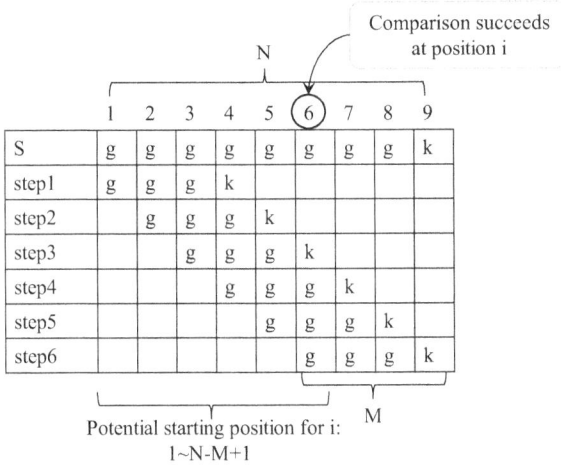

Fig. 4.42: Analysis of the matching under worst-case scenario.

In Fig. 4.42, since all the first three characters of T can be matched in S, but the fourth character of T cannot be matched in S, therefore each failed matching will incur $M = 4$ comparisons, before we move the pointer i to the second character of S. The result is the first three characters of T can find matchings in S, while the fourth character cannot find any matching in S. Continuing our comparison, the total number of comparisons is $N - M + 1 = 9 - 4 + 1 = 6$, while each time we need to compare 4 times ($M = 4$). Therefore, the total number of comparisons is $4 \times (9 - 4 + 1) = 24$.

Discussion on the general case of the worst-case scenario: in Fig. 4.42, each failed matching occurs only after the last character of pattern string T is found to be not equal to the corresponding character in S. Before the new matching begins, the pointer i must backtrace to the position $i - M + 2$.

Under such a situation, if the ith matching is successful, then in the $i - 1$ unsuccessful matchings before, each failed matching incurs M comparisons. Therefore, the total number of character comparisons is $(i - 1) \times M$. The ith matching, which is successful, also incurs M comparisons. Therefore, in total there are $M \times i$ comparisons.

If for all these $N - M + 1$ beginning positions, the probabilities of successful match are equal and are expressed as P_i, then under the worst-case scenario, the average number of comparisons for successful match C_{max} will be:

$$C_{max} = \sum_{i=1}^{n-m+1} P_i \times (i \times m) = \frac{m}{n-m+1} \sum_{i=1}^{n-m+1} i = \frac{m(n-m+2)}{2}$$

If N is much greater than M, then under the worst-case scenario the time complexity of this algorithm is $O(M \times N)$, that is, the magnitude of the product of the lengths of two strings. (Note: Here the uppercase and lower-case n and m have the same meaning.)

Example 4.7: The implementation of BF algorithm on linked string.
Using singly linked list with node size of 1 as the storage structure of strings, to realize brute force matching algorithm. If the matching is successful, then we return the node address pointed to by the effective positional shift. Otherwise we return the empty pointer, as shown in Fig. 4.43.

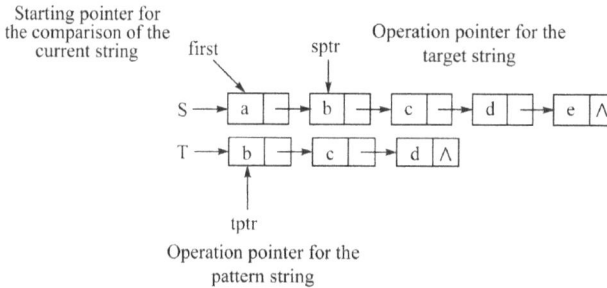

Fig. 4.43: Linked string.

Analysis: When we use singly linked list with node size 1 as the storage structure of the string, it is very easy to implement brute force matching algorithm. It is just that the current positional shift is on node address instead of on integers, and there is not any length information stored in the singly linked list. If the matching is successful, then we return the node address pointed to by the effective positional shift. Otherwise we return the empty pointer.

1. The function framework design is listed in Table. 4.3.

Table 4.3: Function framework design of BF algorithm 2.

Functionality description	Input	Output
BF pattern matching IndexL	Address of main string s	The position of substring in the main string
	Address of substring t	
Function name	Parameters	Function type

2. Description of data structure

```
typedef struct node
{  char ch;
   struct node *next;
} LinkString;
```

3. Pseudocode description is given in Table 4.4.

Table 4.4: Pseudocode for BF algorithm 2.

Detailed description of pseudocode
Suppose sptr points to the position in the main string S where comparison begins, tptr points to the beginning address of the substring;
While (both strings have not been processed to the end)
If (sptr node = tptr node)
sptr and tptr moves to point to the next node
Detailed description of pseudocode
Otherwise first moves to point to the next node to begin comparison with
sptr points to the position in the main string S where comparison begins sptr, tptr points to the beginning address of the substring;
If tptr already points to the end of the link, then the search is finished; we have "match," returns first
Otherwise "No match," return NULL

4. Program implementation

```
/*=====================================================================
Function functionality: The implementation of BF algorithm on linked string
Function input: The beginning address of the target linked list of string, the
beginning address of the pattern linked list
Function output: The address of the matching point
=====================================================================*/
linkstring *IndexL(linkstring *S,  linkstring *T)
// S: Target string T: Pattern string
{
   linkstring *first, *sptr, *tptr;

   first=S;  sptr = first;  tptr=T; // Set comparison address
   while (sptr && tptr)
   // Both strings have not been compared to the end
   {
      if (sptr->data==tptr->data)
      // The characters in two strings are equal
      {  sptr=sptr->next;
         tptr=tptr->next;
      }
```

```
        else                        // The characters in two strings are not
    equal. Reset the comparison address
        {   first=first->next;
            sptr=first;
            tptr=T;
        }
    }
    if (tptr==NULL) return(first); // Match
    else return(NULL);             // No match
}
```

4.3.3.2 KMP algorithm

BF algorithm is simple and easy to understand, but its efficiency is low. The main reason is that when one character is not equal after several characters are matched to be equal, the main string pointer i still needs backtracking, that is, $i = i + 1 - j$. There is a backtracking of j positions.

KMP algorithm improves the backtracking issue. This improved algorithm was proposed together by D. E. Knuth, V. R. Prett and J. H. Morris. Therefore people call it *Knuth–Morris–Prett operation* (abbreviated as KMP algorithm).

1. The basic ideas of KMP algorithm

The following is an actual example of the matching process of KMP algorithm. Observe where the improvement exactly lies. The matching process is shown in Fig. 4.44.

Let S = "ababcabcacbab", T = "abcac."

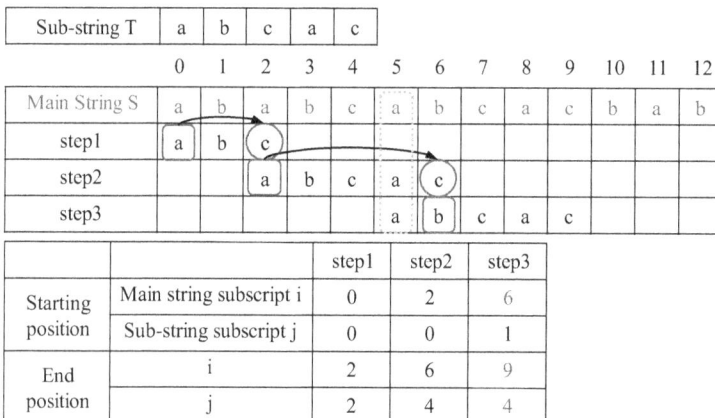

Sub-string T	a	b	c	a	c
	0	1	2	3	4

		0	1	2	3	4	5	6	7	8	9	10	11	12
Main String S		a	b	a	b	c	a	b	c	a	c	b	a	b
step1		a	b	c										
step2				a	b	c	a	c						
step3							a	b	c	a	c			

		step1	step2	step3
Starting position	Main string subscript i	0	2	6
	Sub-string subscript j	0	0	1
End position	i	2	6	9
	j	2	4	4

Fig. 4.44: The matching process of KMP algorithm on string.

Step 1:   When $i = 2$, the comparison ends.

Step 2:   Note that S string starts to be compared with at $i = 2$. This is different from BF algorithm. In BF algorithm, no matter where the last step ended at, the new starting position of i is always one position after the ending position of the last step. In KMP algorithm, i moved for 2 positions.

Why does i start at position 2 in the second comparison, that is, "jumps" for two grids, instead of one?

Because in the comparison of Step 1, we already know that S[1] = "b" and T[0] = "a"; therefore there is no need to compare these two characters again, and we can move i further by another position.

When the starting position $i = 2$ – the ending position of last time, $j = 0$; the ending positions this time are $i = 6$; $j = 4$.

Step 3:   The starting position $i = 6$ – the ending position of last time, $j = 1$.

Note that this time string T does not start comparison from 0, but from 1. Why so?

Because in Step 2, we already compared S[5] and know it to be "a," which is equal to the value at position 3 of T. If we follow the regularity of the ending position of i at the last time, that is, the starting position of this time, then the starting position of S should be 6. In the string T, the character at position 0 is also "a"; thus we would not need to compare it with S[5] again, but start the comparison directly from the position 1 of T.

The idea of KMP algorithm is: try to utilize the already obtained "partial match" result, and not move the "search position" of the main string back to already compared position, but move further onward on this foundation, that is, do not backtrack the positional pointer i of main string s. Thus, the search efficiency is increased.

Another change introduced by this is that the positional pointer j of pattern string T cannot start from the beginning every time, but should be decided by the position when a "mismatch" occurs. This is the key point of KMP algorithm.

Think and Discuss Using the above combination of S and T, we can see that the efficiency of KMP algorithm is increased considerably compared with that of BF algorithm. Does this have anything to do with the arrangement of the S and T in this example, that is, there are some factors of coincidence?

Discussion: We can do further tests with other samples. See the example below.

Example 4.8: Perform matching test on strings with the idea of KMP algorithm.

Let: T = "abcabcacab" S = "babcbabcabcaabcabcabcacabc"

The string matching process of KMP algorithm is shown in Fig. 4.45.

	0	1	2	3	4	5	6	7	8	9	10	11	12	13	14	15	16	17	18	19	20	21	22	23	24	25
T	a	b	c	a	b	c	a	c	a	b																
S	b	a	b	c	b	a	b	c	a	b	c	a	a	b	c	a	b	c	a	b	c	a	c	a	b	c
step1	a																									
step2		a	b	c	a																					
step3					a																					
step4						a	b	c	a	b	c	a	c													
step5									a	b	c	a	b													
step6												a	b													
step7													a	b	c	a	b	c	a	c						
step8																				a	b	c	a	b	c	a	b

		step1	step2	step3	step4	step5	step6	step7	step8
Starting position	Main string *i*	0	1	4	5	12	12	12	19
	Sub - string *j*	0	0	0	0	4	1	0	4
End position	*i*	0	4	4	12	12	12	19	24
	j	0	3	0	7	4	1	7	9

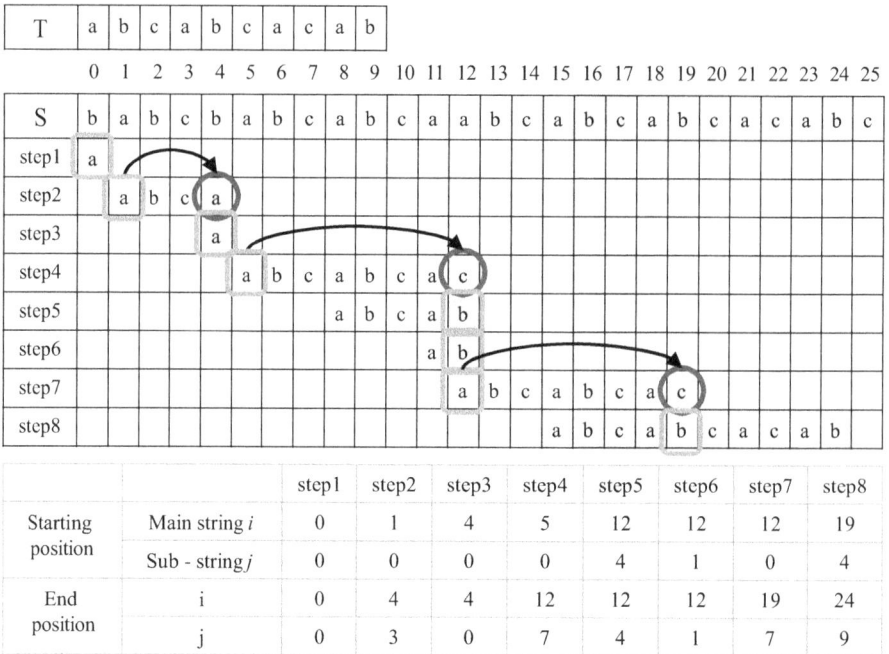

Fig. 4.45: KMP matching test example.

The analysis of steps of matching:

Step 3: The starting position of i is 4, and its ending position is also 4. If $j = 0$, then when the next step begins, we must add 1 to the starting position of i.

Step 5: The starting position of i is 12, the starting position of j is 4. Because in Step 4 the ending position of i is 12, its first 4 characters are "abca," which are the same as the four beginning characters of string T; therefore, in Step 5, we can just set the starting position of j to 4. We can say, when the ending position of string T is 7, the next time the starting position of string T will be 4.

Step 6: Similar to Step 5, when the ending position of string T is 4, the string before is "a," which is the same as the starting prefix of T "a"; therefore the comparison on T next time can start from the "b" after this "a." Therefore the starting position is 1.

Step 8: Repeat the process in Step 5.

Observation: each time after the comparison ends, we can skip the parts that are the same in the already compared substring.

Knowledge ABC The prefix and suffix of strings

The prefix of a string indicates an arbitrary beginning part of the string (excluding the last character). For example, the prefix of the string "abbc" includes "a," "ab," "abb." The suffix of a string is arbitrary ending part of the string (excluding the first character). The suffixes of "abbc" include "c," "bc," "bbc."

"Prefix" indicates all combinations of the head of a string excluding the last character. "Suffix" indicates all combinations of the end of a string excluding the first character.

Through the analysis above, we can summarize the rules for ascertaining the next starting position of string T to be used for comparison: The condition with which string T terminated at a certain position influences its starting position next time. Specifically, it is related to the number of characters found to be repeatedly equal before, that is, when the string before the ending location j has k positions of equivalence between its prefix and its postfix $(0 < k < j)$, then the starting position of the next time will be k.

In Step 4 shown in Fig. 4.45, the ending position of T $j = 7$. The corresponding character is "c," and the content of string before it is "abcabca." The suffix "abca" is found to be in its prefix as well; therefore, $k = 4$. Note that although we also have suffix "a" that is found in the prefix, this time $k' = 1$, $k' < k$, then apparently we will have a higher matching efficiency if we choose the larger k value. The analysis on the relation between the prefix and suffix of the substring of pattern string T can be seen in Fig. 4.46.

Length of sub-string j	2	3		4			5				6					...
Length of pre/postfix	1	1	2	1	2	3	1	2	3	4	1	2	3	4	5	
Prefix of substring	a	a	ab	a	ab	abc	a	ab	abc	abca	a	ab	abc	abca	abcab	
Postfix of substring	b	c	bc	a	ca	bca	b	ab	cab	bcab	c	bc	abc	cabc	bcabc	
The same string length k				1				2					3			

Fig. 4.46: The analysis of the relation between the prefix and suffix of the substring of pattern string.

We can give out the value of the next starting position when each character in string T is used as the ending position, see Fig. 4.47. Here, the j value is the ending position, and the next[j] value is the next starting position.

j	0	1	2	3	4	5	6	7	8	9
T[j]	a	b	c	a	b	c	a	c	a	b
next[j]	−1	0	0	0	1	2	3	4	0	1

Fig. 4.47: The position of next in string T.

Finally, we discuss some special cases.

(1) $j = 0$, $k = -1 - \text{next}[j] = -1$:

It represents when the ending position $j = 0$, the next starting position $j = 0$, $i = i + 1$. The corresponding scenario can be found at the beginning statuses of Steps 2 and 4 in Fig. 4.45.

(2) $j = 1$, $k = 0 - \text{next}[j] = 0$:

Since there is a restriction of $0<k<j$, therefore here the situation of $k = 0$ is an exceptional case.

It represents when the ending position $j = 1$, the next starting position $j = 0$. Without loss of generality, we give the definition of function $\text{next}[j]$:

$$\text{next}[j] = \begin{cases} \max\{k \mid 0, k, j, \text{ and } "t_0 t_1 \cdots t_{k-1}" = "t_{j-k} t_{j-k+1} \cdots t_{j-1}"\} & \text{when this set is} \\ & \text{nonempty Other} \\ 0 & \\ -1 & \text{situations } when\, j \text{ is } 0 \end{cases}$$

Note:
- j represents the ending position of comparison on the substring T. This corresponds to the situation where the first j characters in T are equal. We call it j string. i represents the ending position of the main string S.
- "$t_0 t_1 t_2 \cdots t_{k-1}$" represents the k prefixes of string j, which is represented with jPre.
- "$t_{j-k} t_{j-k+1} \cdots t_{j-1}$" represents the k suffixes of string j, which is represented with jSuf.

Under various scenarios, the meaning of next is listed in Table 4.5.

Table 4.5: The meaning next.

Scenario	Value of j	Value of next[j]	Meaning
jPre = jSuf	Non-0	k	The next comparison starts from si and tk
jPre and jSuf do not exist	Non-0	0	The next comparison starts from si and t0
The first character compared between s and t is already not equal	0	−1	The next comparison will start from si+1 and t_0

Note that there are two methods to obtain the value of next[j].

Method 1: When $j = 0$, next[j] = 0. In other cases it will be 1 – this suits systems whose array indices start from 1.

Method 2: When $j = 0$, next$[j] = \_1$. In other cases it will be 0 – this suits systems whose array indices start from 0.

In the definition of next function, we can obtain the formula for the scenario where the set is nonempty via a list that gives its various potential scenarios, as shown in Fig. 4.48. Here, $t0$ represents $t[0]$ and so on. The values of j and k can be obtained according to the relation $0 < k < j$.

(1) The item $j = 1$ is a special case. Since $0 < k < j$, therefore k cannot be given the value 0, and thus belongs to "other scenarios" in next function. In Fig. 4.48, when $j = 1$, the corresponding value for k is listed as 0. Its meaning should be interpreted as the value of next$[j]$, instead of the value of k.

(2) When $j = 4$, the potential values for k are 1, 2, 3.

When $j = 4$, $k = 1$:

$$jPre = t_0t_1t_2...t_{k-1} = t_0$$
$$jSuf = t_{j-k}t_{j-k+1}...t_{j-1} = t_3$$

When $k = 2$ and $k = 3$, the situations for jPtr and jSuf are shown in Fig. 4.48.

j	0	1	2	3		4			5				...
0<k<j	−1	0	1	1	2	1	2	3	1	2	3	4	
jPtr	/	t_0	t_0	t_0	t_0t_1	t_0	t_0t_1	$t_0t_1t_2$	t_0	t_0t_1	$t_0t_1t_2$	$t_0t_1t_2t_3$	
jStu	/	t_0	t_1	t_2	t_1t_2	t_3	t_2t_3	$t_1t_2t_3$	t_4	t_3t_4	$t_2t_3t_4$	$t_1t_2t_3t_4$	

Fig.4.48: Analysis of the list next$[j]$.

Example 4.9: Give the value of the array next of the pattern string T = "abcac".
Solution: According to the definition of the next function, we can obtain the analysis table for next in Fig. 4.49. After summarizing, we obtain Fig. 4.50.

2. The implementation of KMP algorithm

(1) Pseudocode description of the algorithm
  – The pseudocode for KMP algorithm can be seen in Fig. 4.51.
  – Algorithm design for calculating next.

Previously we have summarized the rule for calculating next – when there are k equivalences between the prefix and the suffix of string j ($0 < k < j$), then the starting position for the next time will be k.

	0	1	2	3	4
pattern string t[ ]	a	b	c	a	c

j	0	1	2	3		4		
0<k<j	−1	0	1	1	2	1	2	3
jPre	/	t0	t0	t0	t0t1	t0	t0t1	t0t1t2
		a	a	a	ab	a	ab	abc
jSuf	/	t0	t1	t2	t1t2	t3	t2t3	t1t2t3
		a	b	c	bc	a	ca	bca
Comparison result		n	n	n	n	y	n	n
next[j]	−1	0	0	0	0	1	0	0

Fig. 4.49: The analysis table for next of Example 4.9.

j	0	1	2	3	4
pattern string t[j]	a	b	c	a	c
next[j]	-1	0	0	0	1

Fig. 4.50: The position of next in the pattern string T.

First-level elaboration	Second-level elaboration
	Let the subscript of main string i = 0; the subscript of the pattern string T j = 0
Start the comparison from the first character of the main string and the first character of the pattern string T	When i, j are respectively smaller than the string lengths of S and T
If the characters are equal, then we keep comparing subsequent characters	If Si matches Tj , then i++, j++
Otherwise, start from the current character of the main string S, and compare it with the next character of the pattern string T	Otherwise, set i, j to the positions that the next matchings are about to begin Main string: i remains unchanged; pattern string: j=next[j]
Return the result	If the scanning on string T is complete, then return "match"
	Otherwise, return "no match"

Fig. 4.51: Pseudocode description of KMP algorithm.

Observe Fig. 4.48, for each position j, the position k will have to go through the changes between $0 < k < j$:

For example, when $j = 4$, j will change in the range 1–3. t_0 needs to be compared with t_1, t_2, t_3:

If $t_0 = t_3$, then $k = 1$.

4.3 String ━━ 265

If $t_0t_1 = t_2t_3$, then $k = 2$.
If $t_0t_1t_2 = t_1t_2t_3$, then $k = 3$.

Therefore, the process of calculating next[j] is a process of matching the prefix of T in string T. The concrete example is shown in Fig. 4.52. At this time, the target string $S = T$, and the comparison starts from s_1. The pattern string starts the comparison at t_0. s_0 will not be compared, and k will be directly set as 1.

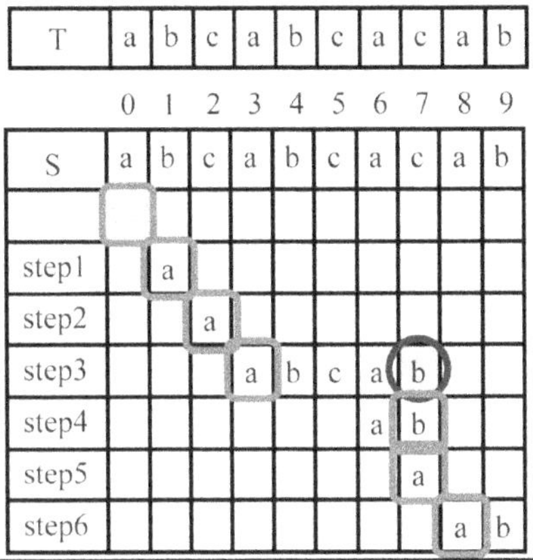

	step0	step1	step2	step3					step4	step5
Subscript j of main string S	0	1	2	3	4	5	6	7	8	9
S[j]	a	b	c	a	b	c	a	c	a	b
Subscript k of sub-string T	−1	0	0	0	1	2	3	4	0	1
T[k]	/	a	a	a	b	c	a	b	a	b
The prefix and the postfix are the same	/	n	n	y	y	y	y	n	y	y
The position to start the next comparison for the sub-string	0	0	0	1	2	3	4	0	1	/

Fig. 4.52: The process of solving next.

Analysis of steps of comparison
Step 0: $k = -1$, it indicates the starting position of the next time; string T starts from 0, string S starts from j++;
Step 1: $s[j]$ is not equal to $t[k]$, then the starting position for the next time: string T starts from 0, string S starts from j++.
Step 2: The same as Step 1.
Step 3: $S[j]$ is the same as $T[k]$, then the starting position for the next time: string T starts from k, string S starts from j++.

We can give the pseudocode for computing array next in a similar manner as we did in KMP algorithm, as shown in Fig. 4.53.

(2) Description of the data structure

```
#define MaxSize 30
//string structure
typedef struct
{    char ch[MaxSize];          // Store the value of string with array
     int len;                   // Length of string
} SqString;
```

Description of the algorithm to calculate next
Initialize the starting positions k=–1, j=0; (k=–1 indicates that for the starting positions of the next time, T will start from 0, S will start from j++)
Within the range of string S
s[j] is equal to t[k] or k=–1
Move j, k by one position
The starting position of the next substring comparison next[j]=k;
Otherwise, set positions to restart the comparisons from: j is unchanged, k obtains the next starting position from the next table

Fig. 4.53: Pseudocode description of the calculation of next.

(3) Structure design of the function

The function framework design of KMP algorithm and the function to calculate the value of next are given in Tables 4.6 and 4.7.

Table 4.6: Function framework design of KMP algorithm.

Functionality description	Input	Output	
KMP matching algorithm KMPIndex	Struct for the target string SqString Struct for the pattern string SqString	int	1: No match
			int value: Position of match
Function name	Parameters	Function type	

Table 4.7: Function framework design for obtaining next value.

Functionality description	Input	Output
Get the value of next GetNext	Struct for the pattern string SqString (address of the next array)	(Address of the next array)
Function name	Parameters	Function type

(4) Program implementation

```
/*======================================================================
Functionality of the function: Obtain the value of next from the pattern
string T
Function input: Pattern string T, (array next)
Function output: None
==================================================================*/
void GetNext( SqString t, int next[ ] )
{     int j=0,  k= -1;
      next[0] = -1;          // Set initial value
      while ( j< t.len )   // Within the range of the pattern string
      {
        //Starting from the beginning position of t, process or
        sequentially compared the main string and the pattern string
        if ( k== -1  ||  t.ch[j]  ==  t.ch[k])
        {
          j++; k++;
          next[j]=k;
        }
        //Reset comparison positions: j doesn't change, k starts from the
        position next[k].
        else  k = next[k];
      }
}
/*======================================================================
Functionality of the function: KMP algorithm - See whether there is a match of
pattern T in the target string S
Function input: Target string S, Pattern string T
Function output: Match successful: Return the position of first occurrence of
pattern string T in S. Match unsuccessful: Return -1
==================================================================*/
int KMPIndex(SqString s,SqString t)
{     int next[MaxSize], i=0, j=0, v;
      GetNext(t,next);   // Obtain the next array
      while ( i<s.len && j< t.len)
      {   if ( j==-1 || s.ch[i] == t.ch[j] )
          //j=-1 indicates this is the first comparison
          { i++;j++; }       // Increment both i and j by 1
          else j=next[j];   //i remains unchanged, j goes backwards
      }
```

```
        if ( j >= t.len ) v = i-t.len;
        //Return the subscript of the first character in the matched string
        else v = -1;       // Return no-match indicator
        return v;
    }
```

Program testing

```
#include <stdio.h>
#define MaxSize 60
typedef struct
{   char ch[MaxSize];
    int len;
} SqString;
int main()
{
    SqString S={"ababcabcacbab",13};
    SqString T={"abcac",5};
    int k;

    freopen("data.in", "r",stdin);
    freopen("data.out","w",stdout);    // Write the output into data.out file

    k=KMPIndex(S,T);
    printf("\n Position of match: %d\n",k);
    fclose(stdin);
    fclose(stdout);
    return 0;
}
```

4.4 Chapter summary

The connection between the main contents on multidimensional arrays in this chapter can be seen in Fig. 4.54.

The connection between the main contents on string in this chapter can be seen in Fig. 4.55.

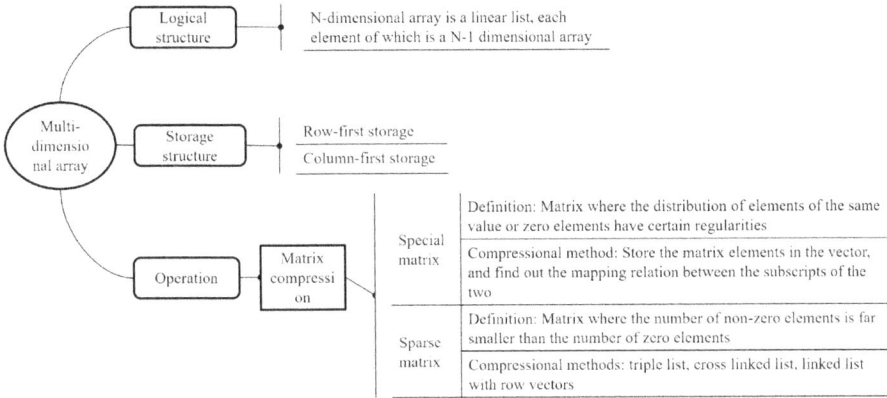

Fig. 4.54: The connection between various concepts on multidimensional arrays.

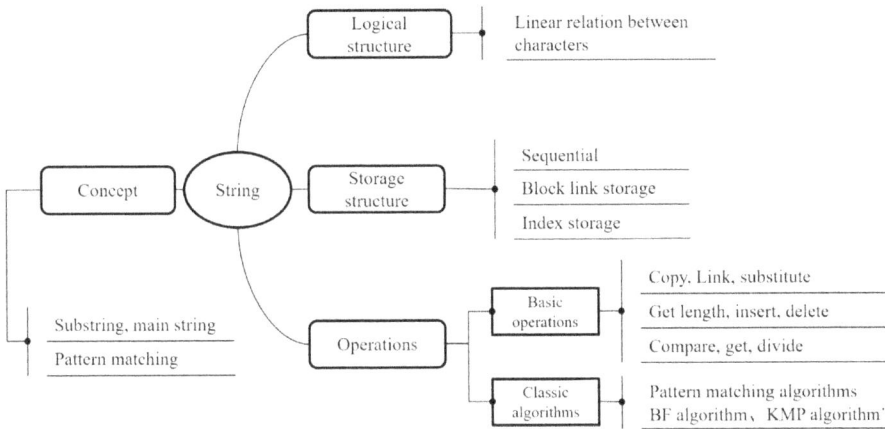

Fig. 4.55: The connection between various concepts on string.

Three key elements on obtaining the address on an array:
- The location of the starting node (base address)
- The number of dimensions and the upper and lower bound of each dimension
- The number of memory units occupied by each array element

Special matrices and their compressions

A matrix can be seen as a two-dimensional array. For certain matrices with special regularities in their data, we usually adopt special storage methods to save storage space.

If the distribution of nonzero elements is regular, then we call this matrix a special matrix. If the number of nonzero elements is far smaller than the total number of matrix elements, then we call this matrix sparse matrix.

The compressional storage of matrix normally involves allocating the same storage space for several elements with the same value. We do not allocate storage space for zero elements. The key points of compression are listed in Table 4.8.

Table 4.8: The key points of the compression of matrix.

Object to compress	High-ranked matrix
Condition of compression	The nonzero elements in the matrix has some regularity in their distribution, or there are a huge amount of nonzero elements in the matrix
Purpose of compression	Reduce the amount of data stored using efficient storage methods
Method of compression	<ul><li>Store the two-dimensional array of the original matrix, compress according to the distributional features of the data, save them to structures such as vector</li><li>The compressional storage of sparse matrix does not only store the value of nonzero elements, but also their locations in the matrix</li></ul>

One-dimensional array entails the one-to-one connection of nodes in a linear list.

Two-dimensional array of $M \times N$ has M rows or N columns of linear lists stored together.

Random access means it takes the same amount of time to access/write to each node.

Special matrices include symmetric matrix, diagonal matrix, triangular matrix and so on. They all have regularities.

Compressional storage entails mapping the two-dimensional array to a one-dimensional space, and the conversion of the two subscripts for row and column into one subscript in one dimension.

Sparse matrices, especially big matrices, have very sparse distribution of non-zero elements.

There are three storage methods: triple list, row linked list and cross-shaped linked list. Their ideas all entail storing the values and positions of nonzero elements.

A string consists of multiple characters concatenated together.

The structure of a string is still the same as that of a linear list.

There are multiple ways to store characters with either arrays or linked strings.

Operations such as obtaining the length of the array, comparison of the sizes and concatenation are all easy.

It is just pattern matching that is quite difficult.

Matching means finding substring in the main string.

The brute-force method needs to check each character one by one.

Its complexity is $O(mn)$, so it is quite slow.

KMP is much better; it carefully observes and skillfully arranges, so that there is no backtracking in the main string. The point of continuation in the substring is to be found in the next table.

The matching is to be checked between the prefixes and suffixes of the various substrings of the pattern string, the biggest length out of which will determine the position of start of comparison for next. It is indeed much faster since its complexity is only O($n + m$).

(Note: The two-dimensional array mentioned above should have M rows and N columns. In the pattern matching mentioned above, the length of the main string is n, and the length of the substring is m.)

4.5 Exercises

4.5.1 Multiple-choice questions

1. String is a special type of linear list. Its specialness lies in that ( ).
   (A) It can be stored sequentially
   (B) It can be stored with a linked list
   (C) The data element is a character
   (D) The data element can be multiple characters

2. String is ( ).
   (A) Sequence with less than one letter
   (B) Sequence of arbitrary number of letters
   (C) Sequence with no less than one character
   (D) Sequence of finite number of characters

3. The length of the string is ( ).
   (A) The number of different letters in the string
   (B) The number of different characters in the string
   (C) The number of the characters in the string, which should be larger than 0
   (D) The number of characters in the string

4. Suppose that there are two strings p and q, the operation which finds the position of first occurrence of q in p is called ( ).
   (A) Linking   (B) Pattern matching
   (C) Getting the substring   (D) Getting the length of the string

5. If the length of a string is smaller than a constant, then ( ) storage method saves the most space.
   (A) Linked   (B) Stack   (C) Sequential

6. A child sequence consisting of arbitrarily many consecutive characters in a string is called a substring of this string ( ).
   (A) Correct   (B) Incorrect

7. If two strings contain the same set of characters, then we say they are equivalent ( ).
   (A) Correct   (B) Incorrect

8. When it takes the same amount of time to store and access any element in the array, such an access is called ( ) access.
   (A) Sequential   (B) Random   (C) Linear   (D) Nonlinear

9. Suppose that the address of the storage unit of the first element of a one-dimensional array is 100, and the length of each element is 6, then the address of its fifth element is ( ).
   (A) 130   (B) 105   (C) 106   (D) 124

10. Suppose that an n-ranked square matrix is a upper-triangular matrix, then the elements that need to be stored is ( ).
    (A) $n^2/2$ (B) $(n(n + 1)/2)$ (C) n (D) n^2

11. The purpose of using compressional storage on some special matrices is to ( ).
    (A) Simplify the expression
    (B) Reduce the cost of unnecessary storage space
    (C) Remove the extraneous elements in the matrix
    (D) Simplify the access to the elements in the matrix

12. Triple list does not include ( ).
    (A) The number of rows   (B) The number of columns
    (C) The value of the element   (D) Total number of elements

13. Suppose the triple list representation of a known sparse matrix is as follows: (1,2,3), (1,6,1), (3,1,5), (3,2,–1), (4,5,4), (5,1,–3), then the third triple in the triple list for its transpose matrix should be ( ).
    (A) (2,1,3)   (B) (3,1,5)   (C) (3,2,–1)   (D) (2,3,–1)

14. If we store a sparse matrix using the triple list compressional method, then we can simply transpose the matrix by switching the row subscript and column subscript of each element. This idea is ( ).
    (A) Correct   (B) Incorrect

15. The size of three dimensions of array A is respectively b_3, b_2, b_1; each array element occupies a storage unit; LOC[0, 0, 0] is the base address. If we select row-ordering as the base order, then the address of element A[i][j][k] would be ( ) (in which $0 \le i < b_3$, $0 \le j < b_2$, $0 \le k < b_1$).
    (A) LOC[0,0,0] + $i*b_2*b_1$ + $j*b_1$ + k

(B) $LOC[0,0,0] + i*b_3*b_2 + j*b_1 + k$

(C) $LOC[0,0,0] + b_3*i + b_2*j + k$

(D) $LOC[0,0,0] + b_3*i*j + b_2*j + k$

4.5.2 Applied problems

1. Suppose the tridiagonal matrix $A_{n \times n}$ is stored with compression in a row-based order in the array $B[3*n-2]$, get:
    The formula for the subscript of k expressed in terms of i, j.
    The formula for the subscripts of i, j expressed in terms of k.
2. There's a known three-dimensional array $M[2 \dots 3, -4 \dots 2, -1 \dots 4]$, and each element occupies two storage units. The initial address is 100. If we store it in a column-based order, get:
    (1) The number of data elements contained in M.
    (2) The storage addresses of M[2,2,2], M[3,−3,3].
3. Let s = "aaab" andt = "abcabaa"; try to obtain the next function of each of them respectively.

4.5.3 Algorithm design

1. There is an array, and we know that one number occurs for more than half of the times in the array. Please find out this number with an algorithm of $O(n)$ complexity.
2. There are 4 billion integers in a file. Each integer occupies 4 bytes. The memory is 1 GB. Please find out an integer not contained in this file with an algorithm.
3. About 1–1000 are stored in an array with 1,001 elements. There is only one element that is repeated. You can only visit each array element once. Design an algorithm to find out this element. Can you design an algorithm which does not use auxiliary memory space?
4. Write a program to produce a random integer larger than 10,000. Output this integer, and then output each number in this integer in the form of English word. For example, if the integer produced is 345,678, then the output should be:

    The value is 345678
    three four five six seven eight

5. On a 5 × 5 matrix, implement via programming:
        Calculate the sum of elements on two diagonals.
        Calculate the product of elements which are on two diagonals and whose row subscript as well as column subscript are even numbers.

6. Calculate the sum of $m \times n$ matrix A and $m \times n$ matrix B with the formula $c_{ij} = a_{ij} + b_{ij}$. a_{ij} is an element of matrix A, b_{ij} is an element of matrix B, c_{ij} is an element of matrix C ($i = 1, 2, \ldots, m$; $j = 1, 2, \ldots, m$).

7. Calculate the product of matrix A and matrix B with the formula $c_{ij} = \sum_{k=1}^{n} a_{ik} b_{kj}$. a_{ij} is an element of the $m \times n$ matrix A ($i = 1, 2, \ldots, m$; $j = 1, 2, \ldots, n$), b_{ij} is an element of the $n \times m$ matrix B ($i = 1, 2, \ldots, n$; $j = 1, 2, \ldots, m$), c_{ij} is an element of the $m \times m$ matrix C ($i = 1, 2, \ldots, m$; $j = 1, 2, \ldots, m$).

8. If there is an element $A[i-1][j-1]$ in the matrix $A_{m \times n}$ that satisfies: $A[i-1][j-1]$ is the smallest value among the elements of row i, and the biggest value among the elements of row j, then we call this element a *saddle point of this matrix*. Suppose that we store the matrix $A_{m \times n}$ with a two-dimensional array, try to design the algorithm that calculates all the saddle points of the matrix, and analyze the worst-case time complexity of the algorithm designed.

Appendix A   Relation graph of data

The meaning of "data structure" encompasses three aspects – the logical structure, storage structure and operations of data. The logical structure of data embodies the relations between data. The storage of data is the embodiment of data in a computer. The processing of data in practical problems first is to abstract the data and relations within the information and select the appropriate storage structure according to the functional requirements and the amount of data of the problem (in Fig. A.1, the "structure selection" part" lists some examples of simple selection principles); second is to divide modules for separate processing according to functional requirements; third is debugging and testing.

https://doi.org/10.1515/9783110595581-005

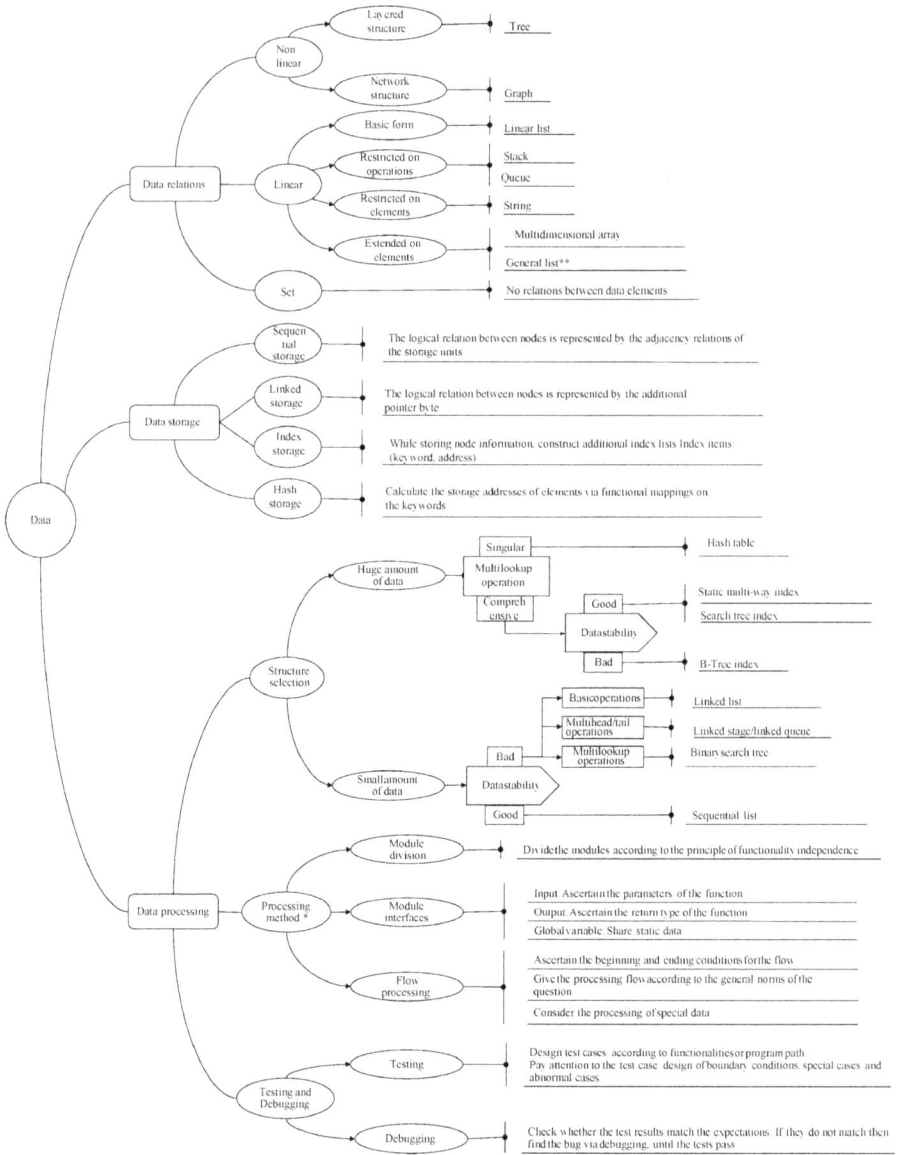

Fig. A.1: Relations between data.
*The data-processing methods here are given in an object-oriented way.
**General list belongsto nonlinear structure; it is an extension of linear list.

Appendix B   How to add custom header files

In Visual Studio IDE, the steps to add custom header files are as shown in Figs. B.1 and B.2.

1. Enter File -> New

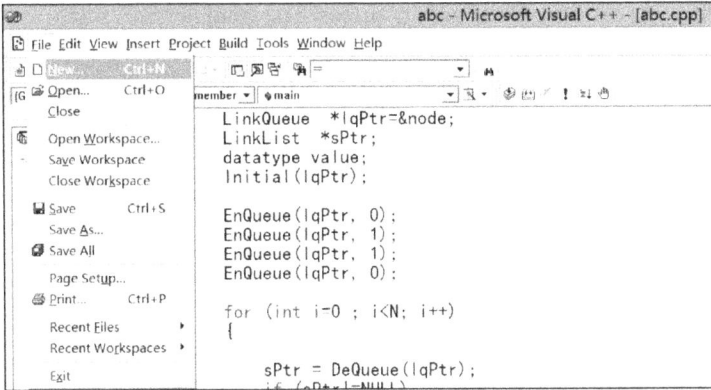

Fig. B.1: File -> New.

2. Select C/C++ Header File

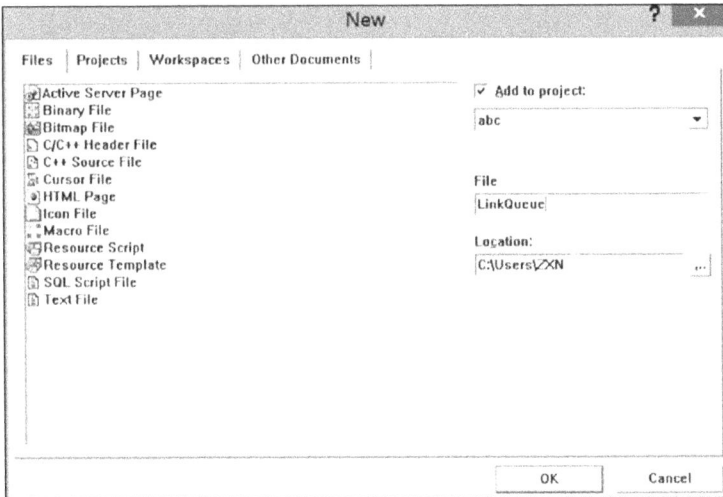

Fig. B.2: Select C/C++ Header File.

https://doi.org/10.1515/9783110595581-006

Note the difference between brackets and quotes when including header files in the code files.

1. Header files that come with the system should be written inside of brackets, so that the compiler can perform the lookup under system paths.

```
#include <xxx.h>
```

2. User-defined files should be written within quotes. The compiler will first try to search the current directory, and then the installation directory of C/C++ (e.g., in VC one can set and modify library file lookup path; in UNIX and Linux one can change it through environment variables), and finally search in system paths.

Appendix C Format of software design manual

Steps to writing huge and complex applications

The "data structure" course sometimes requires a relatively large and complex application. According to classical CS curriculum, how to write large and complex programs is originally comes under the software engineering class. To make it more convenient for readers to understand the related contents, here we briefly introduce knowledge related to large-scale program design. If you want to know about software engineering in detail, you can use this as a clue to look for related books and materials.

Programming is not only writing code. The major problem of program design is to first decompose the large-scale program system into many self-organized and relatively independent components, and then define strict invocation formats/interfaces for the mutual invocations that exist between the components.

From a software engineering perspective, software development is composed of multiple stages, which are requirement, analysis, design, coding, verification and so on.

1. Requirement stage: It is used to describe the information that the programmer must obtain to finish the system functionalities, that is, what the given conditions (inputs) should be, what the functionalities to be completed should be and what the generated results (outputs) should be.
2. Analysis stage: After using "top-down" approach to ascertain the designated aims of the program, decompose the problem into several medium-sized parts that are convenient to process.
3. Abstract design stage: Ascertain the relations between data objects and the operations on the data objects – analyze the logical structure of data.
4. Detailed design stage: Ascertain the storage structure and algorithm design of the data.
5. Coding stage: Code to implement the algorithm.
6. Verification stage: Test with real test data. The data should be able to cover all kinds of scenarios. Debug, find the reasons why the tests might be erroneous through debugging, and correct them.

https://doi.org/10.1515/9783110595581-007

Aspects to consider for program implementation

Normal processing flow	Data	Storage	Linear fashion: Array			
			Discrete fashion: Linked list, hash table, index			
		Transmission	Method	Meaning	Number of data items and way of processing	
			Input	Ascertain parameters	Single	Directly illustrate in the list of parameters
					Multiple	Illustrate separately in the list of parameters
						Make them into a struct and pass the address of the struct
Normal processing flow	Data	Transmission	Output	Ascertain function return type	Single	return (Data)
					Multiple	return (Address)
						The corresponding parameter in the list of parameters is the address
			Global variable	Ascertain static shared data zone	Single	
					Multiple	
	Operation	Algorithm	Algorithm description	Top-down, gradual elaboration		
			Starting condition	Ascertain the conditions for the program to start execution		
			Termination condition	Ascertain the conditions for the program to terminate		
Processing flow for special cases and exceptions				Boundary cases, special cases, abnormal situations		

Format of software design manual

1. Name of the software system
2. Software analysis and design
   - Analyze the problem. Ascertain the way and contents of inputs and outputs of the system. Give the general functionality description of the system.
   - Give the test cases and the list of expected results. Give the test cases in table form according to several categories such as normal, abnormal, boundary, and give the expected results using descriptive language.
   - Give the description of global data structure.
   - Divide modules. Give the functionality of each module and input/output information. Give the processing logics in the form of pseudocode or flowchart.
   - Give the relations between the modules in the form of flowchart.
3. Running environment
   The description of the software and hardware platform for this system.
4. Usage instruction of the software
   - List the operation commands the system provides the user and their functionality illustrations. Also list the response messages of the system and their meanings.
   - Abnormal case processing: Illustrate the method to resume execution from fault point or situations where the software needs to be rerun from the beginning.
5. Source code
   Give the source code and the necessary annotations
6. Testing
   According to test cases, give the test data, test results, debugging and analysis, explanations of remaining issues and so on.
7. Analyze the time efficiency of the algorithm

Appendix D   Answers to selected exercises

Chapter 1 Introduction

1. (A) Logical
2. (A) Correctness
3. (D) Data item
4. (C) Linear structure and nonlinear structure
5. (A) Correlation
6. (A) The logical structure of data is the description of relations between data
7. (C) The finite calculation sequence used to solve problems
8. (B) Feasibility, certainty and finiteness
9. (C) Analyze the efficiency of algorithms to search for improvements
10. (A) Space complexity and time complexity

Chapter 2 The data structure whose nodes share a linear logical relation – linear list

1. (C) Sequential storage structure
2. (A) Visit the ith node $(1 \le i \le n)$ and get the immediate predecessor of the ith node $(2 \le i \le n)$
3. (B) 63.5
4. (A) Has two parts, one for node value and another for pointer showing the relations between nodes
5. (B) Linked
6. (D) Either continuous or noncontinuous is OK
7. (B) Deletion operations will be constantly applied to L
8. (C) is less than 1
9. (A) High storage density
10. (B) If it employs sequential storage, it is easy to perform insertions and deletions
11. (A) Sequential list
12. (D) Singly linked circular list with only rear pointer
13. (B) Randomly access any element
14. (C) For sequential storage of linear lists, the time used to lookup the ith element is proportional to the value of i
15. (A) P->next=h
16. (D) s->priou=p; s->next=p->next; p->next->priou=s; p->next=s;
17. (B) s->next=p->next;p->next=s;
18. (B) head→next==NULL

https://doi.org/10.1515/9783110595581-008

Chapter 3 Linear list with restricted operations – stack and queue

1. (D) cabdef
2. (D) Cannot be determined
3. (D) Stack
4. (D) Potentially modify both the head and the rear pointer
5. (C) Stack
6. (A) (rear-front + m)%m
7. (B) 2 and 4
8. (A) (rear + 1) MOD n = front
9. (C) Only allow element insertion and deletion at ends
10. (C) 3

Chapter 4 Sequential list with special contents – multidimensional arrays and strings

1. (C) The data element is a character
2. (D) Sequence of finite number of characters
3. (D) The number of characters in the string
4. (B) Pattern matching
5. (C) Sequential
6. (A) Correct
7. (B) Incorrect
8. (B) random
9. (D)124
10. (B) $(n(n + 1)/2)$
11. (B) Reduce the cost of unnecessary storage space
12. (D) Total number of elements
13. (A) (2,1,3)
14. (B) Incorrect
15. (A) $LOC[0,0,0] + i*b_2*b_1 + j*b_1 + k$

References

[1]   Google LLC. google.com. [Online]. 2019 [cited 2019 10 19]. Available from: https://www.goo
      gle.com/search?q=data+structures+string.
[2]   Kanade T. Think Like an Amateur, Do as an Expert: Ways to Success in Research (Revised
      Edition). Ma J, Wang G, editors. Electrial Industry Press; 2015. Beijing.
[3]   Liu W. Understanding the "Why", Using Algorithm Study as an Example. [Online].
      http://mindhacks.cn.
[4]   Ries A, Trout J. Positioning: The Battle for Your Mind. McGraw-Hill Inc.; 1985. New York.
[5]   Tewarson RP. Sparse Matrices. New York: Academic Press; 1973.
[6]   Xiao H. CSDN. [Online]. Available from: http://student.csdn.net/space.php?uid=39028&do=
      thread&id=198&page=1.
[7]   Ye C. Discussions on the instruction method for the course "programming languages".
      Computer Education. 2007; (21).
[8]   Zou H. Data Structure: Dazzling Strings of 0 and 1. Beijing: Higher Education Press; 2012.

https://doi.org/10.1515/9783110595581-009

Index

algorithm 1
algorithm efficiency 34
and tree-like structure 20
arguments 26
array 222
Average case 37, 48

Base conversion 164
Best case 37
BF Algorithm 249
Big-O notation 40
binary search 11
Boundary Analysis 6

Caesar Code 61
caller function 27
Circular linked lists 115
computer 1
Constant order 45
constant time complexity 46
Correctness 31

Data compression 228
data element 9
Data Item 18
data structures 1
Decidability 24
declaration 25
definition 25
Deletion 64
delimiter 171
Dequeue 182
diagonal matrix 231
Doubly linked list 119
Dynamic memory allocation 88

Efficiency 32
Enqueue 182
Exponential order 45

Feasibility 24
Finiteness 24
function 25
function header 27

graph structure 20

Hash table storage 22
head pointer 91

Index storage 22
index table 12
induction stage 53
in-fix expressions 171
Initialization 23, 63
in-place algorithm 52
Input 24
Insertion 64
invocation 25
Iteration 64
Iterative algorithm 174

Keyword 10
KMP Algorithm 258

linear list 61, 63
Linear logarithmic order 45
Linear order 45
linear structure 19
Linearly linked list 86
linked list 80
Linked queue 198
Linked stack 141
Linked storage 22
list 11
logarithmic order 45
Lookup 77

Maintenance 5
mathematical induction 173
memory management 81
multidimensional array 221

node 9

operand 171
operation 16
operations on the data 19
operator 171
Output 24

parameter list 26
pattern matching 248

https://doi.org/10.1515/9783110595581-010

pointer 68
Polynomial order 45
pop 139
postfix expressions 171
prefix 261
prefix expressions 171
problem size 36
program 1
programming 1
pseudocode 25
Pseudo-overflow 184
push 139

queue 133

radix sort 209
Random access 65
random access data structure 105
Readability 31
record 11
Recursion 172
recursive algorithms 53
Requirement analysis 4
return type 26
Robustness 32

sequential list 64
Sequential queue 182
Sequential stack 140
Sequential storage 21
singly linked list 86

size of the problem 35
software development 3
Software Engineering 3
software system 3
space complexity 28
space efficiency 49
sparse matrices 221
sparse matrix 232
stack 133
Statement 34
storage structure of data 18
string 240
string-matching algorithm 221
struct 67
suffix 261
symmetric matrix 228

Tail recursion 175
Test case 6, 27
Test result 30
testing 5
the callee function 27
the logical structure of data 18
time complexity 28, 41
tracing 93
triangular matrix 230

Verification 6

Worst case 37
Worst-case scenario 48

www.ingramcontent.com/pod-product-compliance
Lightning Source LLC
Chambersburg PA
CBHW080936220326

41598CB00034B/5797